Fishing Texas

Fishing TEXAS

An Angler's Guide
BY Russell Tinsley

SHEARER PUBLISHING
Fredericksburg, Texas

TM of Fishing Texas, LTD   San Antonio, Texas

Library of Congress Catalog No. 88-090542
ISBN 0-940672-44-8

Published in 1988 by
Shearer Publishing
406 Post Oak Road
Fredericksburg, TX 78624

Printed in Hong Kong
Design by Whitehead & Whitehead

Contents

TO MY WIFE, MARJORIE,
For her encouragement, patience and understanding
over the years.

Acknowledgments

A BOOK SUCH AS THIS wouldn't be possible without a bunch of help and generosity.

For world and state records, my thanks to the International Game Fish Association and the Texas Parks and Wildlife Department.

For scientific and technical information, I am especially grateful to the TP&WD's fisheries staff, both the inland and coastal sections. Also invaluable was the assistance provided by the University of Texas Marine Science Center and the Texas A&M Sea Grant College Program.

For general fishing information, I tip my hat to the fishermen with whom I have shared a boat and whom I have interviewed over the past three decades; many have generously shared their expertise with me.

Thanks also to Nancy McGowan, the artist who painted most of the illustrations. I am privileged to have been able to work with such a talented person.

And finally, thanks to my editor Jean Hardy, who made this book a whole lot better than it would have been without her.

Russell Tinsley.

Introduction

FISHING IS RELAXING AND FUN; that is why it is so popular. But it is even more fun if the angler feels something tugging at the other end of his or her line. This is what the sport is all about.

Hooking a fish, and perhaps landing it, is the culmination of a process, a learned skill. That needs to be understood and stressed.

Successful fishing is knowledge and experience. Many variables come into play. The angler needs to learn the relationship of the parts in order to fit them into a sequence that ultimately will result in that tug on the other end of the line.

I think this book will help you do that. The subtitle is "an angler's guide," which pretty much says it all. It was written—based on interviews and fishing trips with accomplished fishermen over many years, plus material provided by Texas Parks and Wildlife Department fisheries biologists—for the fisherman, not only to aid in identifying both freshwater and saltwater fish, but to explain something about their habits and habitats, along with practical information and tips to help you catch them. Scientific names, as well as common names, are included in order to enable you to learn more by looking up any particular fish and reading about it in books written by ichthyologists.

Some anglers like to specialize, concentrating on one species such as the largemouth black bass or the redfish. Others like to fish for anything that's cooperating. Some people fish from boats, others from shore or when wading, or off piers and docks. Some use natural baits, others artificials. But no matter what species or what method of fishing, there are certain basics: learning where a fish lives in different seasons, its habits, what foods it eats—logical steps in the strategy to first find fish, then fool them into hitting a baited hook.

It is a fascinating challenge.

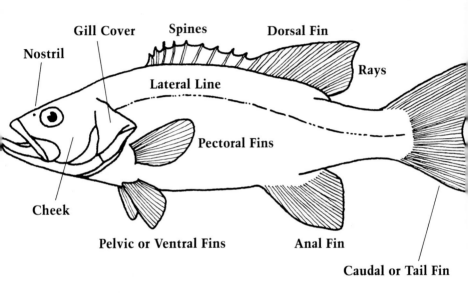

Nostril

Gill Cover

Spines

Dorsal Fin

Rays

Lateral Line

Pectoral Fins

Cheek

Pelvic or Ventral Fins

Anal Fin

Caudal or Tail Fin

Fishing Basics

GETTING FISH TO BITE

THE THEORY OF FISHING is pretty simple. You put something on the end of your line and toss it into the water, hoping to entice a fish to take it.

But simple in application it isn't. You have to be fishing with the right bait in the right place at the right time. You have to know something about the behavior of the fish you are after to do that.

While some fish, such as a male black bass or a bluegill guarding a nest, can be agitated into hitting, trying to destroy the intruder he thinks is preying on the eggs he is guarding, most fish in both fresh water and salt take a bait for one rudimentary reason: They are looking for something to eat. If you are using a natural bait, it should be something that that species normally feeds upon. Or if you prefer an artificial, it should be an imitation of that specific food.

Consider a spoon, one of our oldest known lures. The shiny piece of wobbling metal imitates a small baitfish, a universal food in both fresh water and salt. A lure pulled across the water surface simulates a swimming frog or some other amphibian.

And the type of food can vary greatly. Most scaled fish in fresh water and salt are carnivorous sight-feeders. They eat live food. Channel, blue and bullhead catfish, however, are not very fast or agile, which makes them inefficient predators, and live food such as minnows and crayfish is difficult for them to catch. Thus, they are omnivorous, eating most anything they can catch or find, including rotting meat, algae and moss. As scavengers, they depend primarily on their ability to smell to locate food.

Among the carnivorous fish, there are different feeding habits as well. A black bass, for example, is an ambush feeder.

It hides by or in some type of cover and waits for an unsuspecting minnow, shad or crayfish to come within striking range. This is why a bait should be put by or in the cover since the fish's strike zone is confined. But others like the white bass and striped bass, in fresh water, and the king and Spanish mackerel in salt, are open-water fish that are far-ranging, and they follow the food around. One way to catch them is to troll a bait of their choice until you pass within the sight of prowling fish and you get a strike.

If you want to become a better fisherman, remember this: To catch fish you have to be fishing where the fish are. And the whereabouts of any particular species will depend on food availability. In other words, you hunt the food and not the fish.

Red snapper will be on deep-water reefs or around oil-platform pilings because this is where their food is. The same is true with sheepshead around rock piles, pilings and jetties. Marlin and sailfish roam the 100-fathom curve way out in the Gulf of Mexico for the same reason. This is where they find the food they prefer. And it is the same with all other fish in fresh water and salt.

One of the best places to find largemouth bass is in shallower water with an abundance of food close to deep water, or near a dropoff, perhaps along the edge of an inundated creek channel. In fishing terminology, this break or change in the topography is known as "structure." Deep water provides a sanctuary, where bass can stay until they are ready to feed. Then they move into the shallower water because that is where the food is.

But being in the right place is only part of the challenge. Even a hungry fish has to be enticed to hit. With most species you have to present a bait of the same type and size the fish are accustomed to feeding upon. A so-called "crappie minnow" is about 2 inches long. A crappie has a small mouth and eats small food. The angler handicaps himself by using anything larger. For this same reason, you might cast time and again into a ravenous school of white bass chasing shad at the surface and not get anything but exercise. In all probability you are using a bait too large. It doesn't imitate the size of shad involved in the massacre.

Or in some instances, although you might be fishing the right place, you are fishing the wrong depth. While some fish, particularly reef fish like snappers and groupers, live and feed on or near the bottom, most species can range up and down. For example, someone is standing on a rock jetty and fishing a live shrimp under a popping cork in a deep channel connecting a bay with the Gulf. His bait is suspended only a few feet under the surface. But speckled trout and redfish might be feeding near bottom, much deeper. Consequently, the popping cork needs to be removed and the shrimp allowed to sink to where the fish are. It can be the other way, too; the angler is fishing deep while his quarry is feeding closer to the surface.

Fishing different levels to locate fish is as applicable to fresh water as it is salt water. Where you find fish will usually be dictated by food availability, and there can be considerable vertical movement. But other factors can come into play. An example of this is a school of freshwater striped bass suspended in the summertime. They can't go near bottom because that layer of water in hot weather has inadequate oxygen. They stay at a level where they can find the coolest temperature with oxygen. Even though they still have to eat, the stripers don't move around much at all. You have to put the bait down there where they are—right above them but not below the school. For some unknown reason, a fish will rise to take a bait but seldom will go down after one.

And finally, you have to know the life cycles of individual fish. You wouldn't go after king mackerel in the Gulf in the dead of winter. Migratory kingfish are present along the Texas coast only in the warm-weather months. This cycle isn't limited only to the change of seasons, though. Fish also have daily habits. For instance, sunfish such as bluegills typically move into shoreline shallow water early and late even during a hot summer day. The reason is, they are foraging on various insects, and the most activity with grasshoppers and other insects is near the shore. Again, the fish are going to the food source.

The bait doesn't have to be a grasshopper. It can be a grasshopper imitation. Most sport fish can be enticed into hitting either the real thing or fakes. The choice depends upon the individual fisherman.

But in either case the bait or imitation has to be what the fish prefers to eat, and it has to be presented in the place where the fish will be at that given point in time. In short, you have to know your fish and its druthers. Learn what the fish eats, where it lives, its seasonal and everyday habits.

One shortcut is to fish with a guide. Keep in mind you are hiring his knowledge. He is an instructor as well as a fish-finder. Question him about his choice of baits, the places where he fishes. Accumulate enough information and a picture begins to materialize, a pattern of a fish's behavior. You begin to understand the significance of where to fish, when and how—the basics.

And you are on your way.

INFLUENCES THAT AFFECT FISH

FISH ACTIVITY CYCLES are influenced by such things as barometric pressure, temperature and moon phase. These factors in combination dictate how active fish are and during what periods.

Barometric Pressure

The movement of a barometer's indicator needle is most noticeable right before and after a front. This is why fishing is normally good during these periods. While fish are supposed to bite best on a rising barometer, I also have had good success on a falling barometer, particularly if it is being affected by frontal action.

Otherwise, barometric pressure is determined primarily by the moon's orbit around earth, forcing pressure down in one area, raising it in another. During this natural cycle, fishing does seem to improve when the barometric pressure is rising.

Temperature

Water temperature dictates when freshwater fish spawn. Since their metabolic rates are also influenced by temperature, this affects their feeding and their degree of activity. All fish have what might be called their "comfort zones." For the largemouth it is about 65° to 75°F. Consequently, the fish is most active within this temperature range.

Water temperature also has an effect on saltwater fish. Migratory fish such as kingfish (king mackerel) and ling (cobia) do not show up in Texas waters until the temperature warms to about 70°F. Temperature also triggers the spawning runs of fish such as black drum, flounder and golden (Atlantic) croakers.

Saltwater fish, as a rule, better tolerate warmer water than do freshwater fish. Thus, as we move into summer, saltwater fishing is improving while freshwater fishing is slowing.

Freshwater fish are least active in July and August, or what has long been called the dog days of summer. These fish are most active in early spring and late fall into early winter because the water temperature is fairly stable all over and oxygen is abundant and evenly distributed. But as the temperature rises sharply in the summer, the behavior of fish changes dramatically.

In hot weather, deeper reservoirs become stratified. As the sun warms the surface, there comes a point when the warming makes the water near the surface lighter than that underneath. When this happens, the warmer water remains on top and does not mix with that below, and for some time in the summer, there is no vertical movement of water. This stagnation separates the water into three layers: the upper layer, known as the epilimnion; the colder lower layer, the hypolimnion; and the middle layer, a relatively thin "cushion" called the thermocline, in which temperatures drop rapidly.

The deeper parts of the lake, the lower level, do not have enough oxygen to support fish life for any length of time. This is why it is not unusual for a trotline fisherman to find dead fish on his line in the summer. The fish can go into the lower level for a brief time to feed. What happens then is, a fish gets hooked, and, unable to return to water with adequate oxygen, it suffocates.

Catfish, incidentally, are more active in summer because they can tolerate a water temperature about 10 degrees warmer than most other species. But catfish, along with other species, must remain above the lower level; they become suspended somewhere between top and bottom. This suspended state is most noticeable with striped bass and hybrid stripers. They are normally suspended in the deepest water, that in a reservoir near the dam, or out in the middle in the river channel. They will usually be along the upper part of the thermocline because it contains the most favorable conditions of temperature, oxygen and food supply (schools of shad, making easy prey of themselves, often suspend right above the stripers and hybrids).

The water remains in this state until on into the fall, when cooler night temperatures and wind action slowly reduce the temperature near the surface. This upper water eventually becomes cooler than that below and it sinks while the now-warmer bottom layer starts up, the two mixing along with the thermocline until the water reaches its point of maximum density, when oxygen once again is distributed throughout and the fish become frisky and start moving around again. The mix of water can be gradual or abrupt, depending on how rapidly the temperature drops. As the stagnant bottom water rises in the form of bubbles which burst on the surface, a definite odor is released, a stench from rotting vegetable and animal matter. The lake has turned over.

Moon Influence

Many fishermen depend on daily tables that predict best periods of fish activity, and also on tide tables. All are based to some extent on moon phase, one constant that can be predicted some time in advance.

The moon's orbit, as previously mentioned, establishes barometric pressure. It does the same with tide action.

The moon circles the earth about every 28 days and, since its orbital path is elliptical, its gravitational pull on the seas is not uniform. The sun, to a lesser extent, has some gravitational pull. Both are considered when making tide tables.

When a tide is going in or going out, it affects water depth and the movement of baitfish. When the bait gets active, so do the predatory species.

Tidal movement is most noticeable near and in passes and channels connecting bays with the Gulf. However, there are parts of bays isolated from passes and channels that are influenced at a later time by the water exchange, because of the time needed for tide action to spread into these areas. This is called tidal lag.

Since the moon does not orbit in a perfect circle and gravitational forces are uneven, tides tend to vary in intensity. Gravitational pull of the water is highest when the moon is closest to the earth and in line with the sun. During one complete orbit (synodic month), there are two such periods (called spring tides) one occurring about every two weeks, on the new-moon and full-moon phases. Lesser tides (neap tides) usually occur on the first- and third-quarter moon phases.

USING MAPS AND CHARTS

ONE AID FOR IDENTIFYING promising fishing areas and getting to them is a fishing map or coastal chart. Four different types are readily available.

• A basic lake map.

• A topographic, or bottom-contour, lake map.

• A bay or offshore map with quite a bit of detailed information.

• A nautical chart.

Maps are published for angling purposes; nautical charts are official navigational guides, although they have information pertinent to fishing, such as the location of oil platforms and buoys. Privately produced fishing maps carry this disclaimer: "Not intended for navigational purposes."

Fishing maps are easy to obtain. Some lake maps are free; other lake maps, along with coastal fishing maps, are available at nominal cost in virtually any store that sells fishing tackle.

The basic lake map contains only minimal information: the shape of the reservoir; its size in surface acres; the water level, or normal operating pool, when the reservoir is at full capacity (it can be a few feet above normal), based on the number of feet above sea level where the lake is located; access highways and roads; location of parks, launching ramps and marinas; and a scale representing inches to miles. This type is available from the U.S. Army Corps of Engineers, for the lakes it manages, and in lake-map books. Usually a free map of almost any reservoir is available from the chamber of commerce in the town closest to it. You can find the nearest town on a highway map. For most Corps of Engineers reservoirs, this will be a town with the same name as the impoundment—Belton for Belton Reservoir, Somerville for Somerville Reservoir.

The basic map will help if you've never been on the body of water before. It will direct you to fishing spots such as tributaries, and will provide directions when traveling from one spot to another.

For a few dollars you can buy a detailed bottom-contour map, which has all the information contained in a basic map, along with information about the topography that is hidden under water. These maps are widely used by black bass fishermen, but they can provide a lot of information to other fishermen who expend the effort to learn to read and interpret them. The contour maps show different water depths. Many freshwater fish are attracted to dropoffs, where there is an abrupt break in the underwater topography. Following the contours and noting the difference in depth from one contour to the next will show where these places are. Maybe it will be a point jutting into the lake; the land on the point surface might be exposed, or the water on top of the point will be fairly shallow compared to the water around it. Sometimes fish will be in the shallow water; at other times they will be hanging along the slope on either side or at the end; or they might be in deep water at the bottom of the slope. Another possibility is an inundated stock tank where the water is deeper than that around it. Or perhaps it will be an inundated road bed.

One thing to keep in mind is that these maps show contours for reservoirs at their normal water levels. The contours for a constant-level lake will be accurate. But water in a fluctuating reservoir is seldom at the normal operating level. It might be slightly up, especially in the spring if there has been excessive rainfall, but typically it is at normal pool or below. If the level is down, say, 2 feet, this has to be factored in. In other words, subtract 2 feet from all the contour-curve numbers.

A detailed bay map does not show contours, but it does indicate water depths with numbers sprinkled around. Do not take these numbers at face value; the water depth can vary, depending on the tide. They are close but not always exact. But by comparing the numbers you can get a good idea of an area's general topography, such as the location of a shallow flat. The map will also indicate passes, channels, reefs and oil wells. Most Texas bays are shallow. A fisherman won't have any problems if he stays in a channel, between the markers along either side. He sometimes gets in trouble when he strays out of the channel; if his boat isn't designed to run in very shallow water, he might run aground, or he might get back in a shallow area and not realize the tide is going out and will find himself stranded until an incoming tide brings the water level back up.

There are also offshore maps. These generally show features in that stretch from shore to about 10 or more miles out. Oil platforms and other fish attractors will be indicated, along with compass headings to reach them, and the water depths at various points out from shore. But again, remember that such a map for any part of the Texas coast is for fishing purposes only, not navigation.

A nautical chart is a navigational aid for the fisherman who fishes in the Gulf out of sight of land. Charts are published and distributed by the National Ocean Survey and are available at better marine stores. Four charts exist for the Texas coast. The areas they cover include, roughly, the stretch from Port Isabel to Corpus Christi; that from Port Aransas to Port O'Connor; from Port O'Connor and Freeport to Galveston; and from Galveston to Sabine Pass. There is some overlapping on the charts. The publication date is printed on each chart and you should get the latest one available.

For most fishermen not traveling far out into the Gulf, a chart and compass are all that is needed, if you know the compass heading straight out from the channel. This information for any port along the coast is available from the Coast Guard or from the owner of any tackle store. Actually, anyone who lives in a port will know what this heading is. This heading is used to set your compass. If you are going to an oil platform, for example, you plot the compass heading or course from information on the chart, based on a meridian (vertical line on the chart) or a parallel (a horizontal line), which intersect with a straight line drawn from your starting point to the target point. The angle of the crossing lines, determined in degrees by using a protractor, will tell you how much to adjust your compass heading. When coming back to shore you simply reverse that heading.

An easier way is to find a tackle shop in port that specializes in offshore fishing. Tell the manager your destination and ask the compass heading to reach it. Or ask him to recommend a place to fish and what the compass heading is. But you still should have the chart aboard for reference purposes. Since an elevated object such as an oil platform is visible for several miles in clear weather, the compass heading doesn't have to be exact. It can deviate 5 degrees in either direction and you'll have no problem getting where you want to go. Travel until you sight the platform, then change direction and head to it.

But long runs, as, for instance, to the 100-fathom curve for billfish, require experience and accurate navigation. This calls for the basic marine chart, with numbers superimposed that are used in conjunction with Loran-C. The numbers taken off the chart are programmed into the radio-telepathy directional system to get the correct bearing for any one destination.

A chart also indicates the progressive dropoff in water depths, indicated in fathoms, out from shore. With a chart and depth-sounder, a skipper can compute exactly how far he is from land. He switches on his depth-sounder and takes a reading in feet. Then he converts that figure to fathoms (1 fathom equals 6 feet). Thus, if the water depth is 60 feet, he can look at the 10-fathom mark on the map and know his precise location.

If you are serious about your fishing, it is worth your time to learn to use these fish-finding and navigational aids. A chart or map is one more tool that can refine the process of locating and catching fish. Detailed maps particularly provide a lot of information. If the fisherman knows how to utilize this information, he will greatly improve his angling success.

HANDLING AND RELEASING FISH

HANDLING AND RELEASING FISH are important parts of the angling experience, whether fishing in private or public waters. In private ponds or lakes the angler might release a fish because it is too small or just because he enjoys catching the fish and doesn't want to keep it. Persons who own private bodies of water, or perhaps the people who fish them, make their own rules. Releasing fish is a voluntary gesture.

It also is true in public waters for some anglers—most notably black bass fishermen, who advocate and practice catch and release, fishing only for the sport of catching. All fish they catch are freed. But typically when a fish is turned back, it is because regulations mandate it. Almost all species in both fresh and salt water that come under heavy fishing pressure have minimum-size lengths. A few have maximum retention lengths. There also are slot limits which require releasing fish of certain lengths. (See section on Sport-Fishing Regulations.)

Thus, most fishing situations will involve the routine handling and release of fish, especially undersized specimens.

Many fishermen, I have observed, mishandle fish during the process of removing the hooks and releasing them. Should a fish be abused and eventually die after release, the basic intent of catch and release—to keep that fish in the program— has been circumvented.

Releasing fish plays an integral role in any management plan to improve the fishery, no matter what species is involved. For this reason, proper release becomes important.

Consequently, while a fish is in temporary captivity, it should be treated gently. Don't let it flounce around in the bottom of a boat, on land or on a dock. When handling it, don't exert unnecessary pressure that might result in internal damage. A catfish is hardier than a scale fish such as a crappie; a redfish is more durable than a speckled trout. But if you squeeze a slippery small catfish or redfish tightly around the middle, to keep it from flouncing and jerking free while you remove the hook, your release tactics might be harmful.

With most fish, freshwater fish particularly, there really is no reason to grasp the body; when you have the fish close enough to reach, grab the lower jaw between your thumb and forefinger and clamp down. This immobilizes the fish and keeps it from flopping, and at the same time it naturally forces the fish's mouth open. Free the hook and lower the fish back into the water.

But you have to know your fish. You wouldn't want to try this with a walleye or a speckled trout or any other fish with a mouth full of sharp teeth. When handling one of these fish, you can grasp the body, or hold it by the lower jaw with needle-nosed pliers, or one of those hook removers shaped like a pistol that has pincher-like jaws on the end that close when the handle is squeezed. You can obtain one of these at most tackle stores.

But don't apply too much pressure and damage the jaw. It takes very little force to hold the fish until you can remove the hook and return it to the water.

The less time a fish is kept from the water, the better are

its chances for survival. If possible, play the fish close, grasp it and remove the hook without taking it from the water. Immediate release becomes particularly crucial in the summer when warm water and air temperatures put more stress than usual on the fish.

There is one thing about fish you should keep in mind when handling them. They all have slime coats that afford natural protection. You want to avoid damaging this protective coating. The simple procedure of scooping a fish into a landing net, bringing it aboard and quickly removing the hook and releasing it could be harmful. The net scrubs the protective slime off and perhaps splits the fins and tail, opening the fish to infection and reducing its ability to catch prey. The same thing happens when a fish pitches around in a boat or on a dock. The fish might appear frisky on release, but within a few days a killing fungus attacks areas where the protective coating has been damaged.

If a fish has taken the hook deep, which often happens, especially when using natural bait, be extra careful when removing the hook, to avoid injuring the gills. If you see blood, that fish is probably doomed. If the hook is embedded in the gill area and you can't reach it to gently work it loose, simply cut the line at the hook eye and leave the hook in the fish. Tests have shown that a fish can move around and catch food and swallow it with the hook in its throat. Also, tests have revealed that in a short period of time, maybe a few days, the fish's body chemistry somehow rejects the hook and it simply falls out.

The result is, that fish will be around to reproduce and be available for someone else to catch. It is an investment in the future of fishing.

EQUIPMENT

FISHING CAN BE AS SIMPLE or as involved as you want to make it. A line, a hook and some kind of bait are all you need. The line can be tied to a cane pole or even a trimmed willow branch. I've even watched a native fisherman in Mexico use a 2-liter plastic soft-drink bottle as a reel. The end of the line was tied to the bottle's neck, then it was wrapped around the bottle. On the end was a bait. The fisherman released a short length of line and twirled it above his head, to build up momentum; then he released the remainder of the line, pointing the bottle end in the direction he was throwing. The line peeled off the bottle in the same way it comes off a spinning reel. To retrieve, the fisherman simply rewrapped the line around the bottle.

A rod and reel, though, is much more efficient and easier to use, and there is such a wide range of options, in quality and price, that anyone can afford one. And there is a rod-and-reel combo for every fishing need.

The Rod and Reel

The Texas fishery is diverse, from sunfish a few ounces in size to sharks weighing a half-ton. Habitats range from diminutive ponds to the vast Gulf. There are different methods of fishing, too. Most black bass fishing involves almost continuous casting and this is why the bass angler prefers tackle made from lightweight materials; but when you are trolling for billfish, weight is secondary to strength, since the rod and reel has to deal with the stress generated by several hundred pounds of unleashed fury. Thus, any discussion of tackle has to deal in generalities. There is, obviously, no rod and reel that will handle all jobs.

A rod and reel is selected for a specific need. It is a tool dictated by the job, or species: the fish's size, where it lives, the method used when fishing for it. Then there are the purely technical aspects. Fishing is a subjective sport; the type of reel—spin-cast, spinning or plug-casting—is whichever you prefer. But the reel must be matched to the rod. The key to easy casting is balance: the reel, rod, line and bait all working in harmony. A reel usually has a label recommending the pound-test line that works best on it, while a rod's label will note the range of lure sizes or weights it will handle. You wouldn't, for example, buy a spinning rod and a reel with a 12-pound line and try to use it for fishing a 1/16-ounce crappie jig. It won't work. But the outfit performs admirably when you are using lures weighing a quarter-ounce or more.

Common sense is the best criterion when choosing a rod and reel. Give some thought to how you will use the tackle, and also to how much you want to pay. A graphite rod costs more than one made of fiberglass, but graphite has a combination of lighter weight and heightened sensitivity, and the investment of a few extra dollars might be worth it. High-tech reels are available with many options: graphite frames for lighter weight; calibrated dials for setting reel drags; quick-change handles allowing you to retrieve from either side, right or left; high-gear ratios for fast-speed retrieving; and so on. These extras run up the price. Whether they are worth it is up to you.

If you are unsure as to what you might need, get the advice of someone knowledgeable. Stores that specialize in fishing tackle usually have salesmen who know what they are talking about. But a salesman might try to talk you into buying a high-dollar item. A disinterested party, such as a veteran fisherman, is more apt to steer you right. Also keep in mind that you probably will be using the rod and reel for quite some time; it can be a long-range investment and it shouldn't be a capricious decision simply because you like the looks and feel. You want it to do the job.

While there is no such thing as an all-purpose rod and reel, simply because of the many fishing options, there are a couple of combinations that will serve a variety of needs. For freshwater fishermen, it is what is called "bass tackle." For saltwater fishing, it is what is known as a "popping rod."

Bass tackle normally will include a medium-action rod 6 to 7 feet long with a matching reel filled with line testing from 10 to 15 pounds strength. There are many variations, depending on conditions and circumstances, and this is why most serious bass fishermen carry two or more rods and reels, each outfit designed for a different job. But the one mentioned is a good compromise. It can be used for both natural and artificial baits, to fish for everything from crappies and white bass to largemouth black bass, catfish and even stripers. And it can be called into duty for coastal bay fishing when you are after species like speckled trout and redfish.

The saltwater popping rod is usually 7 feet long and is used in conjunction with a medium-sized heavy-duty reel with line in the 10- to 20-pound range. The handle is long. This rod and reel combination got its name from its wide use for fishing a bait under a popping cork. By gripping the handle with both hands, the angler can make the swift, strong upsweeps of the rod tip to pop the noise-making float on the water surface to attract fish. But it also is used for fishing natural baits on bottom and for casting artificial lures. It can be taken offshore to fish for king mackerel and other species of moderate size. It also adapts well to many freshwater fishing needs. For instance, a popping rod and a freshwater "striper rod" are exactly the same except for the different labeling the manufacturer puts on the rod. This 7-foot rod is also very similar to what bass fishermen call a "flipping rod," one used to flip lures into tight places that would be difficult to hit by conventional casting. Or it can be used simply to cast for bass, or to troll for hybrid stripers and white bass, or even to catch catfish.

These two outfits will serve many diverse fishing situations. For serious anglers whose interests lie outside this general mainstream of reservoir and bay fishing, there are many specialty outfits: fly tackle; ultralight spinning and spin-cast outfits that look like children's toys because of the miniature sizes; heavy-duty, big-capacity reels and stiff, strong rods for going after sharks and other big fish in the Gulf; and others.

The Fishing Line

The performance of premium fishing lines might be too good. It gives a false sense of security and the angler tends to take it for granted. Yet, age and abrasions will weaken even the best line, so that it isn't nearly as strong as its rated strength. Line failure is the primary reason so many bigger fish get away.

Almost all fishermen now use some type of single-strand, mainly nylon monofilament line. In a few circumstances, such as deep-reef fishing for snapper with big sinkers, Dacron is popular because of its negligible stretch.

Keeping a fresh, strong line on your reel is a key element of angling success. Changing line is not that difficult and not that expensive. There is an advantage to having your tackle dealer fill your reel using a line-metering machine because it feeds line evenly and under the proper tension. But you also can buy replacement spools of line and do the job yourself.

Keep in mind, though, that overfilling can be as trouble-some as underfilling. Too much line on the spool causes the line to balloon off and tangle when you cast, especially with a spinning and spin-cast reel, although overloading a casting reel also will make casting more difficult. The line on a spinning reel should stop within 1/8-inch of the lip, while a spin-cast reel should never be filled above the level of the spool. With a casting reel, fill to just slightly below the spool lip.

Filling a Revolving-Spool Reel

Insert a pencil into the supply spool to allow the fishing line to feed smoothly off the spool. Have someone hold each end of the pencil while you turn the reel handle. Keep proper tension on the line by having the person holding the pencil exert a slight inward pressure on the supply spool.

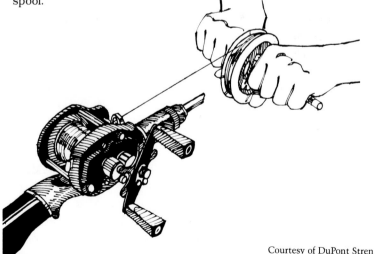

Courtesy of DuPont Stren

Filling a Spinning Reel

You fill a spinning/open-face reel differently than a bait-cast reel because you must allow for the rotation of the pick-up bail which may cause the line to twist.
Follow these steps:

1. Have someone hold the supply spool or place it on the floor or ground.
2. Pull the line so that it spirals (balloons) off the end of the spool.
3. Thread the line through the rod guides and tie the line to the reel with the bail in the open position.
4. Hold the rod tip three to four feet away from the supply spool. Make fifteen to twenty turns on the reel handle, then stop.
5. Check for line twist by moving the rod tip to about one foot from the supply spool. If the slack line twists, turn the supply spool completely around. This will eliminate most of the twist as you wind the rest of the line onto the reel.
6. Always keep a light tension on fishing line when spooling any reel. Do this by holding the line between the thumb and forefinger of your free hand.

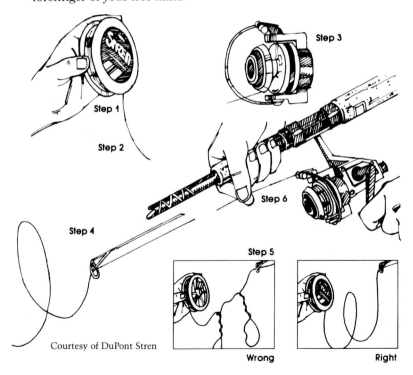

Step 3

Step 1

Step 2

Step 6

Step 4

Step 5

Courtesy of DuPont Stren

Wrong

Right

Filling a Spin-Cast/Closed-Face Reel

Use the same procedure (steps 1 to 6) described for filling a spinning reel. Remember to partially remove the reel cover so you will be able to see the spool and the rotation of the pickup pin. This is critical to ensure that you do not underfill or overfill the spool.

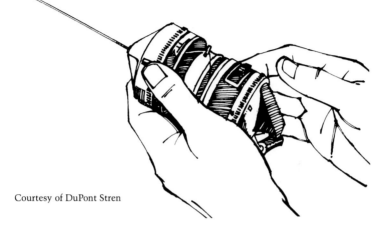

Courtesy of DuPont Stren

What test line you put on the reel will depend on your angling needs. Just remember that the stronger the line, the greater the diameter, and the greater the difficulty in casting.

In addition to the single-strand monofilament, there is also a cofilament line consisting of two or more filaments merged in the manufacturing process into a single unit in a sheath-core relationship. The advantage of this line is less stretch and greater resistance to abrasion because of the protective sheath.

While there are a variety of lines made for specific fishing situations, such as trolling for blue-water fish way out in the Gulf of Mexico or casting for largemouth bass in heavy cover, most of us can get by with an all-purpose premium line, one with the important characteristics of abrasion resistance, high-tensile breaking strength, and a moderate amount of controlled stretch, yet limp enough for casting ease—features incorporated into a leading manufacturer's signature brand, a line such as Berkley Trilene XL or DuPont Stren. Since nylon monofilament absorbs water, it changes once it becomes wet. Wet

World's Fair Knot

The winning knot in Du Pont's Great Knot Search

Created by Gary L. Martin of Lafayette, IN, this terminal tackle knot was selected by a panel of outdoor writers as the best new, easy-to-tie, all-purpose fishing knot from 498 entries in the Du Pont Great Knot Search. Martin named it the World's Fair Knot because it was first publicly demonstrated by him at the Knoxville '82 World's Fair.

1. Double a 6-inch length of line and pass the loop through the eye.

2. Bring the loop back next to the doubled line and grasp the doubled line through the loop.

3. Put the tag end through the new loop formed by the double line.

4. Bring the tag end back through the new loop created by step 3.

5. Pull the tag end snug and slide knot up tight. Clip tag end.

breaking strength is always less than dry breaking strength, about 15 percent less on the average. But it can be much less when abrasion comes into play. Nicks caused by a fish's teeth, gill covers, or the line rubbing against rocks or brush or the bottom of a boat will weaken the line. Any damage will normally affect the few feet right above the hook or lure. Check this section of line regularly, particularly if you've caught a fish or two or if you have felt the line rubbing against some obstruc-

King Sling

This knot is used for putting a loop in line that is attached directly to lures.

1. Insert end of line through lure eye and double back about 10 inches.

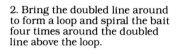

2. Bring the doubled line around to form a loop and spiral the bait four times around the doubled line above the loop.

3. Bring the lure down and through the loop.

4. Tighten it by pulling from both ends.

tion. If you detect any roughness, break off three or four feet of line and retie.

There are also other factors to consider. The knot, unless it is tied properly, will slip or snap before the breaking strength of the line is reached. Also, while you fish, regularly check the line directly above the hook or lure. If you feel roughness, break that segment of line off and retie.

If the line becomes tangled or twisted, a common occurrence on spinning and spin-cast reels after the monofilament has been used for some time, it is also more prone to break and more difficult, if not impossible, to cast. You can straighten it

The Uni-Knot System

Here is a system that uses one basic knot for a variety of applications. Developed by Vic Dunaway, author of numerous books on fishing and editor of "Florida Sportsman" magazine, the Uni-Knot can be varied to meet virtually every knot tying need in either fresh or saltwater fishing.

Tying to Terminal Tackle

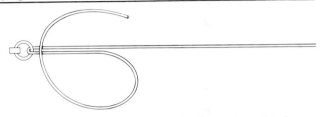

1. Run line through eye of hook, swivel or lure at least 6 inches and fold to make two parallel lines. Bring end of line back in a circle toward hook or lure.

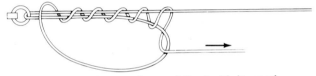

2. Make six turns with tag end around the double line and through the circle. Hold double line at point where it passes through eye and pull tag end to snug up turns.

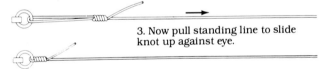

3. Now pull standing line to slide knot up against eye.

4. Continue pulling until knot is tight. Trim tag end flush with closest coil of knot. Uni-Knot will not slip.

some by removing whatever you have tied on the end and letting out a considerable amount of line behind a moving boat, pulling the free monofilament through the water. This drag of water resistance causes the monofilament to turn in the opposite direction of the tangles and removes them, although a line has a "memory" and therefore a tendency to easily tangle again. That's when you need to replace the line.

Another consideration when buying new line is color or visibility. Unless a person is really serious about fishing,

Snelling a Hook

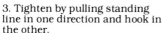

1. Thread line through hook eye about 6 inches. Hold line against hook shank and form Uni-Knot circle.

2. Make as many turns through loop and around line and shank as desired. Close knot by pulling on tag end of line.

3. Tighten by pulling standing line in one direction and hook in the other.

Line to Reel Spool

1. Tie loop in end of line with Uni-Knot; only three turns needed. With bail of spinning reel open, slip loop over spool. (With revolving spool reel, line must be passed around reel hub before tying the Uni-Knot.)

2. Pull on line to tighten loop.

matching a specific color to a fishing situation only adds to confusion in most instances. Unless you know exactly what you need, get premium clear or green line and be confident you've made the right choice. Either color has a proven track record of low visibility when fishing in fresh or salt water.

Setting the Reel Drag

Many of the more expensive reels have a calibrated drag adjustment. If you are using 14-pound test line, you set the dial at 14. But on most reels, new and older models, the fisherman still must set the reel drag manually based on his own judgment. This requires some knowledge of different fish species and various fishing conditions.

As anyone who has taken high school physics knows, it

Joining Lines

1. Overlap ends of two lines of about the same diameter for about 6 inches. With one end, form Uni-Knot circle, crossing the two lines about midway of overlapped distance.

2. Tie Uni-Knot around leader with doubled line. Use only three turns and snug up.

3. Pull tag end to snug knot tight around line.

4. Pull knots together as tightly as possible and trim ends and loop.

5. Pull the two standing lines in opposite directions to slide knots together. Pull as tight as possible and snip ends close to nearest coil.

takes more force to put a stationary object into motion than it does to maintain the motion. Consequently, a line is more vulnerable in a moment of sudden stress, as when a fish strikes or when the angler heaves back to set the hook. Unless the reel drag responds instantly, the stress can exceed the breaking strength of the line.

Even so, there's another factor—the fish's personality. A largemouth black bass doesn't strike with all that much sudden force. It flares its gills to create a suction to suck prey into its mouth. With a larger bass the hit feels like nothing more than everything coming to an abrupt halt. The drag is more crucial after the fish is hooked. Since bass like to live in or around some sort of cover such as brush, once hooked the fish tries immediately to return to the cover. With the drag set tightly, the bass has to work to move the reel spool.

On the other hand, fish like freshwater striped bass or saltwater Spanish and king mackerel are slash-type strikers. When one hits on the run, near or at top speed, the stress factor at the moment of impact is compounded, like a meter indicator needle jumping all the way over and then right back, the stress peaking just that quickly. To compensate for this, you should have a lighter-set reel drag so that line is released easily and instantly to reduce stress. For these open-water fish, then, the strike is more a factor than is the ensuing fight, so far as the reel-drag setting is concerned. (But braking action increases as the spool empties, and if a runner like the king mackerel makes a long dash, the braking action might be too much and the line will snap, if the drag isn't set where it will release line easily.)

Knowing how tightly the drag is set, simply by pulling on the line, comes with experience. But there is something else to consider. The lighter the line the more critical drag adjustment becomes.

For most fishing situations, no matter what type of reel you are using, the drag should be set at about 1/3 of line test. This, with the combined bend of the rod and friction of the guides, will allow for an effective drag that will still slip when required rather than break the line.

Yet even a light-set drag won't release line with impunity. To get some idea as to how your tackle performs, try this simple backyard test. Put the reel on the rod and run the line through the guides. While holding the rod at a 45° angle, as if you were fighting a fish, have a friend pull on the line, bending the rod naturally. As he does this, adjust the drag-setting knob or wheel until the line flows at a moderate line tension. If you need additional drag while playing a fish, you can place your hand against the reel spool to slow the flow of line, letting off or adding tension as is necessary. This is better than trying to tighten the reel drag as you play the fish. In the excitement the tendency is to adjust the drag too tightly and then only bad things can happen.

Once you have gone through this simulated fishing situation, you can now grasp the line near the reel and pull on it to get some idea how much tension you need. Consequently, you will know about how tight to set the drag as you fish. Also, it is a good idea periodically to test the drag release. Some drags have a tendency to "load up" after you've caught a few fish. If the drag becomes too tight, it is unable to respond properly.

And one more thing. If you are using an open-faced spinning or closed-face spin-cast reel, don't reel while the drag is surrendering line. One closed-faced model I am familiar with has a slip-clutch to prevent this; but on most reels, turning the handle while line is going out only puts twists in the line, which weaken it. Also, you will realize how serious that can be when you try to make your next cast. The line will come off the reel in tangles.

Hooks and Sinkers

The familiar hook design has not changed much since 1832 when the English hook-making business was flourishing and the venerable Mustad Company was organized. The most notable change has been the alteration of some hook shanks for specialty fishing, such as bending the shank to make a plastic worm run straight in the water. But the basic designs are still used for most fishing situations.

Hook sizes are designated by a numbering system. In the straight-number system (smaller hooks), a No. 1 is the largest, the hooks getting progressively smaller with each larger number, a No. 2 being larger than a No. 4, and so forth. Yet with the No./o-series, it is the other way. A No. 1/o is the smallest (yet slightly larger than the No. 1), with larger numbers indicating larger hook sizes, a No. 4/o being larger than a No. 2/o. The numbering system applies to both single-shank and treble hooks.

There are several different hook styles with names like

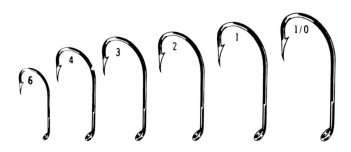

HOOK SIZES
Hooks pictured are true to size.

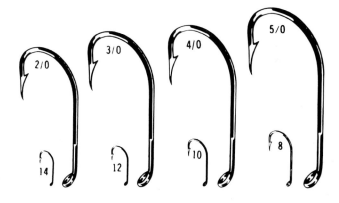

Aberdeen, Kirby and O'Shaughnessy. With some styles there are also options of short shank, long shank, extra light and extra strong. When shopping, compare the different styles and pick the one you like; or ask the tackle-store manager which one he recommends for the type of fishing you intend to do.

There is a tendency to use too large a hook, especially when fishing a natural bait. A larger hook has more bulk, making it more difficult to hide; and more weight, which stifles the action of a live bait.

A good rule of thumb is to match hook size to the mouth

PARTS OF A HOOK

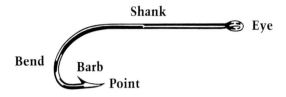

size of the species you are after, or, put another way, to match it to the food the fish is accustomed to feeding upon. For use with larger baits for larger fish with large mouths, such as bass in fresh water and offshore species in salt water, you can get by with larger, stronger hooks. Such hooks are made mostly of carbon steel, although some are manufactured from nickel-steel alloys and stainless steel. But for any of the smaller specimens, such as sunfish or crappies or saltwater croakers, you need a small hook, preferably of very light weight, since you will be using smaller baits.

With sinkers, there is also the tendency to add too much weight. Never use a sinker unless you absolutely have to, and then put on the smallest sinker you can get by with. Sinkers accomplish three things, two of them bad. First, the positive: A sinker takes a bait to bottom, or maybe only to near bottom if you are fishing in a current. That's the idea. Now, the negatives: Anything you add to the line is going to rob the bait of some of its natural look; and with weight on the line, it is harder to detect a bite.

If you must add weight, a slip sinker is your best bet. This sinker, either bullet- or egg-shaped, has a hole through it. You put the sinker on your line, then tie on a small barrel swivel, and tie about a 15-inch leader with a hook on the other end of the swivel. The swivel acts as a stop, preventing the sinker from sliding down against the hook. With the 15 inches of free line, a bait can move around naturally. And when a fish picks up the bait, the line runs freely through the sinker. There is less resistance for the fish to detect. Also, you have more control of the situation because, with the line having freedom of movement, you are feeling the pull of the fish and not the weight of the sinker.

Any sinker you clamp or pinch on the line could weaken the monofilament. A better choice is a core-lock sinker. This slender sinker has a slit lengthwise along the side and a rubber center, with tips protruding from both ends of the sinker. You put the line in the slit and grab the ends of the rubber core and twist them in opposite directions to clamp the sinker in place. With the rubber wrapped around the line, there is no stress to weaken it.

Artificial Baits

Walk into a major tackle store and you will be bewildered by shelves lined with artificial baits of every style, size, shape and color imaginable, lures for both freshwater and saltwater fishing.

This is an instance when you absolutely must know your fish and what it eats at different times of the year in order to know which baits to buy. Size and color are always important considerations, along with the depth at which the bait should be fished—or whether it floats on the surface or runs shallow or deep. Entire books have been written about the various baits for one species, such as the largemouth bass, or one method of fishing—fly fishing, for example. Don't be overwhelmed, and don't assume you have to try them all. If you want to learn more, the opportunity is there. Check your local library for fishing books. There are also many instructional videos. Fishing programs are shown regularly on television. Make it a point to learn the names of knowledgeable fishermen in your hometown and go to them for advice. If there is a fishing club, join it.

Fishing is knowledge, and the information isn't dumped on you all at one time. You pick it up in bits and pieces. And as long as you fish, you will never stop learning. There always is something new.

Downriggers

For fishing at precise depths, either trolling or drift fishing, one aid that many fishermen rely on is the downrigger. It is particularly popular with anglers after striped bass and hybrid stripers in reservoirs. To a lesser extent it is used in offshore coastal fishing for species like king mackerel, although downriggers are getting more popular for saltwater fishing all the time.

A downrigger is mechanically simple to use. A reel holding wire cable is attached to a bracket which in turn is mounted on the side or stern of the boat. This reel is on the same plane as a boom, usually less than 36 inches long, which extends over the water. Cable goes from the reel end of the boom where a pulley feeds it straight down into the water. At the end of the cable snapped into a holding clip is a weight, normally shaped like a cannonball, weighing typically from 5 to 8 pounds. The weight is lowered and raised either manually (a hand crank on economy models) or electronically, by simply pressing a button. A calibrated scale shows exactly how deep the weight is lowered. You lower it to the depth at which you wish to fish.

A tube-shaped holder atop the downrigger holds the rod and reel. Somewhere on the weight or on the cable just above it is a line release. This device holds the line until a striking fish jerks it free. The line, with either an artificial or natural bait on the end, trails the weight, sinking slightly below it. Once a fish hits and yanks the line from the release, the downrigger has done its job and the angler has direct contact with the fish.

The angler has the choice of a lightweight portable model that can be taken on or off, designed for the recreational fisherman, or a heavier permanently mounted downrigger, preferred by fishing guides.

Downriggers can be used in conjunction with paper-graph or liquid-crystal depth-sounders, which show fish on the display, revealing their precise depth. The downrigger puts a bait down in the strike zone of the fish, slightly above them, where they will rise to hit. If the downrigger ball is lowered too deep and pulled through a school, it will spook the fish.

THE FISHING BOAT

USING THE GENERIC NAME "fishing boat" is like saying the "family automobile." Any boat can be used for fishing just as any automobile can be used to transport the family.

In either case, though, some do a better job of it than others. Some boats are designed and made specifically for fishing. The best known perhaps is the so-called bass boat, although there are quite a few others, such as the scooter, a raft-shaped contraption designed to run on shallow flats—bay water only inches deep.

Fishing boats come in all sizes and shapes, from the aluminum flatbottom less than 15 feet long to cabin cruisers more than 50 feet in length that go way out into the Gulf after billfish. But no matter the size, if a boat is operated in public waters, it and its occupants must adhere to certain rules dictated by federal and state laws.

If it is more than 14 feet long and/or powered by an outboard of 12 horsepower or more, it must be titled with the Texas Parks and Wildlife Department and it will be assigned an identification number. This number must be displayed on both sides of the bow. Also, when the motorboat is in operation, the certificate of number or a facsimile must always be aboard and available for inspection by a law-enforcement officer.

All powerboats are required in addition to have various safety devices aboard, depending on the size of the boat. Every powered boat is required to carry one U.S. Coast Guard–approved life jacket of the correct size and type and in good condition for every person aboard. Such life jackets are technically known as Personal Flotation Devices (PFDs), and the "Coast Guard Approved" label is clearly visible on them. State law further dictates that in every Class A and Class 1 boat that is underway, any occupant 12 years old or younger must actually be wearing a life jacket.

For regulatory purposes, motorboats are classified by four types:

Class A—Boats less than 16 feet in length.

Class 1—Boats 16 feet or over and less than 26 feet in length.

Class 2—Boats 26 feet or over and less than 40 feet in length.

Class 3—Boats 40 feet and over.

For Class A boats, one approved life preserver of any type—buoyant vest, ring buoy or buoyant cushion—is required for each person aboard.

For the other three classes, PFD requirements call for one Type I (offshore life jacket), Type II (near-shore life vest), or Type III (flotation aid) for each person aboard, plus one Type IV (throwable device such as a cushion, ring or horseshoe) immediately available for emergency use.

If operated at night, the boat must have lights. Most power-boats come from the dealers equipped with the necessary lights. Class A and Class 1 boats are required to have two white running lights, one fore and one aft. Class 2 and Class 3 boats must have two white lights, one on the stern and one on the bow, along with a red light on the port (left) side and a green light on the starboard (right) side.

Most smaller boats are not required to have fire extinguishers, but it is good insurance to have one aboard. Boats, particularly those of fiberglass construction, can burn, and burn rapidly.

Any boat less than 26 feet in length is required to have a fire extinguisher of the B-I type aboard if one or more of the following conditions exist: 1. Closed compartment under thwarts and seats where portable fuel tanks are stored; 2. Double bottoms not sealed to the hull or which are not completely filled with flotation material; 3. Closed living spaces; 4. Closed storage compartments in which combustible or flammable materials are stored; 5. Permanently installed fuel tanks.

A Class 2 boat must carry two B-I types, or one B-II type. A Class 3 boat is required to have three B-I types, or one B-I and one B-II.

Each approved fire extinguisher, incidentally, is classified by a letter and a Roman numeral according to the type of fire it is designed to extinguish and its size, or capacity. The B classification is for gasoline, oil and grease fires.

Class 2 and Class 3 boats must also have an efficient whistle or horn or other sound-producing mechanical device.

One item not required but one that every boat should carry is a sturdy anchor with the appropriate length of line (10 times as many feet of line as the depth of water you fish in). If not enough line is out, the anchor won't bite and hold, especially if there is much wind. If you get in trouble—as when your engine won't start—put the anchor out and wait for help.

One emergency that can be avoided is being caught in dangerous weather. Coastal waters can get extremely rough and treacherous, but inland waters can, too. Listen to weather reports before you go fishing.

Coastal weather warnings are unique because of the special relationship between wind and waves. The longer the wind blows in a steady direction and the greater the distance over the water, the higher the waves. A wind of 35 knots can create 6-foot waves in just 2 hours. Driving a boat in such conditions is not the most pleasant of experiences. It can be hazardous, too.

Every boat that goes offshore should have a VHF radio. The Coast Guard monitors Channel 16. You can never know when something might go wrong, whether mechanical failure or a sudden storm. You can avoid surprises by tuning in to the National Weather Service, which issues marine forecasts every 6 hours for all coastal areas.

In addition to monitoring the weather, there are a few other things to keep in mind:

• Never overload the boat—or overpower it. Check the capacity plate attached to the boat and use this as a guide to proper power and loading.

• Tell someone on shore about your plans: where you are going and when you will be back.

• Before starting out, check the fuel supply.

• And if you are trailering your boat, properly attach the safety chain every time you tow the trailer, even for short distances. The safety chain on the trailer is designed to prevent the tongue from dropping to the road if the trailer coupler separates from the hitch ball for any reason.

FINDING FISH ELECTRONICALLY

DEPTH-SOUNDERS ARE REMARKABLE MACHINES that take much of the guesswork out of fishing. While some of the delicate instruments actually pinpoint fish schools or even individual fish, perhaps their greatest asset is being able to "read" the bottom contour.

There are five types of depth-sounders for the recreational fisherman, and although they are all sonar units, they differ in the way they display information. Sonar is the acronym for sounding, navigation and ranging, developed in World War II for the Navy.

Sound waves travel faster and better through water than in air. In sonar, an electrical pulse is fed into an underwater device attached to the boat bottom called a transducer, which converts electrical pulses to sound pulses. These ultrasonic sound pulses travel through the water until they strike an object or the bottom, and they bounce back and are picked up by the transducer as an amplified echo that can be measured and converted into information, such as the distance to the object and its size, or the distance to the bottom, giving the water's depth.

This information is displayed in one of five ways:

• A digital read-out, or numbers displayed on a small screen. This unit, which is normally mounted on the boat console, is called digital or computer sonar. It scans the bottom and provides instant information in tenths of a foot. The fisherman can watch the unit and know the exact water depth, either while fishing or speeding across the water from one place to another.

• The flash of a neon bulb on a revolving disc, or what is called a flasher unit.

• A tracing burned on the surface of a special paper by a

moving stylus, a system known as the paper graph or chart recorder.

• A marking with pixels (dots) on a liquid-crystal display, an LCD unit.

• An image shown on the face of a cathode ray tube, or what is called video sonar.

These machines have come a long way since Carl Lowrance developed the Lo-K-Tor flasher unit, or what became known as the Little Green Box, in the late 1950s. In fact, the flasher unit, as a depth-finding accessory to be mounted anywhere on a boat, is no longer made. The only flasher available is one that mounts in a boat console. The advancement in technology of liquid-crystal units with high-speed performance has rendered the flasher obsolete for general angling use.

Like the digital sonar unit, a flasher console unit is used for safety purposes when going from one place to another. The fisherman can glance at the unit and get an immediate reading concerning water depth, even when running at high speed. It can also be used as a reference when moving around and looking for a specific water depth to fish. With either type, though, an immediate reading is all the fisherman gets. With digital sonar or a flasher, once a place is passed, the information is gone. There is no recall or memory.

The other three units provide much more detailed information, actually showing individual fish or schools of fish, and, consequently, have become known as "fish-finders."

A paper graph almost paints an underwater picture in explicit detail, similar to a black-and-white line drawing, showing everything from bottom to surface. But its larger size, mechanical moving parts, higher cost, and the need for fairly expensive paper puts it out of reach of most casual fishermen, although guides and serious anglers, especially those who fish deep water, love it.

A liquid-crystal display unit generally is much less expensive and its no-moving-parts simplicity makes it durable even in a boat pitching wildly in rough water. The better models with more pixels (dots) have high resolution, displaying the bottom contour in such detail that small objects like stumps and rocks can be identified. Additionally, anything not attached to the bottom is identified by a flashing dot or one or more dots displayed in color, depending on the unit. These signals usually indicate individual fish or a school of fish. An LCD unit also has a recall or memory, which makes it possible for the angler to take another look at something he has just passed, to see if it is worth going back to, or to store information, such as an underwater hump out in a lake that he might want to find again. This is possible because of a split-screen display. A picture recalled from memory is locked in on the left side of the screen, and on the other side, there is a scrolling look at the bottom as the boat eases along. When the picture on the right side matches the one on the left, you've found your place, maybe that hump.

Video-sonar units, especially those that display in 6 colors, perform a myriad of jobs, such as reading boat speed and surface temperature, along with the other things such as recording depth and finding fish. The display is similar to a TV screen, and while this is one of the advantages, giving quality resolution, the displayed picture has reduced visibility in bright sunlight, making it almost mandatory that a video-sonar unit be mounted inside a boat cabin.

A problem with any of these units is that you have to watch one almost constantly to see what's down there in the water. You will spend more time studying the depth-sounder than you will actually fishing. For this reason, you should also have one or more markers in the boat. This way, when a likely spot is located, or even a fish concentration, a marker can be thrown overboard to show precisely where the place is, giving a visual reference point. You don't have to consult the depth-sounder every few minutes to see if you've strayed from the spot.

A few paper-graph units interface with loran (long range navigation), which employs a highly sensitive radio receiver to pick up signals transmitted from shore stations, for navigating out of sight of land. Loran-C (which replaced an earlier system in 1980) makes it possible for an experienced boat captain to find a rather small object, such as a rock outcropping, even if he has to run 50 or more miles to get there. Loran-C is accurate to within about 250 feet. Thus, once the captain gets this close, or even closer, he switches to the paper graph to find the exact spot. Some of these paper-graph units measure depths to more than 1,000 feet in segments as small as 1 foot. The captain also can use the unit to scan the water below as he travels, looking for bottom features or schools of fish.

Another navigational aid, one that eventually will replace Loran-C, is called GPS (Global Positioning System). Unlike Loran-C, which utilizes shore stations, GPS depends on a U.S. Department of Defense network of 24 navigational satellites. A GPS receiver with a liquid-crystal display is like Loran-C in that it checks your present location, calls up the location of your way point, then draws an imaginary straight line from where you are to where you want to go, whether you are out in the Gulf of Mexico or on an inland lake. You know precisely where you are at all times. Like Loran-C, it can also be utilized for establishing position, usually less than 100 feet from the way point, before calling on a depth-finder to locate the exact spot to fish. The fisherman has the option of a hand-held portable GPS receiver, used in conjunction with a depth finder, or a permanent-mount GPS/sonar unit for pinpoint location.

Your choice of which style depth-sounder to buy depends on your needs and what you are willing to pay. You should go look at the various units and be better informed about the capabilities of each type. But whichever type you select, read through the instruction manual time and again until you understand all the functions. It takes considerable study and experience to understand properly what is being viewed on the display. In a way it is like learning to use a computer. It seems awfully complicated at first, but once you master it, you will wonder how you ever got by without the machine.

Be reminded, though, that it is a tool, nothing more. It is no guarantee of angling success. The underwater world operates in mysterious ways. Fish are unpredictable and the angler never knows what to expect. That is why it is called "fishing" and not "catching."

SPORT-FISHING REGULATIONS

FISHING HAS EVOLVED from a rather simple sport into one involving all types of sophisticated equipment. Yet it remains a subjective pastime. Fishing in all its various forms is still just that—fishing. No method, no tools, no elitist status makes the catching of a carp or a sheepshead a lesser delight than catching a trophy largemouth black bass or a wild-leaping tarpon. Thankfully, we continue to have a choice.

In most cases, though, we do not have a choice as to what size fish we can catch and how many we can keep. We must adhere to rules and regulations established by the Texas Parks and Wildlife Department. And while there are general regulations for both fresh and salt water, there are many exceptions. Each year the department publishes its "Fishing Guide," and you can pick up a free copy wherever fishing licenses are sold. Every angler should obtain a copy and read it diligently (and it is not a bad idea to keep a copy in the boat or tackle box). Regulations can change, and many do from one year to the next, typically rules concerning a specific body of water or a specific fish species. Keep in mind the old saying: "Ignorance of the law is no excuse."

General Regulations

No state laws govern the taking of fish from private waters. If you are fishing a farm or ranch pond or a private lake, for instance, you do not need a fishing license, you can fish using any method you please, and what you catch and want to keep is up to you.

But it is like driving a vehicle: once you leave private property and get on a public road, your behavior is dictated by law. You have to play by the rules.

Anyone between the ages of 17 and 65 who fishes in public

waters must have a fishing license, along with a stamp, such as a Freshwater Trout Stamp or a Saltwater Sportfishing Stamp, if one is required. Additionally, a person 17 years or older must, while fishing, have in his or her possession a driver's license or a personal identification card issued by the Texas Department of Public Safety. All sport-fishing licenses and stamps are valid only from September 1 through the following August 31, except lifetime licenses and temporary licenses, both resident and nonresident, issued for a specific number of days. A resident is a person with U.S. citizenship, or an alien who has officially declared intent to become a citizen, and who has resided in Texas for more than six months immediately preceding application for a license.

The lone exception is the first Saturday in June, the annual free sport-fishing day. No person fishing public waters is required to have a fishing license or stamps for this one day.

Size and Creel Limits

All of the popular game fish in fresh and salt water are regulated by laws restricting the catch. These restrictions assume various forms: legal minimum length; maximum size; catch and release only; slot limit; and creel and possession limits.

With minimum legal lengths being pretty much the norm, a measuring stick is an important piece of equipment. A minimum length is self-explanatory; if a fish such as a saltwater speckled trout has a 15-inch minimum length, it has to be longer than that to be legal. It is the same with maximum length; if the fish is longer than the maximum it cannot be retained. Catch and release is just that; every fish caught must be released. Slot limits take two forms. An outside slot is widely used in black bass management. With a 15–21 slot, for example, any fish less than 15 inches or longer than 21 must be released. Then there is an inside slot used in redfish management. With a 20–28 inside slot, only fish 20 to 28 inches long can be kept. A creel limit is how many fish of any species—those of legal length—can be retained in one day of fishing. The possession limit is twice the daily limit.

Use these guidelines to measure fish correctly:
1. Place the fish on its side with the jaw closed.
2. Squeeze the tail fin together or turn it in a way to obtain the maximum overall length.
3. Measure a straight line from the tip of the snout to the extreme tip of the tail fin.

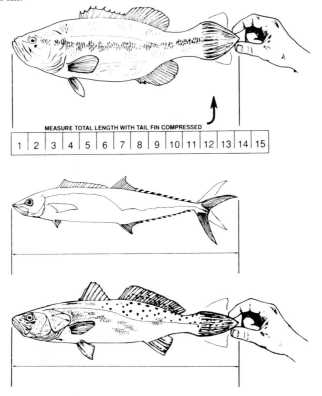

Saltwater regulations are general for the entire coast and are relatively easy to understand. There are legal minimum sizes, some maximum lengths, and daily creel limits. The regulations for any fish species are the same no matter where you fish.

Freshwater regulations, however, can vary from one body of water to another, particularly those involving largemouth black bass. It is not unusual for three reservoirs in the same region to have three different sets of regulations concerning bass. And the regulations for any lake can change from one year to the next.

At the same time there are general uniform statewide regulations for largemouth bass along with other species such as catfish, crappie, striped bass, and white bass. These regulations, which apply to waters without specific laws (exceptions), mandate legal minimum length and the daily creel limit. General laws concern most public waters.

The general laws along with the exceptions are explained in the Texas Parks and Wildlife Department's "Fishing Guide."

Another way fishing has changed, especially over the last couple of decades, is this more structured set of rules involving more fish species. Changes have been dramatic. The days of catching and keeping a lot of fish are gone.

Many factors determine the supply of fish to be caught, but according to fisheries biologists, one crucial factor is harvest or catch. Laws of just a few years ago didn't address the problem of overfishing except for a few species. As a result, many fish stocks in both fresh and salt water suffered the consequences of fishermen catching and keeping too many fish, especially undersized fish. Natural reproduction couldn't keep up. Fishing success declined. This led to numerous changes in our fishing regulations.

Attitudes had to change, too. Consider the Gulf of Mexico. In this vast sweep of water it seemed inconceivable that abundant fish stocks such as king mackerel (kingfish), red snapper, and sharks could be threatened. But we underestimated the efficiency of commercial and sport fishermen, mostly commercial fishermen armed with modern technology. Millions of tons of fish were being caught, fish of all species, from Spanish mackerel to marlin. The pressure took its toll. Sport fishermen suddenly found they were catching only a fraction of the fish they were accustomed to catching. Declining fish stocks led to regulations for commercial and recreational fishermen in both state waters (out nine nautical miles) and federal waters (nine and beyond) that dictate how we fish today.

In fresh water, it was the same story with such species as white bass and crappies. Some years ago even biologists argued that sport-fishing pressure had no significant impact on the numbers of these prolific fish. But subsequent studies proved otherwise. Over the state fewer fish were being caught, and the fish being caught were smaller. Now, as with other freshwater fish, there are legal minimum lengths and creel limits for white bass and crappies.

But laws are not the total answer. To do any good, regulations must have the cooperation of fishermen, and to give regulations support, fishermen must be sold on their intent: to improve the fishery.

Size limits are intended to protect fish in a way that maintains a strong population of fish considered to be prime spawners. Size equates to age and sexual maturity, and minimum lengths keep fish in a body of water long enough to let them spawn at least once before they become legal length to catch. (Maximum lengths with some saltwater fish serve the same purpose.)

Daily creel limits also help neutralize fishing pressure. Since fewer fish are being taken from a body of water, there are more fish left for future fishing trips. It is sort of a tradeoff. While a fisherman might be limited in number as to how many fish he can keep and take home to eat, there also are more fish left to be caught, keeping the fishery healthy.

The basic control factor, however, is legal length limits. Over time, fish of a certain size become stacked, particularly school-type fish such as crappies, white bass, and saltwater speckled trout. With a 15-inch minimum length, for instance, fish become "stacked" at about 14 inches or slightly longer. On a fishing trip when the fish are biting, a fisherman might catch many fish, but most will be just shy of the legal limit. Few if any will pass the minimum-length test. This is a result of fishing pressure skimming off the 15-inch keepers.

We are, in many cases, talking in fractions of an inch. Consequently, you must first know what the legal length is for the species you are after and then what the proper procedure is when measuring fish. If there is any doubt about a fish's length, release it. A fraction of an inch could prove expensive if you're stopped by a game warden.

And one more thing. Handle a fish gently while measuring. The tendency is to push down on the fish while it is on a measuring board, trying to stretch the fish to its maximum length. This could prove harmful. Don't bother to measure a fish that's obviously not long enough. Release it immediately.

APPLYING FOR A RECORD

STATE AND WORLD RECORDS for a species are noted at the end of each individual fish profile in this book. You will note that in several cases the state record exceeds the world record for a species. If you catch a fish weighing more than either one of or both the listings, you can submit it for possible record recognition. But since records are constantly changing, you might check to see if you have a record for that species before processing the paperwork.

There are various ways to get your name on a record list or lists. State records include only the greatest weights of the various species in both fresh and salt water. World-record lists not only recognize the largest all-tackle records, they also have listings for different line classes (including one listing for fly-tackle only). It is possible for the weight of a line-class record taken on 4-pound line to exceed in weight the same species of fish caught on 12-pound line. So check not only the all-tackle listings to see if the fish you caught is a record, but also consult the line- class records. For the most part, the two world-record lists compiled by two different organizations are virtually identical, since once necessary documentation is completed, the information is sufficient to get recognition from both record keepers.

The two most common and well-known lists are the all-tackle records (world records) and the Texas state records.

Other lists include world line-class records; fly-fishing all-

World and state records in this guide are listed as recognized on May 1, 1993.

tackle records; fly-fishing tippet (leader) records; state private-waters rod-and-reel records; state public-waters records (the biggest fish species caught from individual public lakes, rivers, bay systems, and the Gulf of Mexico); and state public waters, unrestricted category (the biggest fish caught by means other than rod and reel).

For more information concerning record books and procedures, write:

State records: Texas Parks and Wildlife Department, 4200 Smith School Rd., Austin, TX 78744.

World records: The International Game Fish Association, 3000 E. Las Olas Blvd., Fort Lauderdale, FL 33316 (freshwater and saltwater); and the National Fishing Hall of Fame, P.O. Box 33, Hayward, WI 54843 (freshwater only).

Requirements are essentially the same for all three (some Texas records and all-tackle world records are the same), although when you apply for a possible line-class world record, the first 25 feet or more of the line used in the catch must be included with the application.

The standard "Form for Submitting Record Fish," available from many tackle stores or any TP&WD office, is preferred since it has all the questions with appropriate blanks to be filled in to make the application official.

These requirements are: species; weight; length; where caught; tackle used; other details of catch; name of angler, permanent address, home and business telephone numbers; location of scales; type and capacity of scales; Texas Department of Agriculture certification number and date; weightmaster's name and address; name, signature and address of one disinterested witness to weighing; notarized statement signed by angler that the fish described was hooked, fought and landed by him or her personally (although help is permissible when netting or gaffing the fish), and all the other information submitted is true and correct; and a clear photograph showing full length of the fish in relation to a recognizable object, preferably a yardstick. An additional photo with angler and his catch is also desired. Spotted bass and sunfish specimens (only) must be examined (may be frozen) by a TP&WD fish biologist. Shark record submissions must include teeth, patch of skin, or other verification of species.

With the exception of those fish eligible for unrestricted state-records classification (such as those taken by trotline, bow and arrow, speargun, or other device), all fish submitted for freshwater and saltwater divisions (both state and world records) must be caught on rod and reel, and—this is crucial—taken by the person making the application with no help from anyone else in fighting the fish. If an angler hooks a fish, then hands the rod to someone else, he is disqualifying himself.

WANT TO HAVE IT MOUNTED?

EVERY FISHERMAN is after the big one, the fish of his dreams. As long as a fish is of legal size, the angler can have it mounted and hang it on the wall. But the bigger it is, the more the mount will cost. With fish, taxidermists charge by the inch.

There is another thing you should know about taxidermy. The mount may look like the fish you caught, but most fish mounts today are replicas. With a replica, all the taxidermist has to do is order a pre-molded fish of the right size and species from a supplier and then add artificial skin, paint, and glass eyes.

You can still have it mounted the old-fashioned way, using the fish's skin and head and maybe even the fins and tail. Some taxidermists who specialize in fish still prefer to use the real fish, particularly when making unusual custom mounts. But most prefer to work with artificial skin and parts because fish typically have some damage to the skin and fins that is hard to repair, and also because making a replica eliminates the tedious job of skinning the fish, treating the skin with some sort of preservative, and letting it dry for weeks before painting it. And despite what you may have heard, using the fish's parts won't enable the taxidermist to make the mount larger or smaller than the fish you caught. Fish skin won't stretch, nor will it shrink, after it has been tacked onto the form, or "mannequin," to dry.

A mount can be, if you prefer, a combination of the real thing and a lookalike. For example, it might be a body replica of your sailfish fitted with the fish's bill. The only problem with this approach is that it still involves killing the fish. Releasing it and buying a mount to match the size makes more sense.

For the best replica, take precise measurements of the fish—the size of the head in relation to the body, the size of the mouth, the belly (if the fish is a female with eggs), and any other unusual features.

Whether made from real or artificial parts, however, the final product depends on the paint job to make the fish appear realistic. Fish, with their blends of many colors, are difficult to render, and some taxidermists have more talent than others. An accomplished fish taxidermist has to be an artist, blending shades of lacquer with a spray gun and adding detail with a brush to attain the right look. So if you have a camera with you, take several close-up photographs of the fish immediately after it is caught. When a fish has been out of the water for any length of time, its coloration fades. A photo will give the taxidermist a color guide to make the mount look as much like the actual fish you caught as his talent will permit. Otherwise, he will have to depend on color illustrations in a book.

A Guide to the Freshwater Fish

TEXAS possibly has more fish in a wider variety than any other state. Nature is only partly responsible. Man has given her a helping hand.

Back when I was growing up, fishermen went to streams and rivers close to home. If there was a reservoir nearby, that was a bonus. Only a few man-made lakes existed, such as Buchanan on the Colorado River and Possum Kingdom on the Brazos.

There still are stretches of rivers—an estimated 16,000 miles—that provide quality fishing, but access to most rivers is usually through locked gates and is not available to everybody. The same is true of farm and ranch ponds, which have proliferated over the past three decades. Those private fishing holes that are managed properly produce fish in both quantity and quality. But a majority of anglers do their fishing in lakes and reservoirs open to the public.

There are a lot of them to be fished—approximately 650, varying in size from urban lakes not much larger than a couple of acres to giants covering thousand of acres, constituting almost 1.8 million surface acres, according to the Texas Parks and Wildlife Department. During the dam-building boom of the 1960s and 1970s, reservoirs were created on every major watershed. Some of them are huge bodies of water, such as Toledo Bend, Sam Rayburn, Falcon, and Amistad.

These big lakes somewhat overshadowed the smaller reservoirs, most covering less than 2,000 acres, that were being built at the same time. These were power-plant reservoirs to be used in generating electricity. A bonus byproduct was some quality fishing, especially for bragging-sized largemouth black bass. Because access could be controlled at these fenced-in reservoirs, which are owned by municipalities, river authorities and utility companies, the fishing resource could be managed.

As some of the lakes began to age, though, productivity slackened. The Parks and Wildlife Department's Inland Fisheries Division, headed by the late Bob Kemp, turned things around with a grandiose plan: import species with better genetics, such as the Florida-strain largemouth bass, or those that would fill a certain niche. Striped bass, brought here from South Carolina, began to prowl the open waters of large reservoirs, preying on the abundance of gizzard shad that had grown too big for white bass to eat. Smallmouth bass, using broodstock obtained from Arkansas, were introduced into steep-sided, rocky lakes where largemouth bass, which prefer weedy, shallower reservoirs, were not reproducing in sufficient numbers and growing to provide quality fishing.

The results have been spectacular. Anglers regularly catch Florida bass weighing more than 12 pounds from many different reservoirs. Smallmouth bass are thriving in the deep, clear impoundments in the central and western portions of the state. Striped bass in the 30-pound class are breaking lines and have many fishermen mumbling to themselves. Hybrid stripers, a cross between the striped bass and white bass, are providing a lot of angling sport in numerous reservoirs. Walleyes are being caught at Lake Meredith in the Panhandle, as well as at a few other lakes. Saltwater red drum (redfish) are doing quite well and growing to big sizes in some warmer-water power-plant reservoirs.

At the same time, native species such as northern largemouth bass, sunfish, white bass, crappie and catfish are holding their own, as management tools including minimum-size restrictions and daily catch limits are being used to control angling pressure.

Thanks to the combination of these factors, plus the awareness of fishermen toward the need for protecting our natural resources, the future of Texas' inland fishing does indeed appear bright.

Freshwater Fish

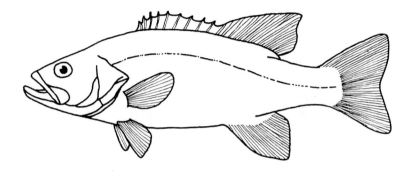

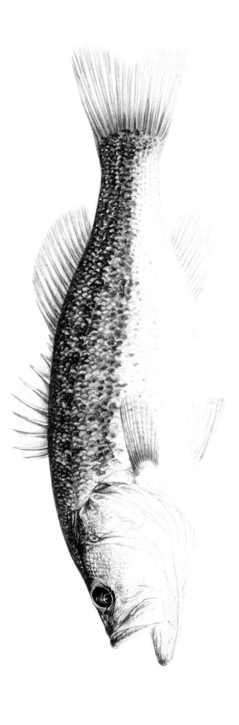

LARGEMOUTH BASS
(*Micropterus salmoides*)

DESCRIPTION: Also called black bass and bigmouth bass, the largemouth is not a true bass but rather is the largest member of the sunfish family, Centrarchidae. Its basic color is green, with an irregular stripe, called the lateral line, lengthwise along its sides. The back is dark green shading to a lighter green, sometimes almost white mouth bass spawn at a temperature range of 65° to 68°F. Spawning activity occurs in quiet water 2 to 8 feet deep, on a firm bottom rather than mud. Bass do not nest in colonies as do the smaller sunfishes such as bluegills. The male fans out a nest and attracts a female that may lay from 2,000 to 26,000 eggs, depending on her size, which are fer-

with a yellowish tint, on the underside. Richness of the green varies with water clarity. The largemouth is distinguished from the smallmouth and spotted bass by several characteristics, most notably its large mouth. The maxilla, or upper jaw, extends to a point back beyond the eye, while the jaw of the smallmouth or spotted bass goes only to the eye. The forward (spinous) portion of the dorsal fin is almost completely separated from the rear (soft-rayed portion) of the dorsal fin by a notch. Average size is 1 to 5 pounds, although in places where the Florida largemouth bass has been introduced, it is not unusual for the fish to exceed 10 pounds.

HABITS/HABITAT: A very adaptable fish, the largemouth bass is found in large reservoirs, farm and ranch ponds, rivers and creeks statewide. It grows fastest in shallower lakes with good water clarity, abundant vegetation, and adequate forage species such as small sunfish and shad. It tends to inhabit shallow water in spring and fall, deeper water in winter and summer. This bass likes to hang along dropoffs between deep water and shallow, in or near some type of cover. It is most active when water temperature is 65° to 75°F. Large-

tilized immediately. The female is chased away and the male guards the eggs and maintains a constant circulation with fin movement to prevent their suffocation. The fry hatch in about 5 to 10 days and remain in a compact school guarded by the male. The first food is microscopic animal life called plankton, and insect larva. Upon reaching a length of about 2 inches, fingerling size, they become active predators, eating most anything they can catch, even other bass. At 1 year the fish will measure about 12 inches and weigh about a pound, maybe an ounce or two more. Life expectancy is about 6 to 8 years, but some fish reach age 10, although a fish this old is uncommon.

REMARKS: This is the most-sought fish in the state, as it is found in great numbers in such a variety of waters, from private ponds to large lakes. It will take both natural and artificial baits and can be caught in all seasons.

STATE RECORD: 18.18 pounds. Lake Fork. January 24, 1992. Barry St. Clair. Klondike.

WORLD RECORD: 22 pounds, 4 ounces. Montgomery Lake, Georgia. June 2, 1932. George W. Perry.

SMALLMOUTH BASS
(*Micropterus dolomieui*)

DESCRIPTION: The smallmouth bass also is a member of the sunfish family, Centrarchidae. The fish is not as deep-bodied as the largemouth bass and grows to only about half the size. The spinous dorsal fin is not as high as that of the largemouth, and the notch between the 2 parts is shallow. The mouth is smaller, and the maxilla extends back only to the eye. Coloration is to 10 days, and protects the fry until they are capable of making it on their own. Growth rate will depend on the habitat, but in a reservoir, a smallmouth will be 8 to 9 inches long at 1 year old and will weigh about half a pound. It lives about as long as the largemouth.

REMARKS: The smallmouth bass is not native to Texas. It was first introduced in the early

greenish-bronze shading to a whitish underside, with barlike markings along the back and sides. Adults tend to be uniform in color, almost a rich golden hue with bar markings. In clear water with a dark background the fish is darker in color; in silty water, it is lighter. Average size runs from about 1 to 2 pounds in reservoirs, less than a pound in streams.

HABITS/HABITAT: The smallmouth bass likes deep-sided, rocky, clear reservoirs; gravel bottoms and cooler water; and fast-flowing rivers in the western part of the state. A principal food source is the crayfish. It is not as inclined to hang around floating or submerged vegetation and generally is found in deeper water than the largemouth. The fish is most active in spring, fall and early winter. Smallmouth bass spawn in the spring when water temperature is between about 59° and 65°F. While the largemouth likes quiet water, the smallmouth prefers some current. Also, the smallmouth typically nests in slightly deeper water than does the largemouth. The male prepares the nest and attracts a female that will lay between 1,000 and 10,000 eggs. The male smallmouth then fans the nest until the eggs hatch, in about 4

1970s, originally using broodstock from Arkansas, later from Tennessee. It has adapted best in steep-sided, clear, rocky reservoirs such as Meredith, Texoma, and Whitney. Fish weighing more than 5 pounds are now being caught. A smallmouth bass is a stronger fighter than a largemouth of comparable size.

STATE RECORD: 7.72 pounds. Lake Whitney. November 20, 1988. Ron Gardner, Whitney.

The teeth of a hooked fish or the sharp edges of some underwater obstruction can nick a fishing line and weaken it. These nicks are normally near the end of the line and invisible to the eye. Sometimes you can feel any roughness by running the line through your fingers. Even better is to run it through compressed lips, which are more sensitive. If you detect any roughness, break off that segment of line and retie your hook or lure.

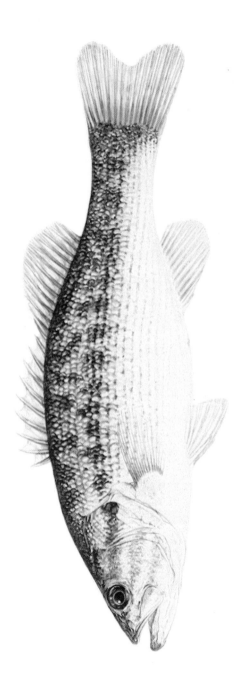

SPOTTED BASS
(*Micropterus punctulatus*)

DESCRIPTION: The spotted bass, also called the Kentucky spotted bass, is a member of the sunfish family and sometimes is confused with the smallmouth bass, since body configuration and coloration are similar. Varying shades of green color the back and sides, and there is a whitish underside. In a way it resembles a cross between its largemouth and smallmouth cousins. It has the irregular lateral line of the largemouth and the small mouth of *M. dolomieui*. Also, the max- back into a reservoir. Like the smallmouth, it prefers some current when spawning. Although there is a spurt of early growth, the overall growth rate is not as rapid as either the largemouth or smallmouth. At age 1, the fish will average 7 to 9 inches and weigh a half-pound, perhaps less.

REMARKS: Spotted bass are most abundant in eastern reservoirs and rivers like the Sabine, Neches and Cypress. It is a strong fighter for its size, and is highly sought as food.

illa does not extend back beyond the eye, and the dorsal fin is not as deeply notched as the largemouth's. It does, though, have its own distinctive markings: a series of black dots or splotches below the lateral line, and an elliptical spot resembling a rough growth on the tongue. Open the mouth and you can see the spot, or run your finger over the tongue and it feels like sandpaper. Average size is about a pound or less, with anything over 3 pounds being considered unusually large.

HABITS/HABITAT: Native to the Colorado River drainage system and waters eastward, the spotted bass prefers the deeper water of reservoirs. It also likes clearer streams with gravel bottoms where riffles and pools are present. The fish's preferred diet is crayfish supplemented by smaller prey fish and insects. Like other members of the family, the spotted bass is most active in spring and fall. Spawning occurs at about 65°F in a manner similar to that of the largemouth and smallmouth. There is some evidence, however, that the spotted bass is more migrant than its cousins, moving upstream to spawn in small tributaries, then drifting downstream into deeper pools or

STATE RECORD: 5 pounds, 9 ounces. Lake O' the Pines. March 13, 1966. Turner Keith, Austin. WORLD RECORD: 9 pounds, 4 ounces (tie). Both from Lake Perris, California. February 24, 1987; Steven M. West. April 1, 1987; Gilbert J. Rowe.

A weak line is the fish's ally. After some time on a reel, monofilament takes a set, coming off in loops instead of in a smooth flow, and it can become brittle, particularly if exposed to direct sunlight. Change line at least once a year, preferably more often, depending on how much you fish.

One place where fish like to gather—and one that is sometimes overlooked by the fisherman—is the area around a bridge piling. The shade attracts everything from black bass and sunfish to crappies.

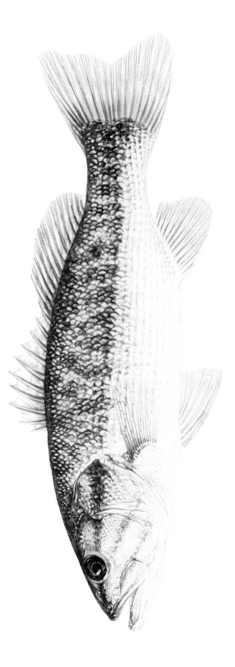

GUADALUPE BASS
(Micropterus treculi)

DESCRIPTION: The Guadalupe bass is the smallest of the sunfish-family bass found in Texas. The fish is a slim specimen that looks almost identical to the spotted bass, including the more blotched, irregular lateral stripe, and the small, rough tooth patch. There generally will be 12 separate spots or spots along the side. These spots on a spotted bass normally are loosely connected fished on or near the bottom. Spawning habits closely correspond to those of the spotted bass, in about the same places and at the same water temperature. The Guadalupe is a very slow-growing fish. At age 1 it will be no more than 6 inches long, if that. Any fish weighing more than 2 pounds is rare, particularly in its river habitat.

REMARKS: The Guadalupe bass is the offi-

and number fewer than 12. The only true identification, though, is through scientific liver analysis. Average size is a half-pound or less, although Guadalupes in reservoirs are typically larger than those in streams.

HABITS/HABITAT: The Guadalupe bass is found in the fast-flowing streams and deep reservoirs of central Texas and no place else in the world. It is the predominate spotted bass in Hill Country lakes and rivers, and if you catch a spotted-type bass in these waters, it is more than likely a Guadalupe. The fish thrives in swift, clear rocky rivers with pools and riffles, and also in deep and clear reservoirs. It tends to hang around steep rocky banks and rock jumbles instead of near aquatic vegetation. Like the smallmouth and spotted bass, it is more of a deep-water resident than is the largemouth, feeding primarily on underwater food rather than that found on or near the surface. The staple diet is crayfish and small prey fish like minnows, although hellgrammites rate high with stream fish like the Guadalupe bass. These fish are most active in spring and fall but they are not inclined to come into shallow water to feed. The most productive baits will be

cial state fish of Texas. It was long thought to be a subspecies of the spotted bass, but in 1955 it was declared a distinct species after extensive scientific analysis. Guadalupe bass prefer a clean, clear-water environment and are most abundant in the Guadalupe River and the Colorado River drainage, including the Llano and Pedernales rivers and the Highland Lakes chain, particularly Lake Travis just west of Austin. The Sabinal River in the Lost Maples State Natural Area in Bandera County is a Guadalupe bass sanctuary. Only catch-and-release fishing is permitted.

STATE RECORD: 3 pounds, 11 ounces. Lake Travis. September 25, 1983. Allen Christenson, Jr., Austin.

WORLD RECORD: Same.

> When fishing a surface lure for bass, cast your bait toward the sun and bring it by your target—a stump maybe—so that the fish can turn and hit the plug away from the sun. Bass seem to strike the lure better going away from the sun than they do going into the sun.

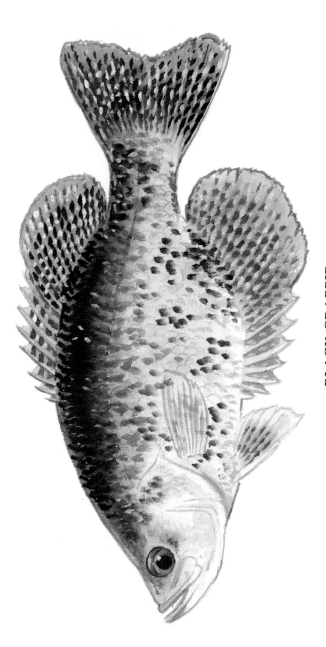

BLACK CRAPPIE
(*Pomoxis nigromaculatus*)

DESCRIPTION: The black crappie, sometimes called speckled perch, belongs to the sunfish family, Centrarchidae. Coloration is silvery-green, sometimes with a yellowish tint, with an nest in colonies, as do white crappie, although black crappie usually spawn a bit earlier, when water temperature is about 60°F. Young black crappie tend to seek more cover than do white crappie.

overlay of irregular dark blotches. The fish tends to be more deep-bodied than the white crappie, and the markings on the sides of the black crappie are irregular (jagged) while the bars on the white crappie are distinct and vertical. The black crappie has 7 or 8 spines in its first dorsal fin, compared to only 6 on the white crappie. The male black crappie does not assume breeding coloration in the spring, unlike the white crappie male, which turns much darker. Average size is three-quarters of a pound or less, with any fish more than 1 1/2 pounds considered large.

HABITS/HABITAT: The black crappie is limited mostly to the clear, acid-type waters in the eastern part of the state. It moves into shallow water in the spring to spawn but otherwise is a deep-water fish, doing best in larger bodies of water. It is very cover-oriented, a school of crappies, often a large number of fish, will gather in and around brush piles, submerged trees and rock piles. Except when spawning, crappies are seldom found in water less than 12 feet deep. Their primary diet is minnows and shad, although adult black crappies feed on more insects and crustaceans than do adult white crappies. Black crappie

The growth rate of the black crappie is slightly less than the white crappie's. The fish does not do well in ponds because it is fecund, quickly over-populates, consumes all the available food, and dies out. The fish is short-lived; a 4- to 6-year life-span is about maximum. Slow growth coupled with a short life expectancy is the reason a black crappie typically does not grow very large.

REMARKS: Crappies are cyclic, particularly in smaller lakes, with populations fluctuating greatly. The crappie is better appreciated for its superior table quality than its value as a sport fish.

STATE RECORD: 3 pounds, 11 ounces. Toledo Bend Lake. January 17, 1985. Fritz Gowan, Poplar Bluff, Missouri.

WORLD RECORD: 4 pounds, 8 ounces. Kerr Lake, Virginia. March 1, 1981. Carl Herring, Jr.

Lowering and raising an anchor spooks fish. When you move into an area you intend to fish, ease the anchor down slowly. Don't pitch it overboard with a mighty splash.

WHITE CRAPPIE
(Pomoxis annularis)

DESCRIPTION: The white crappie, widely known as the white perch, is the other crappie species in the state, and it also belongs to the sunfish family. Its coloration is silvery-green shading to a darker green along the back, with several vertical dark bars on either side. The first dorsal fin

Adults feed almost entirely on minnows and shad. Life expectancy is 5 to 6 years.

REMARKS: White crappies will be in deep water, often along a dropoff such as an inundated creek channel, except when they are spawning. They can be caught both day and night. Where an

has a maximum of 6 spines, while that of the black crappie has 7 or 8. During the spawning season the male white crappie turns darker, more black than white, making identification confusing. But the fairly uniform vertical bars along the sides of the white crappie and the dorsal spine count distinguish it from the black crappie. Average size is a pound or less; any white crappie exceeding 2 pounds is rare.

HABITS/HABITAT: The white crappie, found statewide, spends most of its life in deep water except in the spring, when it goes into sloughs, coves and tributary streams to spawn in shallow water. Like other members of the sunfish family, it is a nest builder. White crappie normally nest in colonies over a gravel or sand bottom in water 2 to 6 feet deep and at a temperature of about 65°F. They spawn deeper in clear lakes than they do in murky water. An adult female is highly prolific, laying up to 150,000 eggs. The fry hatch in about 5 days and begin feeding on microscopic animal life. Once they reach fingerling size, the school begins to roam, eating tiny baitfish and insects. Growth is slow, about 3 to 5 inches the first year, with a 2-year crappie being 7 to 8 inches long.

angler takes one, he will usually catch several. The best bait is a small live minnow, but crappies will hit tiny jigs. The white crappie is thought by some to be one of the finest fish you can put on the dinner table.

STATE RECORD: 4 pounds, 9 ounces. Navarro Mills Lake. February 14, 1968. G. G. Wooderson, Corsicana.

WORLD RECORD: 5 pounds, 3 ounces. Enid Dam, Mississippi. July 31, 1957. Fred L. Bright.

Should you be fishing for crappies and action suddenly ceases, that doesn't mean the fish have quit or left. A school of crappies has the tendency to move vertically, up or down. Try fishing deeper or shallower and you might locate the fish again.

An electric knife makes filleting fish quick and easy. Use it as you would a conventional fillet knife.

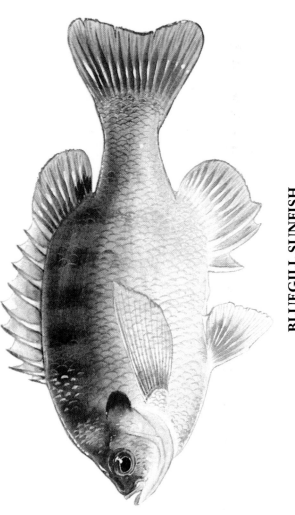

BLUEGILL SUNFISH
(*Lepomis macrochirus*)

DESCRIPTION: The bluegill, also called a perch or bream, is the best known of the smaller members of the sunfish family, Centrarchidae. It is often confused with other family members of similar size because these fish are much alike in

in summer, normally early and late in the day, its presence marked by dimples on the surface as it feeds on insects. Bluegills spawn over an extended period of time, with some activity occurring through the summer, beginning when the

shape, fin formation (the forward spinous dorsal fin is contiguous with the second soft dorsal) and habits. The bluegill, though, can be identified by several distinguishing characteristics: a deep, compressed body that's almost round; a dark spot at the base of the dorsal fin; small mouth; the ear flap has a flexible rear edge and is short, broad and dark to the margin; the pectoral fin is long and pointed; and there are vertical bars on the sides. Coloration can vary greatly depending on water clarity, but the sides are generally green with some lavender, brown, copper or orange tint. The throat is often yellowish, even rust-colored. The breeding male is usually more brilliantly colored, the fore-part of the belly being orange-red or orange-yellow. Average size is about 4 to 6 inches, with anything over a half-pound being considered large.

HABITS/HABITAT: The bluegill is an adaptable fish that thrives in a variety of waters, from small ponds to large reservoirs. But it does best in East Texas lakes that have a lot of shallow water and vegetation. The fish is most active in spring and fall, but it often prowls the shoreline shallows water temperature reaches about 70°F. They nest in colonies, or what some fishermen call "brim [bream] beds." Numerous bluegills can be caught when the spawning fish are concentrated. As many as 50 nests are sometimes crowded into a small area. At such times, one of the most effective baits is the gray cricket. Since all carnivorous fish feed on the bluegill, nature has made this species highly prolific, with a single female laying from 12,000 to 65,000 eggs. The eggs and fry are tended by a very protective male. Thus, bluegills in waters where predation is not adequate can soon over-populate, resulting in numerous stunted speci-mens. Insects are the bluegill's principal food. At age 1, a typical bluegill is about 4 inches long.

REMARKS: Ounce for ounce, the bluegill is probably the "fightingest" fish in fresh water. It is delicious to eat and is often fried whole.

STATE RECORD: 0.86 pound. Corpus Christi. April 18, 1993. William Smith, Mathis.

WORLD RECORD: 4 pounds, 12 ounces. Ket-ona Lake, Alabama. April 9, 1950. T. S. Hudson.

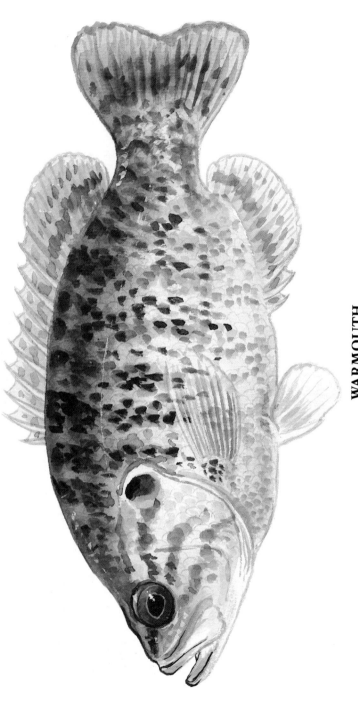

WARMOUTH
(*Lepomis gulosus*)

DESCRIPTION: The warmouth, nicknamed goggle-eye and stumpknocker, is a member of the | times in one season. A female will lay from 4,500 to 65,000 eggs. The male guards the nest and eggs,

sunfish family. The body shape is similar to that of a small black bass, including the largemouth. The eyes are large and have a tinge of red. Coloration ranges from a grayish-green back with a light-yellow belly to a darker appearance: mottled brown on the back and sides, with golden belly and lower sides. The male has a bright orange spot on the dorsal fin. Average size is about 4 to 6 inches, with a half-pound fish considered large.

HABITS/HABITAT: The warmouth is found statewide, although it is most abundant in the eastern portion of the state. It is essentially a lake or pond fish, preferring quiet, weedy water over a soft bottom. An adult warmouth is more carnivorous than other sunfishes; crayfish, snails and small fish comprise a major part of its diet. The warmouth is a nest builder, but it seldom congregates in "beds" as other sunfish do. Nests are built in a varying range of water depths and at varying distances from shore. The fish seem to prefer weed beds, sunken logs and rubble in silty water over a soft bottom rather than open water. Spawning activity begins at about 70°F, with incubation taking about 34 to 35 hours at 72°F. The warmouth may spawn an indefinite number of but once fry depart the nest area, they get no parental care. Because newborn fish immediately seek the sanctuary of thick weeds, the survival rate is high, resulting in overpopulation, particularly in ponds. Young warmouth feed on insects. The first-year growth is normally 4 inches or less.

REMARKS: The warmouth likes to hang around stumps and cypress knees, normally feeding at a greater depth than most other sunfish. It will readily hit small artificial lures like a spinnerbait. The warmouth is edible, but it should be skinned before cooking because the skin often has a muddy taste.

STATE RECORD: 1.30 pounds. Town Lake. July 19, 1991. Ralph Manns, Jr., Austin.

WORLD RECORD: 2 pounds, 7 ounces. Guess Lake, Florida. October 19, 1985. Tony Dempsey.

> One of the most effective artificial baits for taking a variety of freshwater fish is the leadhead jig. All game fish like a crayfish, and a jig resembles a crayfish.

GREEN SUNFISH
(Lepomis cyanellus)

DESCRIPTION: The green sunfish, also called a goggle-eye or rock bass, belongs to the sunfish family. It is greenish in color with an orange or yellowish border on the dorsal, anal and tail fins. sively. He also protects the fry until they are able to make it on their own. This results in a high survival rate of a very prolific species, which leads to overpopulations in most bodies of water. Conse-

There are faint vertical bars on the sides of the bass-shaped body. Some scales are tipped with turquoise, giving the appearance of rows of color. The eyes are large and prominent, and the mouth is large. The back of the upper jaw extends to the middle of the eye. The pectoral fin is broad and rounded. Typical weight is 4 to 6 ounces, although some specimens might grow to a half-pound or more.

HABITS/HABITAT: The green sunfish, found statewide, is primarily a stream fish, although it also inhabits reservoirs and ponds. It normally hangs along the edge of a sluggish current. While it seems to show a fondness for a silty or mud bottom, it can also be found in clear-running small rivers and creeks with sandy beds. Adults feed on insects and small fish. Green sunfish nest in colonies in late spring and through the summer, with spawning activity beginning at about 70°F. Each nest may be 6 inches to about 2 feet in diameter, depending on the size of the male that builds it, over a bottom of gravel or sand. The female lays from about 12,000 to 65,000 eggs. The male hangs over the nest, keeping the eggs alive with gentle motions of his fins, and defends the nest aggres-

quently, the fish seldom reach a size desirable to fishermen.

REMARKS: With its larger mouth and greenish color, a green sunfish looks something like a miniature largemouth bass. It will readily hit small natural baits like a grasshopper, along with tiny artificial lures. The fish is edible but very bony.

STATE RECORD: 0.65 pound. Joe Pool Lake. May 12, 1990. Richard A. Collins.

WORLD RECORD: 2 pounds, 2 ounces. Stockton Lake, Missouri. June 18, 1971. Paul M. Dilley.

Although fish in medium and small rivers and even creeks typically are not large by lake standards, they pull hard in the running water. I like to match my tackle to the fish, using light or ultralight spinning or spin-cast gear. Light tackle gives the fish more of a fighting chance, making big fighters out of little fish.

REDEAR SUNFISH
(*Lepomis microlophus*)

DESCRIPTION: The redear sunfish, also known as the shellcracker, is dark olive above, yellow to green on the sides, shading to almost white on the belly. The mouth is small, about the same size as that of the bluegill, although the redear's body is more elongate. Pectoral fins are very long and pointed. The most notable characteristic is the red edge on the opercle flap (ear) of the male and the flexible orange ear flap of the female. During the spawning season the coloration of the male redear becomes much more vivid and bright, but the color quickly fades once the fish is taken from the water. Average size is 6 ounces or so, although 8-ounces-plus fish are not uncommon from some waters.

HABITS/HABITAT: The redear sunfish, found statewide, does best in small lakes and ponds. It is more of a bottom fish than the bluegill and other, smaller sunfishes. It feeds primarily on worms, aquatic insects, small crustaceans and mollusks. Like the bluegill, the redear nests in large colonies. Because the redear spawns in deeper water, it does not have the prolonged spawning season of most other sunfish. Males prepare the nests when water temperature reaches about 70°F. One or more females might deposit several thousand eggs in the same nest. The male guards the nest. Incubation period is from 5 to 10 days. Average growth is about 3 inches the first year. Life expectancy is about 4 to 6 years. The greatest number of fish are caught in spring and early summer during the spawn. Since the redear spawns in deeper water, the "beds" can be hard to locate. Persistent bubbles rising to the surface in a small area often reveal a colony of nests. Productive baits are tiny crayfish, earthworms or gray crickets. Redears can be caught at other times of the year but the angler has to fish near bottom with natural baits to take them with any consistency.

REMARKS: Redear sunfish, available from commercial fish growers, are widely stocked in combination with largemouth bass in farm ponds and stock tanks. Most larger redears that are caught come from ponds with strong bass populations that prevent the sunfish from overpopulating. The redear is delicious but has numerous small bones.

STATE RECORD: 0.69 pound. Cleburne State Park Lake. April 9, 1993. David Owens, Cleburne.

WORLD RECORD: 4 pounds, 13 ounces. Merritt's Mill Pond, Florida. March 13, 1986. Joey M. Floyd.

LONGEAR SUNFISH
(*Lepomis megalotis*)

DESCRIPTION: The longear sunfish is probably the most colorful member of the sunfish family. The male is a brilliant orange or, in some clear water are easily seen; the many oval-shaped depressions are tightly bunched and rimmed by sand, silt or debris. Spawning activity commences

instances, scarlet. Because of a bluish tint on the head it is sometimes confused with the bluegill, but it can be identified by several characteristics, especially the wide, long, flexible opercle flap or "ear," which is always trimmed in white. The pectoral fin is short and rounded, and the cheeks usually carry wavy turquoise markings. Average size is only about 4 inches.

HABITS/HABITAT: The longear, a very adaptable fish, is common statewide, except in the Rio Grande Valley, where it is rare. It occurs in about the same places as the bluegill and is most abundant in reservoirs and ponds. The major difference between the two is that the bluegill grows larger, making it more desirable among fishermen. The longear eats a wide variety of foods, but its main diet is aquatic and flying insects. It often moves into the shoreline shallows to feed, dimpling the surface as it picks off insects. The greatest number of fish are caught, though, when they are "bedding" for the spawn. A colony of longear sunfish nests is often mistaken for a group of bluegill nests. Like the bluegill, the longear spawns in large "beds" over a prolonged period of time, from late spring through most of the summer. The nests in at about 70°F, with males preparing the nests. A single female will deposit thousands of eggs, and one or more females might share the same nest. The male keeps the eggs alive with fin action, at the same time guarding the nest against any intruder. The male also aggressively protects the newborn fry, which hatch in about 5 to 10 days. Growth is slow, the fish barely reaching 4 inches after 2 years. As with other sunfish, overpopulation and stunted specimens are common.

REMARKS: The longear sunfish is edible but bony.

STATE RECORD: 0.18 pound. Lake Texoma. September 14, 1992. John Hardin, Farmers Branch.

WORLD RECORD: 1 pound, 12 ounces. Elephant Butte Lake, New Mexico. May 9, 1985. Patricia Stout.

A fisherman is no better than his tackle. When it fails, he fails. Invest in quality tackle. It will pay off in the long run.

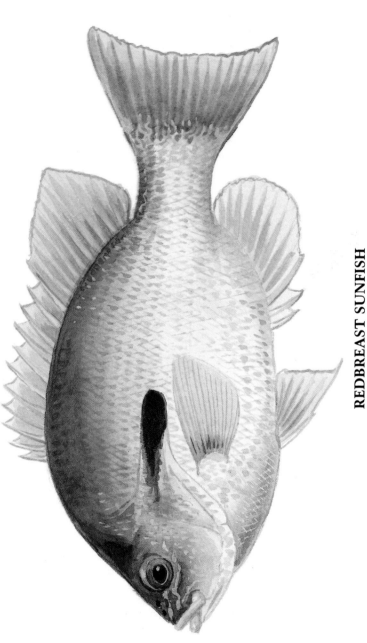

REDBREAST SUNFISH
(*Lepomis auritus*)

DESCRIPTION: The redbreast sunfish, also called the yellowbelly perch and sunperch, has a | before scattering. The fish will grow about 4 to 6 inches the first year. Life expectancy is generally

bluish-black back shading to a belly that is an orange or reddish, sometimes yellow, color. The lighter shades of belly color turn much more brilliant during the spawning season. The narrow black ear flap grows to a length of about an inch or more on an adult fish. The mouth is moderate in size. The redbreast is one of the state's larger sunfishes, occasionally attaining a weight of almost 1 pound, but the average fish weighs about a half-pound.

HABITS/HABITAT: The range of this adaptable fish is statewide, although it is uncommon in the western third of Texas. At home in reservoirs, ponds, rivers and bayous, it tolerates faster water than most other sunfish species and is probably the dominate sunfish in the fast-flowing clear rivers and creeks of central Texas and in other parts of the state. It feeds on insects, worms, crustaceans and small fish. When spawning, the redbreast resembles the other true sunfishes, although a typical colony of redbreast nests won't be as large as that of bluegills. Also, the typical redbreast female does not lay as many eggs. The male prepares the nest and protects the eggs and fry. After hatching, the young may remain schooled for several weeks thought to be about 4 to 6 years. The redbreast is most active in spring and fall, but it can be caught in the summer, hitting natural baits like worms and grasshoppers and small top-water poppers and plugs. Because of its larger size and aggressive nature, it is very popular with fishermen, especially fly fishermen.

REMARKS: The redbreast is delicious to eat, sometimes growing large enough to fillet.

STATE RECORD: 1.25 pounds. Guadalupe River. May 2, 1987. Rock Layne Hamilton, Dallas.

WORLD RECORD: 1 pound, 12 ounces. Suwannee River, Florida. May 29, 1984. Alvin Buchanan.

Fly fishing is easy to learn when you understand that balanced tackle is the key to effortless casting. Rods and lines are labeled with numbers and you want to match them. Thus, for a 6-system rod, buy a 6-weight line. In fly fishing, you are casting the line, not what's on the end of the line.

HYBRID SUNFISH
(*Lepomis microlophus* × *Lepomis cyanellus*)

DESCRIPTION: The hybrid sunfish is a cross between a redear female sunfish and a male green sunfish, and any offspring can have varying characteristics of both parents. The hybrid typically has the large mouth and orange-fringed fins of the father, but also has the red ear tab of the mother. It is deep-bodied and thick through the shoulders. Young hybrid sunfish tend to be pale in color, but adults become much more colorful. Average weight is about 12 ounces, with some specimens attaining more than a pound.

HABITS/HABITAT: The hybrid sunfish was developed for small lakes and ponds where sunfish tend to overpopulate. There is some reproduction between hybrid sunfish and native stock, if there are any true sunfishes in the lake or pond, but it is minimal. Ideally, the hybrid sunfish should not be stocked in waters where other sunfish species are not found. It is intended to be a put-and-take fishery, replenishing with another age class after about half the original fish that were stocked are caught.

REMARKS: Hybrid sunfish are available only through commercial fish producers for private

stocking purposes. The fish is quite adaptable and under most conditions it seems to grow larger and faster than either parent since it is capable of taking advantage of a wider variety of foods. It is fine eating, with most specimens being large enough to fillet.

STATE RECORD: None.

WORLD RECORD: 1 pound, 3 ounces. Walker Farm Lake at Olive Branch, Mississippi. April 6, 1986. Troy M. Wright.

If you are fishing with a live minnow or some other baitfish, keep in mind that if the fish is hooked through both lips, it tends to swim down; hook it in the back slightly behind and above the dorsal fin, though, and the tendency is for it to struggle upwards. But avoid running the hook through the spine, the middle part of the body. That will paralyze the minnow.

ROCK BASS
(Ambloplites rupestris)

DESCRIPTION: The rock bass, also called the redeye bass or goggle-eye, is a member of the sunfish family. The fish has a large red eye and they hatch, in about 5 to 7 days; he protects the young for a short period afterwards. Growth is slow, and a year-old fish usually will be no more

rounded pectoral fins. Coloration is bronze with small dusky spots. Juvenile fish tend to have irregular dark vertical bars on the sides. A dark blotch is usually located at the upper edge of the gill cover. It can be distinguished from the warmouth and other sunfishes by the 6 spines in the anal fin. Also, it normally has 11 spines in the first dorsal fin while other sunfishes have no more than 10. Average size is 5 to 6 ounces.

HABITS/HABITAT: Rock bass live primarily in streams and rivers in the central part of the state, although a few are in the deeper, clear reservoirs of the Edwards Plateau. The fish likes clear water with rocks and gravel bars. Although the rock bass can be caught throughout most of the year, spring and fall are the better periods. The staple diet consists of insects and small crayfish and fish. One of the better baits for catching it is an earthworm, although it will hit a wide variety of small artificials, such as spinnerbaits and diving plugs. Spawning begins when the water temperature is about 60° to 70°F, normally over a gravel bottom. The male fans a circular nest, encourages a female to lay her eggs (which will range from 5,000 to 10,000) then guards the eggs until

than 3 inches long. The rock bass is not nearly as abundant and widely distributed as are other sunfishes.

REMARKS: The rock bass is found in about the same places as Guadalupe and smallmouth bass. Most rock bass are caught accidentally while fishing for other bass. The fish is not generally sought for food because of its small size and numerous small bones.

STATE RECORD: None.

WORLD RECORD: 3 pounds. York River, Ontario, Canada. April 1, 1974. Peter Gulgin.

Grasshoppers are good fish bait, but sometimes they are difficult to catch. Try hunting at night, using a bright light to look for grasshoppers on weed stems or Johnson grass. The light blinds a 'hopper and you can pick it off. Another prime time is early of a summer morning. A grasshopper's wings are damp with dew and it is not nearly as elusive.

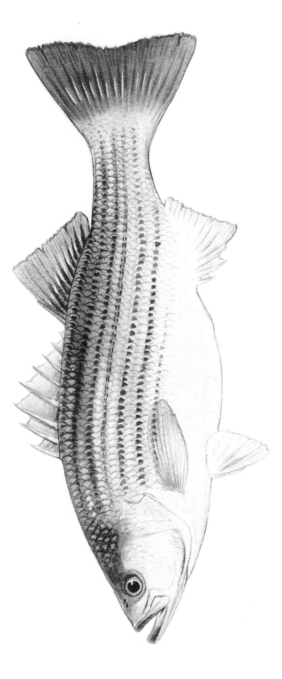

WHITE BASS
(Morone chrysops)

DESCRIPTION: The white bass, commonly called the sand bass, is a freshwater representative of the temperate bass family, Percichthyidae. The dorsal fin is composed of 2 separate parts, with the front spiny portion distinctly separated or log. They are not guarded. The current keeps them alive until they hatch, in only 2 or 3 days. If no running water is available, white bass will spawn on windswept sandy beaches. The young fish will grow to about 8 inches during its first

from the rear soft-rayed portion (one spine is located at the anterior of the soft dorsal). The anal fin has 3 spines, the first only half as long as the second, and the second only half as long as the third. Coloration is dark along the back, silvery on the sides, and white underneath. The sides are streaked with several longitudinal, incomplete dusky lines. Average size is a pound or less, but in some waters, 2-pound specimens are not unusual, although fish this size are considered large.

HABITS/HABITAT: The white bass is primarily an inhabitant of large reservoirs statewide where its principal food, gizzard and threadfin shad, is most abundant. Except when in tributary streams to spawn, white bass prefer the open waters of a lake. Most spawning activity is from February into April, depending on area of the state and water temperature (58° to 62°F). The fish does not build a nest; it is a "free spawner." Males precede the females into tributary streams. Spawning activity is mostly at night in shallow, running water. The adult female releases her load (she is capable of laying more than a half-million eggs) and the male fertilizes the eggs. They drift and sink until they contact some object such as a rock

year. Life expectancy is about 4 years, one reason the fish doesn't grow any larger than it does.

REMARKS: The white bass spends most of its time in deeper water, but when feeding, particularly early and late in the day during summer and fall, a ravenous school of them can be seen chasing shad at the surface, chopping water with their frenzied action. The white bass is highly desired as food.

STATE RECORD: 5 pounds, 9 ounces. Colorado River below Longhorn Dam in Austin. March 31, 1977. David S. Cordill, Spicewood.

WORLD RECORD: 6 pounds, 13 ounces. Lake Orange, Virginia. July 31, 1989. Ronald L. Sprouse.

> Varying the retrieve can make a difference in angling success. If you are getting no action, try slowing your reeling. The common tendency is to retrieve too rapidly. But sometimes it also can be the other way. Speeding up the retrieve will turn the fish on.

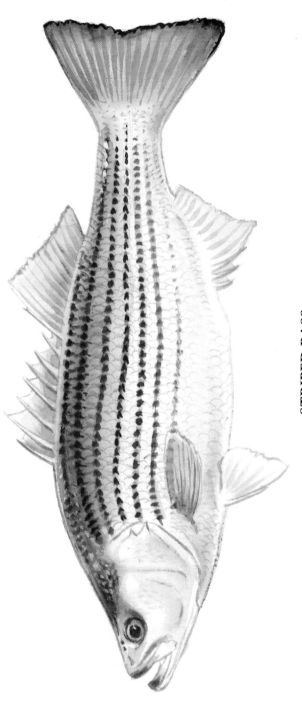

STRIPED BASS
(Morone saxatilis)

DESCRIPTION: The striped bass, also called the striper, belongs to the family Percichthyidae. Identification of large specimens is easy, but smaller striped bass are sometimes confused with white bass, since coloration is essentially the same or at night during hot weather. Stocked stripers will be 11 to 12 inches long after the first year, but after that, growth is rapid. Life expectancy is about 10 years, maybe slightly longer for females.

REMARKS: The striped bass is an anadro-

same. There are differences, however. The horizontal black stripes along the sides of the striped bass are uninterrupted. The striped bass has 2 razor-sharp points on each gill cover while the white bass has only 1. The striped bass has 57 to 67 scales in the lateral line, the white bass 52 to 58. The striped bass tends to be slim while the white is deep-bodied with an elevated back. Average size is 5 to 10 pounds, although fish more than 20 pounds are not uncommon.

HABITS/HABITAT: Since striped bass require a tremendous amount of food, they are stocked statewide only in large reservoirs. Primary food is gizzard shad. The fish is most active from late fall through the winter into spring. It can tolerate colder water better than most other fishes. Schools of striped bass are prowling about in shallow water in cold weather and can be caught on topwater plugs. During the summer, stripers tend to suspend in deep water, in the coolest water to be found with adequate oxygen, normally in the lower part of a reservoir near the dam and often over some sort of structure such as submerged trees. The suspended fish will be in schools and be of similar size. They typically feed early and late in the day,

mous species, meaning that it lives in both fresh and salt water. It is not native to Texas waters, but has been widely introduced into many reservoirs since the mid-1970s. For the most part, the striped bass is a put-and-take fishery; there is no consistent natural reproduction, the one exception being in Lake Texoma. Stripers need a stretch of water about 50 miles long in a major tributary like the Red River (which feeds Texoma) to keep the eggs in motion until they hatch. The fish is good to eat, but any red meat in a fillet should be trimmed out, since this part has a strong flavor.

STATE RECORD: 45 pounds, 8 ounces. Town Lake. March 1, 1993. Morris Boyd, Austin.

WORLD RECORD: 67 pounds, 8 ounces. O'Neill Forebay, St. Luis, California. Hank Ferguson.

In any fishing, concentration is essential. You have to concentrate to fish a bait properly and to detect a bite. Also, your strike trigger is cocked and you can react much more positively to set the hook.

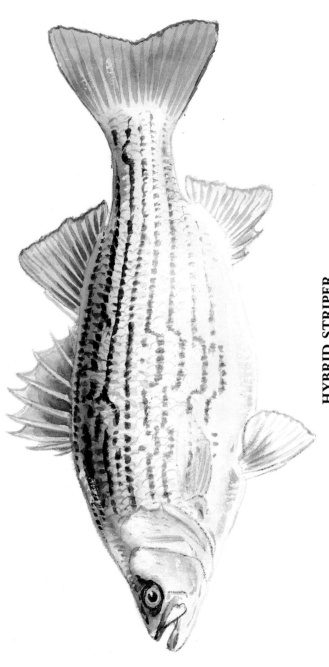

HYBRID STRIPER
(*Morone saxatilis* × *Morone chrysops*)

DESCRIPTION: The hybrid striper is a cross between the female striped bass and the male white bass. The hybrid possesses some characteristics of both its parents. The coloration is basi- water timber. It also becomes active at night, around lights. Although natural conditions prevent it from reproducing successfully, the hybrid striper does go through the motions in the spring.

cally the same for all, silvery-white with narrow black stripes. But the hybrid striper, with its deeper body and arched back, more closely resembles the white bass than the striped bass in configuration, especially when comparing smaller specimens. Usually, the fish can be identified by the stripes along the side. A striped bass has unbroken, distinct stripes; the hybrid striper's are distinct but usually broken (ragged) or chainlike. The white bass is characterized by much less distinct horizontal stripes. Average size is about 2 to 6 pounds, with any fish better than 10 pounds considered large.

HABITS/HABITAT: The hybrid striper is found in many reservoirs statewide. It has adapted quite well to warmer power-plant reservoirs along with smaller (less than 3,000 acres) conventional impoundments. The fish is most active from fall through the winter into spring, when it is roaming about in search of shad, its basic food. It normally prowls in schools of varying sizes. Generally, it will possess some of the behavioral patterns of both its parents, schooling to chase shad on the surface when the water temperature is cool, suspending in deep water in the summer. The hybrid striper is more inclined to suspend right in under-

A typical female will be heavy with eggs. The fish also will migrate upstream to seek the running water of a tributary. Initial growth of stocked fish for the first few years is much more rapid for hybrid stripers than it is for striped bass.

REMARKS: Hybrid stripers are generally stocked in smaller reservoirs where striped bass won't do as well. The fish is a very strong and determined fighter. It is good to eat, but any red meat in a fillet should be cut out.

STATE RECORD: 19 pounds, 10.56 ounces. Lake Ray Hubbard. June 20, 1984. John Haney, Dallas.

WORLD RECORD: 24 pounds, 3 ounces. Leesville Lake, Virginia. May 12, 1989. David Lambert.

Any change in the weather that moves the barometer either up or down usually triggers fish feeding activity. The change doesn't have to be abrupt. Sometimes it is only a change in wind direction, such as that which results from the passage of a weak cold or warm front.

YELLOW BASS
(Morone mississippiensis)

DESCRIPTION: The yellow bass belongs to the temperate bass family, Percichthyidae, and is not feed as readily near the surface as do white bass. One of the prime times to take them is in

often confused with the white bass of similar size, although the white grows larger. Any fish in question that weighs about a pound is almost without exception a white bass. There are other, more reliable, identifying features, however. The yellow bass is dark olive above, silver to golden on the sides, and white to yellow on the belly. The golden color becomes more vivid on a spawning male. The dorsal fins of the yellow bass are joined. The second anal spine is as long or longer than the third. The body stripes of the yellow bass are more prominent, and the lower two below the lateral line are irregular or broken near the tail. Average size is about 5 inches, with maximum size being about 10 inches.

HABITS/HABITAT: The fish is native to waters in the northeastern part of the state, including Caddo Lake, the Cypress, Sabine and Red rivers, and reservoirs along these river systems. Some have been transplanted over the years into impoundments on the upper Trinity River watershed. Good numbers are caught in spring and summer in places like Lake Fork, Caddo Lake and Lake Tawakoni. The smallish fish normally roam in large schools, similar to white bass, but they do early spring, when they are moving into tributary streams to spawn. They feed primarily on insects, crustaceans and small fish. A live minnow or any tiny lure that resembles a fish is a productive bait. Since they normally feed considerably below the surface, the bait must be presented deep. Yellow bass spawn in the current of tributaries or along wind-blown lake shores, although the fish are not as dependent on moving water for spawning as are other members of the bass family. The eggs are extremely small and are distributed at random over gravel and rock. There is no parental care of eggs or newborn. Fry feed primarily on insects. Growth rate is slow, reaching a size of 4 to 5 inches the first year, growing only 1 or 2 inches a year thereafter.

REMARKS: Yellow bass are not actively sought because of their size, but they are fun to catch on ultralight tackle, using the same methods that work on white bass. The fish is edible but bony.

STATE RECORD: None.

WORLD RECORD: 2 pounds, 4 ounces. Lake Monroe, Indiana. March 27, 1977. Donald L. Stalker.

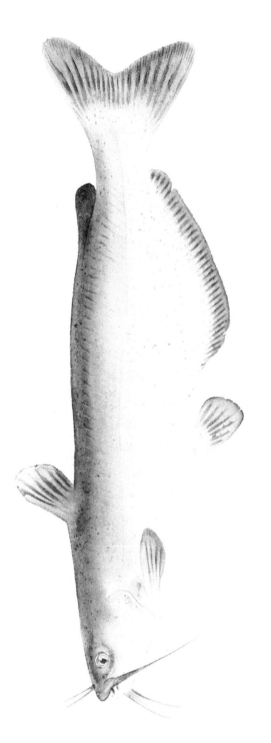

CHANNEL CATFISH
(Ictalurus punctatus)

DESCRIPTION: The channel catfish, sometimes called the spotted cat or fiddler cat, belongs to the family Ictaluridae, as do all the other catfishes. The head is small and narrow. Coloration of smaller specimens is silvery-white, and normally the sides are marked with numerous black dots. Older fish turn darker and the color along female away, guards the entrance to the nest and may devour the eggs if they are disturbed. Normal incubation takes from 6 to 10 days. The newborn, protected by the male, feed mostly on aquatic insect larvae. Growth is rapid, about 10 inches the first year.

REMARKS: The channel catfish not only is

the back is more silvery-gray, shading to a silvery-white along the belly. On larger adults the spots are either obscured or absent. The anal fin always has 24 to 29 rays. The stiff spines on the dorsal and pectoral fins are needle-sharp and bear a toxic substance. Average size is 1 to 2 pounds, but some catches of 10 pounds or so are possible. Any channel catfish larger than 20 pounds is unusual.

HABITS/HABITAT: The channel cat is the most abundant of all the catfishes, being found statewide in all our streams and reservoirs. It has been widely stocked in small private lakes and ponds. The fish are caught most readily in spring and fall, although they are taken through the summer, especially at night. The channel catfish is both a predator and scavenger, the food ranging from fish, both alive and dead, to insects, mollusks and vegetable matter—just about anything it can find. Commercial stink baits and blood baits are popular with fishermen after channel catfish. The fish spawn when the water temperature reaches 75°F. The nests are in an underwater cave, hollow log or rock crevice. A female weighing about 2 to 4 pounds lays about 4,000 eggs per pound of body weight. The male, after chasing the

sporty to catch, but it is also highly prized as food. It is the catfish grown commercially in aquaculture. An angler should be cautious when taking a fish off the hook. The sharp fin spines can inflict painful punctures that might become inflamed and even infected.

STATE RECORD: 36 pounds, 8 ounces. Pedernales River. March 7, 1965. Mrs. Joe L. Cockrell, Austin.

WORLD RECORD: 58 pounds. Santee-Cooper Reservoir, South Carolina. July 7, 1964. W. B. Whaley.

A catfish has a very sophisticated sense of taste or smell that permits it to locate food without actually seeing it. The "nose" is composed of the barbels, or what some people call whiskers. There are 8 of these appendages around the mouth and nostrils. This ability to smell is why you can catch catfish from muddy water.

BLUE CATFISH
(Ictalurus furcatus)

DESCRIPTION: Also called the hump-back cat or sea cat, the blue catfish is often confused with its close relative the channel catfish. Body configuration is similar, although the blue cat tends to be more blocky. Both have forked tails. Coloration is also similar; especially confusing is will eat most anything that is available, alive or dead. Initial growth is slow, about 6 inches the first year, but the growth rate picks up dramatically about the third or fourth year. This, along with a life expectancy of 10 years or longer, is why blue catfish attain large sizes.

that a channel cat can have a "blue" color phase. The coloration of the blue catfish is slate-blue above, shading to white on the underside. Adults have no black spots on the sides. The blue catfish has a larger head than does the channel catfish, and the upper jaw protrudes slightly beyond the lower. The anal fin is long. The most reliable way to identify the fish is to count the rays in the anal fin. The blue catfish has 30 to 36, the channel cat only 24 to 30. The blue catfish also has a strong sharp spine along the anterior edge of its dorsal and pectoral fins. Average size is 5 to 10 pounds, although blue cats commonly reach sizes exceeding 25 pounds.

HABITS/HABITAT: The blue catfish is found statewide in rivers and reservoirs. Fish are caught in greater numbers in spring and fall, and some are taken during the summer months, mostly at night. Spawning habits are similar to the channel cat, at a water temperature of about 70° to 75°F. A popular spawning spot in a reservoir is a rock crevice in the riprap of the dam. Incubation period is about 10 days. The young feed on insect larvae and a variety of vegetable matter, while adults

REMARKS: The blue catfish, unlike the channel catfish, does not frequent the smaller streams, preferring instead the big, deep rivers with sluggish currents. It has been widely stocked in reservoirs and is highly prized as food.

STATE RECORD: 82.5 pounds. Lake Texoma. February 20, 1993. Jason Holbrook, Howe.

WORLD RECORD: 109 pounds, 4 ounces. Cooper River, South Carolina. March 14, 1991. George Lijewski.

Despite the conventional wisdom, catfish in a reservoir are not always found on or near the bottom. Sometimes they will be suspended closer to the surface. When you start fishing, use two rods and fish baits at different levels, one near the bottom, another about halfway up. Vary the depth periodically until you locate fish. Then you can hold one rod and fish at that level.

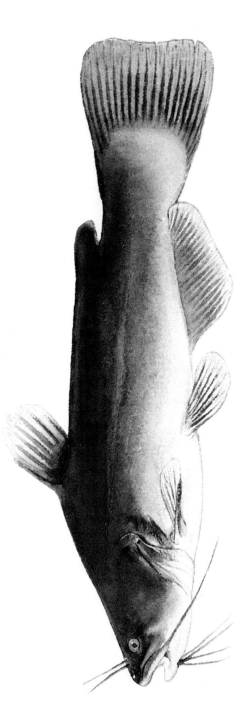

BLACK BULLHEAD CATFISH
(Ictalurus melas)

DESCRIPTION: The black bullhead catfish is commonly called the mud cat or polliwog. Coloration is black to greenish-black on the back, shading to gray or white on the belly, although a fish from muddy water might be more yellowish than black. The tail is square, the chin barbels black. There are 17 to 24 rays in the anal fin. Aver-

REMARKS: The state has another bullhead species, the yellow bullhead catfish (*Ictalurus natalis*). It is similar to the black bullhead in shape, size, habitat and range. Coloration is light yellow to olive-green on the back, shading to white on the belly. The head is relatively large and the chin barbels are white. There are 23 to 27

age size is 6 to 8 ounces, occasionally a pound or more.

HABITS/HABITAT: The black bullhead is mostly found in small lakes and ponds statewide. Bullheads prefer murky or muddy water. The fish is a scavenger and is particularly active in hot weather. Almost any kind of bait, rancid or otherwise, will take bullheads. The bullhead is different from other more-popular catfishes in that the pectoral fin is minus strong barbs, although it is capable of finning the careless fisherman. Bullheads often show up in ponds where they are not wanted. They can survive in a habitat that is more mud than water, and, unlike the channel cat, can reproduce in ponds and quickly overpopulate. Spawning occurs in late spring or early summer in saucer-shaped nests constructed by the parents on a mud bottom. There will be 2,000 to 12,000 eggs and both parents guard the nest. Incubation lasts 4 to 6 days, depending on water temperature. Compact schools of baby bullheads may be seen swimming on the surface, giving the appearance of a small, dark cloud in the water. Bullheads do not do well in clear water.

rays in the anal fin. Because the typical bullhead is small and the soft flesh tends to have a muddy taste, it is not generally sought as food.

STATE RECORD: 4.02 pounds. Navarro Mills Lake. June 10, 1984. Roy Calame, Wortham.

WORLD RECORD: 8 pounds. Lake Waccabuc, New York. August 1, 1951. Kani Evans.

World record yellow bullhead: 4 pounds, 4 ounces. Mormon Lake, Arizona. May 11, 1984. Emily Williams. (No state record.)

River catfish usually can best be caught on natural foods. Their diet is varied, depending on what is available. The grasshopper, for example, is a summer food. Crayfish are high on the spring diet because the crawdads are small and soft-shelled, just the way catfish like them. Other top baits include worms, hellgrammites, minnows, frogs and store-bought shrimp.

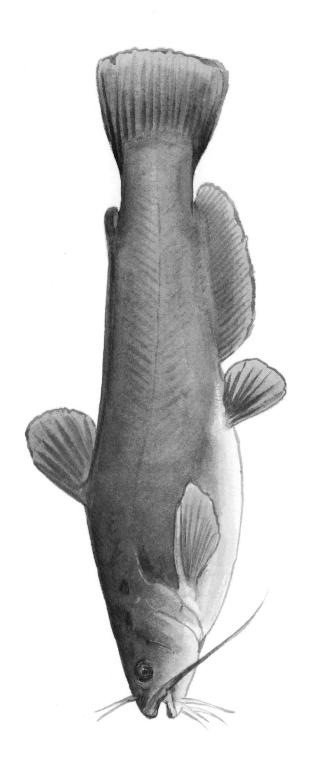

Yellow Bullhead Catfish
(Ictalurus natalis)

If you plan to anchor in one spot to fish, put out an anchor at either end of the boat, with the bow pointed into the wind, to better hold it in position. Should you plan on fishing at night, get on the water before dark so you can better pick a prime spot and see what you are doing. Or scout in the daylight, mark a spot with a sealed plastic jug, and return to it after dark. Lights for night fishing are most effective when there is no moon.

Want to improve your odds of catching catfish? Try baiting a hole. It's easy. Put some grain sorghum (maize) or wheat in a bucket, cover the grain with water, and set it in the sun for a few days until it becomes mushy and soured. Scatter some of the stinky stuff in the area you intend to fish. It will bring catfish in.

If you buy a carton of catfish bait and use only a part of it, don't throw the rest away. Seal the container tightly and put it in the freezer. The bait will last indefinitely.

Knot failure is one reason the big fish always seem to get away. After you've tied a knot, check it before making a cast. Monofilament can be difficult to tie, especially in dim light, and unless it is tied properly, the knot will slip and give easily.

A pair of needle-nosed pliers or a pistol-shaped hook remover is better than fingers when you are trying to free a hook that a fish has taken deep in its throat. You can usually reach the hook and remove it without injuring the fish.

FLATHEAD CATFISH
(Pylodictis olivaris)

DESCRIPTION: The flathead catfish, better known as the yellow cat or Opelousas cat, has a body configuration unlike that of other members of the catfish family: the shovel-like head has a projected lower jaw; the mouth is as wide as the head, the anal fin is short, having only 12 to 18 rays; and the tail is not forked. Coloration varies long will typically lay from 7,000 to 11,000 eggs. The young hatch in 4 to 6 days and immediately seek shelter under rocks or brush—in flowing water, if available. Fingerlings, which are virtually black in appearance, feed on living larvae during their first year, then become fish eaters. Adults feed almost exclusively on fish, taking

with water quality. In clear water the adult is dark to olive-brown with dark brown, mottled markings on the side; the belly is light yellow or creamy white. In muddy waters it is lighter yellow, sometimes losing the mottled appearance. Also, after a fish has been on a line for some time, stress turns the color from dark to a vivid yellow. Average size is 5 to 10 pounds, but fish weighing more than 40 pounds are regularly caught.

HABITS/HABITAT: The flathead catfish is found statewide in all major river systems and reservoirs. The fish does best in large rivers and reservoirs with a strong forage (fish) base. Flathead catfish are caught from spring through the fall, more regularly in late spring and fall. The bigger specimens are normally taken on devices such as trotlines and limblines. A live sunfish is a favored bait. Spawning runs from late spring through midsummer. A male selects an underwater cave, hollow log or rock crevice for spawning, his preference being for a rocky area. After enticing a female to lay her eggs, the male runs her away and stands guard at the mouth of the cave or crevice. He is a vicious defender. A female about 2 feet

whatever is available, even other catfish. Initial growth is slow, about 6 inches the first year, but on into the third or fourth year, growth accelerates. A 50-pound specimen is about 10 years old. Some fish live as long as 18 to 20 years.

REMARKS: A big flathead catfish is a prized catch. Since the fish is a predator that feeds on fish, one occasionally will hit an artificial lure. It makes fine table fare because of its preference for good water quality and its natural-food diet.

STATE RECORD: 98 pounds. Below Lewisville Lake Dam. June 2, 1986. William O. Stephens, Lewisville.

WORLD RECORD: 92 pounds, 4 ounces. Lake Lewisville, Texas. March 28, 1982. Mike Rogers.

Flathead catfish often feed at night just before the moon comes up. Find out when the moon will rise and be on the water an hour or two before that. If the moon rises late, around midnight or later, that's really a prime time.

FRESHWATER DRUM
(*Aplodinotus grunniens*)

DESCRIPTION: Also known as the gasper-gou or gasper, the freshwater drum is a member of the family Sciaenidae. It is silvery-gray on the top, males gather on a spawning ground, the females deposit their eggs while males simultaneously fertilize them, and the eggs are allowed to drift

shading to silver sides and white belly. One taken from murky water tends to be more of a metallic grayish hue. The body is deep and laterally compressed with a round, overhung snout. The tail is rounded. Average size is 1 to 3 pounds, although specimens weighing more than 10 are not unusual.

HABITS/HABITAT: The freshwater drum is found statewide in all major rivers and reservoirs. It is a stream fish that has adapted to impoundments in large numbers, and does as well, if not better, in murky rivers as it does in clear ones. Drum feed on the bottom because that is where they find preferred foods such as freshwater clams, mussels and crayfish. The drum's pharyngeal teeth and powerful jaws permit it to crush the tough shells of the invertebrates it eats. Drum can be caught year-round, but one of the prime times is in the spring, when water temperature reaches the mid-60s. Drum move upstream to find running water where they can deposit their eggs. If a dam gets in the way, they mill about below the structure, sometimes concentrating in large numbers, and a lot of them are caught. The crayfish is a productive bait. The drum, like the white bass, does not build a nest for spawning. Females and wash until they stick to vegetation and underwater obstructions where they remain until they hatch. The adults make no effort to guard the eggs or the resulting offspring. The young feed on bottom insects. Growth is relatively slow for a fish of its size. At a year of age it will be about 10 inches long and weigh 5 or 6 ounces. The fish has been known to live for more than 15 years.

REMARKS: The drum, a distant relative of the saltwater croakers, is one of the few fishes capable of making a sound. It has lower throat bones covered with coarse, blunt teeth, and a very large air-bladder. A combination of these features permits it to make its deep croaking or drumming sound. Another characteristic is a pair of "lucky stones." These two bones are located on each side of the head, slightly back of and above the eyes. Each has a distinctive L etched on it. Carry these stones and they are supposed to bring luck.

STATE RECORD: 31 pounds. Lake Arrowhead. May 4, 1978. Larry D. King, Wichita Falls.

WORLD RECORD: 54 pounds, 8 ounces. Nickajack Lake, Tennessee. April 20, 1972. Benny E. Hull.

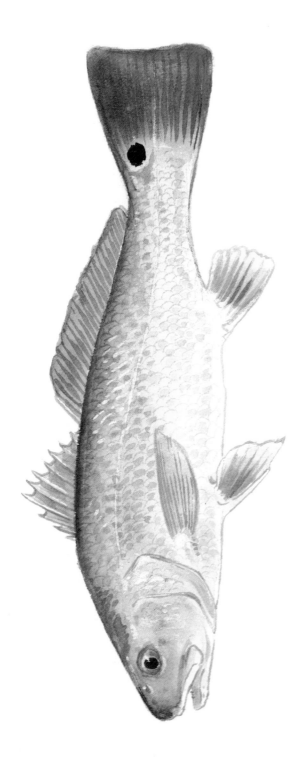

FRESHWATER RED DRUM
(*Sciaenops ocellatus*)

DESCRIPTION: The snub-nosed red drum, better known as the redfish, is elongated in shape and thick through the shoulders. The dorsal fin is contiguous, and the scales are large. Typical coloration is a vivid coppery-red shading to a white also is productive at times. Generally, though, at some time of the day the fish leave deep water and move into the shallows near shore, and bank fishermen catch them with regularity, using chicken livers as a favorite bait. The growth rate of freshwater red drum is generally faster than redfish in their natural saltwater habitat. A year-old fish might be 12 inches long or more. Life expectancy is more than 5 years and fish of 30-pounds-plus are possible.

REMARKS: In power-plant reservoirs around the state where it has been stocked, the red drum has become one of the most-sought fishes. The fish not only grows to large sizes but is a very strong fighter. It is prime table fare.

STATE RECORD: 30.25 pounds. Braunig Lake. October 14, 1989. Jack Talbert, San Antonio.

WORLD RECORD: None.

A plastic worm or grub is usually thought of as a bottom bait, to be bounced along in stop-and-go jerks. For a change of pace, fish a worm or jig with a twister-type tail as you would a diving plug. Cast, let it sink to the desired level, then retrieve steadily. The fluttering tail provides all the action you need.

---

belly, although the color turns flat or dull rapidly after the fish is caught. There is no other fish in freshwater that looks like it, in either shape or color. The most notable marking is a large black spot on either side of the caudal peduncle, just forward of the tail fin. Occasionally, a specimen might have multiple spots. Average size is 5 to 10 pounds, although fish larger than 20 are not unusual.

HABITS/HABITAT: The red drum is a saltwater species (see page 134) that has been introduced into fresh waters statewide. It does best in reservoirs that have a warmer year-round water temperature and a higher level of salinity. It is a put-and-take fishery, since the fish do not reproduce in fresh water. Survival rate of stocked fish, however, is very high. Red drum stocked in fresh water have shown a tendency different from their saltwater counterparts, which spend most of their time in shallow water. The fish stay mostly in water about 15 to 20 feet deep off points, and fishermen use deep-running plugs and downriggers to get down to them. Winter fishing is normally slow. The prime period is from mid-spring through the summer into fall. Drift-fishing with live bait

YELLOW PERCH
(Perca flavescens)

DESCRIPTION: A member of the perch family, Percidae, the yellow perch has a distinctive coloration: a yellow or olive-yellow body overlaid with dark or blackish vertical bands. The belly is pale and the anal fin orange-pink. The fish has no not spawn in Texas every year. But only irregular spawns are needed since the fish is fecund, the female laying from 10,000 to about 50,000 eggs, depending on her size. Large schools spawn in small areas, such as shallow coves and sloughs. Growth

canine teeth in the jaws or roof of the mouth. Average size is 6 to 8 ounces, with any fish weighing more than a pound considered large.

HABITS/HABITAT: The yellow perch's natural range includes much of Canada and the northern U.S., but it has been stocked in Panhandle waters such as Lake Meredith and Greenbelt Reservoir. It is a school fish that likes the open waters of a reservoir. While the fish will move into shallow water in the winter, once the water heats up, they migrate into greater depths, out of the fishermen's reach. The late-winter to early-spring spawning season is a prime time to catch them in numbers. The yellow perch is primarily a fish eater, including shad and minnows. The most productive bait is a small live minnow. But even during the winter in shallower water a bait must be presented near the bottom, since the fish seldom are distributed vertically. Yellow perch need a water temperature of 45° to 50°F to spawn. It takes around 12 to 21 days for incubation. If the temperature rises too rapidly, the fertilization process will be aborted. Thus, yellow perch may is relatively slow, with a year-old fish measuring about 3 inches. Life expectancy is about 8 years.

REMARKS: Since the yellow perch needs cold water to reproduce, it is generally not found south of the Panhandle region. It is delicious to eat.

STATE RECORD: None.

WORLD RECORD: 4 pounds, 3 ounces. Bordentown, New Jersey. May 1865. Dr. C. C. Abbot.

Want to catch fish like the pros? Roland Martin, all-time leading money winner on the Bass Anglers Sportsman Society's (B.A.S.S.) tournament trail, offers this simple advice for starters: "Go early and stay late. You have to be on the water to catch fish. There really is no substitute for being out there, actually fishing. And you can learn by fishing with and observing other good fishermen. If you can afford it, hire a guide one time. He can teach you a lot."

WALLEYE
(Stizostedion vitreum)

DESCRIPTION: The walleye is commonly called a walleyed pike, but it is not a pike; it is a member of the perch family, Percidae. The fish is elongate but stockily built, almost cylinder-shaped. Coloration is olive-green to brown on the top shading to yellowish sides with a white belly. The sides have an irregular pattern of small, dark

After spawning, the parents immediately return to deeper water. The eggs hatch in about 10 days and the fry feed on microscopic life. Growth is rapid, however, and once walleyes reach fingerling size, they become effective predators, their diet being primarily small fish, including other small wall-eyes. Adult walleyes feed on fish almost exclu-

blotches. The mouth is large, with sharp canine teeth lining the jaws. The eyes are large, almost bug-eyed, and opaque. They appear to glow at night in the illumination of a light. There also is a distinctive white tip on the lower lobe of the tail. Average size is 1 to 3 pounds, although specimens weighing more than 5 pounds are caught regularly in some places.

HABITS/HABITAT: An occasional walleye might be caught in any of several lakes around the state, but the fish is most plentiful in Panhandle reservoirs and some other lakes in the northern part of the state, where the water temperature remains cold long enough to accommodate spawning. The fish is most active in the winter and also in early spring, when it is spawning. Among the more productive baits are live minnows and nightcrawlers, fished on or near the bottom in deeper water, sometimes trolled very slowly with a Colorado spinner just forward of the natural bait. The walleye spawns in early spring when water temperature reaches 45° to 50°F. Spawning occurs at night, randomly over gravel of a tributary stream, along a wind-blown shoreline, or in the riprap of a dam. There is no parental care of eggs or young.

sively. A walleye will grow about 12 inches its first year and will weigh slightly more than a pound.

REMARKS: The walleye is an import, first brought from Iowa in 1965 and stocked in Lake Meredith in the Panhandle. Later, stocking was greatly expanded to include other reservoirs. The walleye, with its flaky white meat, is considered a delicacy.

STATE RECORD: 11.88 pounds. Lake Meredith. February 26, 1990. Hank L. McWilliams, Jr., Borger.

WORLD RECORD: 25 pounds. Old Hickory Lake, Tennessee. April 1, 1960. Mabry Harper.

> After a front passes, when the barometer is rising, fish are often active, but once barometric pressure gets high and stabilizes, the winds usually turn around to the south, resulting in a bright sky, and the fish turn off. It might take two or three days for them to return to their normal routines.

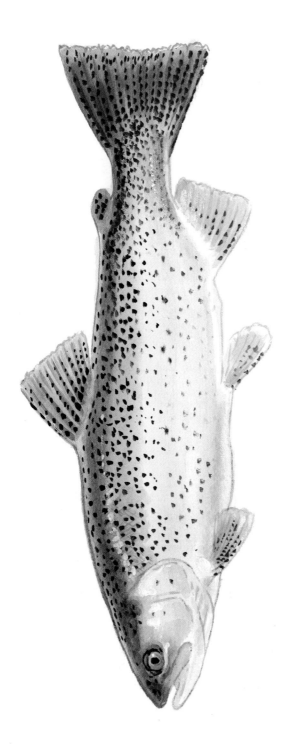

RAINBOW TROUT
(*Salmo gairdneri*)

DESCRIPTION: The rainbow trout, a member of the Salmonidae family, has the familiar trout shape. It is unrelated to the saltwater trouts, which belong to the family Sciaenidae. Immature fish are not as colorful as adults. A pinkish band often extends along the body from across the temperatures, although some catches have indicated that a few fish have survived for several years.

REMARKS: A few brown trout (*Salmo trutta*) and brook trout (*Salvelinus fontinalis*) have also been stocked periodically in the Guadalupe River

gill cover to the tail, and the sides are profusely spotted. The tail is forked. Average size of rainbow trout stocked in Texas waters is 8 to 10 inches.

HABITS/HABITAT: Texas has no native freshwater trout species. The rainbow trout's natural range includes many northern and western U.S. areas. Stockings are made at regular intervals through the winter months in the Guadalupe River below Canyon Lake; the Brazos River below Possum Kingdom Lake; Boykin Springs Lake in the Angelina National Forest; Foster County Park in San Angelo; and in small lakes in six state parks: Buescher, Tyler, Meridian, Bonham, Cleburne and Daingerfield. Recently, stocking sites have been expanded considerably. Rainbow trout are caught in the winter while stocking is ongoing. While they can be taken on artificials, the most popular bait is common canned yellow corn. The basic diet of smaller trout is mostly nymphs and insects. This is a put-and-take fishery with no reproduction, despite the stocking in recent years of the redband strain of rainbow trout, which is more tolerant of warmer water and temperature fluctuations. There is very little carryover from one winter to the next, due to hot summer water

below Canyon Lake by clubs and individuals. The tail of the brown trout is square, and the upper jaw extends well back beyond the eye. Coloration on the upper part is olive-brownish, lighter below. The brook trout can be distinguished by the worm-like markings along the back and dorsal fin. All trout are delicious to eat.

STATE RECORD: 7 pounds, 4 ounces. Guadalupe River. Februry 4, 1993. Ron Weigle, Canyon Lake.

WORLD RECORD: 42 pounds, 2 ounces. Bell Island, Alaska. June 22, 1970. David Robert White.

OTHER STATE RECORDS: Brown trout—7 pounds, 2 ounces. Guadalupe River. February 7, 1986. Jeff DeLong, San Marcos. Brook trout—10.6 ounces. Guadalupe River. February 19, 1984. J. Bryan Hendricks, Lake Jackson.

When wade fishing, learn to slide and shuffle your feet instead of picking them up and stepping. This way you are less likely to step off into a deep place or stumble over some underwater obstruction.

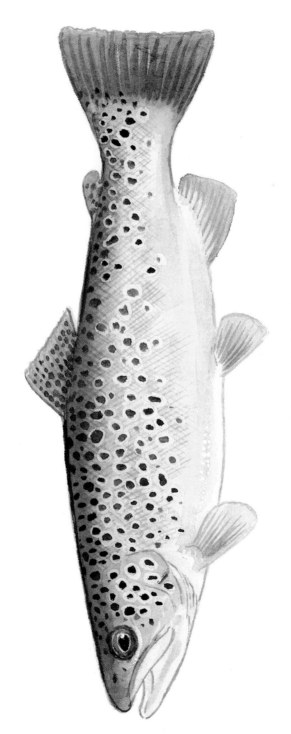

BROWN TROUT
(Salmo trutta)

To net a fish, simply lower the net into the water and lead the fish into it. Always net a fish head first. If you try to scoop it from underneath, you won't get it into the net and you risk knocking the fish off the hook, or if you hit its tail, that fish will try to make another run and you might lose it.

When a right-handed person uses a casting reel, the normal procedure is to cast with the right hand, then shift the rod to the left hand in order to reel with the right. If you can make the change, buy a left-handed casting reel and learn to reel with your left. The master hand, or right hand, has more sensitivity and quicker reflexes. By holding the rod in the right hand you can work lures better and you have more strength or hook-setting power. You also save time since you don't have to bother to shift the rod from your right to left hand every time you make a cast.

If you want to catch panfish, such as any of the sunfish species, you probably can find bait without much effort. You can dig earthworms, or even grow your own. Red wigglers, for example, are easy. An old foam ice chest with a drain hole cut in the bottom is good for this. Mix 1/3 top soil with 2/3 peat moss and keep the mixture moist but not wet. Feed them table scraps. Another good bait is a small grasshopper. You can capture grasshoppers and keep them indefinitely in your home freezer. Just thaw them out when you are ready to fish. They work about as well as fresh grasshoppers.

When fishing with a plastic worm, set the hook the moment you feel anything suspicious or see your line hesitate or jump forward. The longer you let a fish have a worm, the better the odds you are not going to hook that fish.

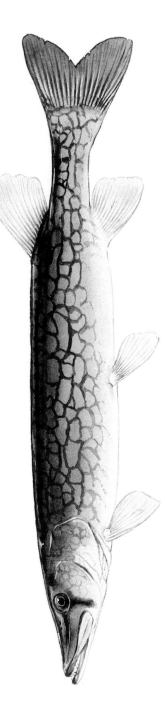

CHAIN PICKEREL
(Esox niger)

DESCRIPTION: The chain pickerel, also known as the jackfish or jack, is a member of the pike family, Esocidae. The body is elongated and thin. Coloration is a deep olive-green on the back, shading to a creamy yellow on the belly and overlaid with a horizontal chainlike pattern of dark bands on the sides. This pattern, however, is not as distinct on a juvenile fish, which might have vertical bars. The mouth is very large, with long, pointed teeth. The dorsal and anal fins are set well

favored spawning areas. The fertilized eggs adhere to underwater vegetation or to the bottom, with incubation lasting from a week to 10 days, depending on water temperature. The young feed primarily on insects until they are capable of catching and eating small fish. The chain pickerel will grow from 12 to 14 inches the first year to about 18 inches on its second birthday. Life expectancy is only about 4 to 5 years.

REMARKS: The chain pickerel is a flashy

to the rear of the body, just in front of the tail. Average size is about a pound, with a maximum length of about 26 inches and maximum weight of 3 to 4 pounds. Because of the slim body, length is out of proportion to weight.

HABITS/HABITAT: The chain pickerel is found in the Cypress River drainage, including Caddo Lake, Lake O' the Pines and Lone Star Lake, in the northeast part of the state. The fish likes weedy areas of quiet, sluggish waters, such as the headwaters of Caddo Lake. Adult fish feed almost exclusively on other fish. Chain pickerel are most active in the winter, when the greatest numbers are taken, although they can be caught with some regularity at other times of the year, principally early spring and late fall. Favored feeding times are early and late in the day. One of the more productive lures is a small spinnerbait, resembling a baitfish. Live minnows and small sunfish are also good. The chain pickerel is different from other native fishes in that it spawns in the winter, when water temperature is 47° to 50°F. It does not build a nest. A 2-year-old female will lay up to 30,000 eggs. Weedy areas close to shore are fighter, often jumping in spectacular leaps. When taking one off the hook, the angler should be wary of the very sharp teeth. It is edible but very bony.

STATE RECORD: 4 pounds, 10 ounces. Caddo Lake. June 12, 1986. Deborah Throusedale Morris, Woodlawn.

WORLD RECORD: 9 pounds, 6 ounces. Homerville, Georgia. February 17, 1961. Baxley McQuaig, Jr.

If you want to bait an area around a dock or a spot out in the lake, soak a bale or two of alfalfa hay and sink them. They need to be pre-soaked or otherwise they will float away. The hay attracts minute aquatic life which in turn attracts minnows, along with crappies and other fish. Hay bales are biodegradable and will eventually disappear. But while they are in the water they release nutrients that help enrich the habitat.

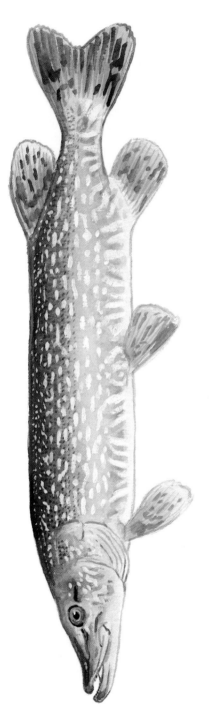

NORTHERN PIKE
(Esox lucius)

DESCRIPTION: The northern pike belongs to the same family as the chain pickerel, but there isn't much chance of confusing the two since they come from different parts of the state. The northern pike has a slim, elongated body, a "duck bill" with a mouth full of sharp teeth, and a distinctive color pattern. The body is greenish with pale, elongate blotches and a white belly. There usually are dark markings on the anal and dorsal fins,

REMARKS: The northern pike was brought to Texas in hopes that it would be a biological control on undesirable rough fish. It is a vicious striker and strong fighter. Be careful handling the fish because it has a nasty disposition and the needlelike teeth can inflict painful injuries.

STATE RECORD: 18 pounds, 4.5 ounces. Town Lake in downtown Austin. August 29, 1981. Michael D. Sharpe, Austin.

which are located far back on the body near the tail. Average size is 2 to 4 pounds, although specimens over 10 are occasionally caught. Because of its long and slender shape it gives the impression of weighing more than it really does.

HABITS/HABITAT: The problem with the northern pike is that it likes cold water, and this has restricted its stocking in Texas. The only place where it has adapted with any degree of success has been Greenbelt Reservoir near Clarendon, in the Panhandle east of Amarillo. This predacious species likes waters with abundant vegetation. It is a voracious feeder that begins preying on other fish when it is only 4 to 6 inches long. Adults feed heavily on shad and other forage fish, which comprise almost their entire diet. The northern pike spawns at a colder temperature than any native fish. Migration into shallow-water spawning areas begins when the water temperature is about 46°F. The fish spawn at random, building no nest. The adhesive eggs are spread over underwater vegetation and hatch in about 14 to 30 days. A small female weighing 3 to 4 pounds will lay about 10,000 eggs.

WORLD RECORD: 55 pounds, 1 ounce. Lake of Grefeem, West Germany. October 16, 1986. Lothar Louis.

Birds can help fishermen find school-type fish like white bass, hybrid stripers and striped bass when they are chasing shad. Seagulls move to inland reservoirs in the greatest numbers in the fall. Carry a pair of binoculars and watch open expanses of water, especially over sand flats nearer shore. If you see a bunch of gulls circling and diving, hustle that way. You've found a school of fish feeding at the surface. Also, do not ignore any gulls sitting on the water. Often they are over a school of fish and are waiting for the action to start. Use a spoon or white jig and work the bottom under the gulls. A bird or two on the water has led me to cooperative fish many times.

ALLIGATOR GAR
(*Lepisosteus spatula*)

DESCRIPTION: The alligator gar, along with other gars, belongs to the family Lepisosteidae, generally regarded as being "prehistoric." The head of this gar resembles that of an alligator, hence the name. The body is tubelike, with scales that resemble tank armor plating. The stubby snout is full of sharp teeth. Eyes have an evil, truculent glint. Coloration ranges from olive-green, on smaller specimens, to a dull, dark gray. Any alligator gar under 25 pounds is considered freshwater fish in the state. The unrestricted state record (taken by means other than rod and reel) weighed 302 pounds, caught in 1953 on a trotline in the Nueces River of South Texas. Because of its size, strength and teeth, any alligator gar should be handled with extreme care. It is not sought for food.

STATE RECORD: 279 pounds. Rio Grande. 1951. Bill Valverde, Mission.

WORLD RECORD: Same.

small; specimens weighing more than 100 pounds are not uncommon.

HABITS/HABITAT: Alligator gars, found statewide, are most abundant and grow largest in waters in the eastern and southern parts of the state. The fish likes big, sluggish rivers and reservoirs. It also is found in the mouths of rivers along the coast, and in brackish water more salty than fresh. It can survive because of its unique auxiliary breathing system, which has an air bladder that partially serves as a lung, permitting it to exist in water of very low oxygen content. During hot weather a gar regularly surfaces to "breathe" this auxiliary air. Alligator gars like warm weather and are most active from spring through early fall. Most are caught on juglines using a large live fish, their favorite food, or a chunk of cut bait. A snap is tied to the jug, and once a fish is hooked, the snap is attached to a loop in the line of a rod and reel, the jug is cut free, and the fisherman is in direct contact with the fish, to play it down. Not much is known about the fish's habits except that it spawns in late spring. Life expectancy is more than 20 years.

REMARKS: The alligator gar is the largest

Ever wonder what to do with the leavings after you've cleaned your fish? Use them to bait a hole to attract catfish. Grind up the leftovers, put them in a milk carton, and freeze. Next time you go fishing, use it as chum. Tear off the carton and pitch the frozen block into the water. It will sink, thaw and attract catfish.

While trolling for largemouth black bass, try different levels of water. Maybe you will use a deep-running plug while your buddy ties on one that runs at a medium depth. Also, if you are not getting any action, vary the trolling speed. While sometimes bass will go for a faster-moving bait, the tendency is to troll too fast. Throttle your outboard down as slow as it will go. To go even slower, troll in reverse.

LONGNOSE GAR
(Lepisosteus osseus)

DESCRIPTION: The longnose gar is better known as the needle-nosed gar. Coloration of the long and slim body is mostly olive-green, and the snout is much longer than that of the alligator gar. The longnose gar has only 1 row of teeth, while the alligator gar has a double row of teeth in the upper jaw, arranged in 2 rows along both sides. The longnose grows to weights better than 10 pounds, although the average weight is less.

HABITS/HABITAT: The longnose gar is the most widespread and most abundant of all the gar species, being found in all the major rivers, reser-

guished from the shortnose gar, which it closely resembles, by the large spots on the head. The shortnose has no spots. Gars are edible but very bony. There are no state or world records for the shortnose gar.

STATE RECORD: 50 pounds, 5 ounces. Trinity River. 1954. Townsend Miller, Austin.

WORLD RECORD: Same.

State record spotted gar: 0.98 pound. Shawnee Creek. September 2, 1992. John Hardin, Farmers Branch. (World Record: 8 pounds, 8 ounces. Illinois.)

voirs, and their tributaries. It is an adaptable fish that can live most anywhere. Longnose gar migrate upstream in the spring to spawn, moving into tributary streams or concentrating below dams. A female will deposit a large number of eggs that are greenish in color and reported to be toxic. Young gar feed on insects, but once they reach fingerling size they become voracious predators and their diet is almost exclusively other fish. Longnose gar can be caught on rod and reel if the tackle is rigged right. A prime time is summer when the fish are surfacing and a school is easily located. A piece of nylon rope about 3 inches long, is an effective lure. No hook is needed in that the fibers become entangled in the fish's teeth and it can't get away. The lure should be fished very slowly. Sometimes a Colorado-shaped spinner attached just forward of the nylon will attract more strikes.

REMARKS: Texas has two other, smaller gar species, the shortnose gar (Lepisosteus platostomus) and the spotted gar (Lepisosteus oculatus). The shortnose gar can be distinguished from a longnose gar of comparable size by the length of the snout. The spotted gar can be distin-

If you see a school of white bass or hybrid stripers chasing shad at the surface, don't rush right into the activity. Instead, get where the wind is at your back, cut the boat engine well away from the feeding frenzy, and drift close. If the fish sound and disappear before you get within casting range, just wait and watch for a few minutes. They likely will surface again nearby.

A black bass likes to snuggle next to some sort of cover, such as a stump, in order to hide and ambush prey. It prefers darker areas where it is not easily seen. On a sunny day, cast to the shady side, or dark side, of the stump, as close to the fish's hiding spot as possible. If the lure drops too far out, the bass probably won't come out to grab it.

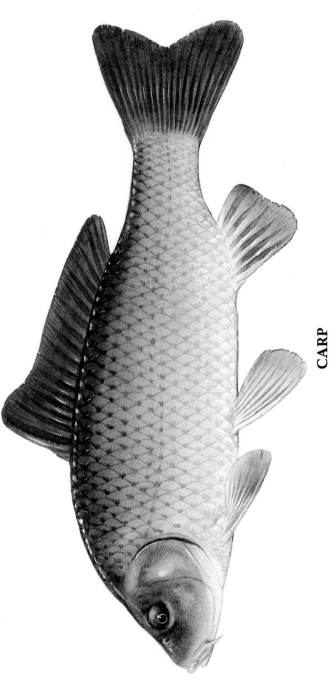

CARP
(Cyprinus carpio)

DESCRIPTION: The carp belongs to the family Cyprinidae, which includes the minnow. Although the coloration will vary with water clarity, a carp normally has a color ranging from can be made by mixing 100% Bran Flakes with Big Red soda water to a thick consistency, molding it into a small ball, and putting it on a treble hook. Wheaties mixed with water is another good

brassy-green or bronzy to a golden tone. The robust body is deep and humped. The mouth is small. Both the dorsal and anal fins have a heavy toothed spine. The upper jaw has two barbels on each side, easily distinguishing the carp from other sucker-like species, including the goldfish. Average size is 2 to 8 pounds, but specimens exceeding 20 are fairly common.

HABITS/HABITAT: The carp, abundant statewide, can survive and thrive in about any water conditions, and although it is found in all the river systems, it flourishes best in off-colored shallow lakes. In many bodies of water, the carp is the dominant species. The carp is primarily a warm-water fish and it can be caught through the summer when most other fishes are inactive. Carp root along the bottom with their suctionlike mouths, in search of food. They are omnivorous, the diet including both animal and vegetable matter. Thus, a bait should be put right on bottom and not moved. Carp can be drawn to a fishing area by pitching range cubes, which can be bought at any feedstore, into the water. An effective bait

bait. Carp spawn in very shallow water of sloughs and coves in the spring, when the water temperature is about 65°F. The adults can often be seen thrashing about, their backs breaking the surface, turning the water muddy. A 15-pound female may carry up to 2 million eggs, which hatch without parental care in about 5 to 10 days. Growth is rapid. Where adequate food is available, a year-old fish might weigh more than a pound. Life expectancy is long, more than 25 years.

REMARKS: A carp, while not flashy, is a very strong fighter. In addition to the common carp, which is sometimes called the scaled carp, there are 2 genetic variations: the mirror carp, which generally has only 3 rows of large, irregularly shaped scales; and the leather carp, which is scaleless. All carp are edible but very bony.

STATE RECORD: 22.22 pounds. Lake O' the Pines. March 10, 1991. David Click, Harleton.

WORLD RECORD: 75 pounds, 11 ounces. Lac de St. Cassien, France. May 21, 1987. Leo van der Gugten.

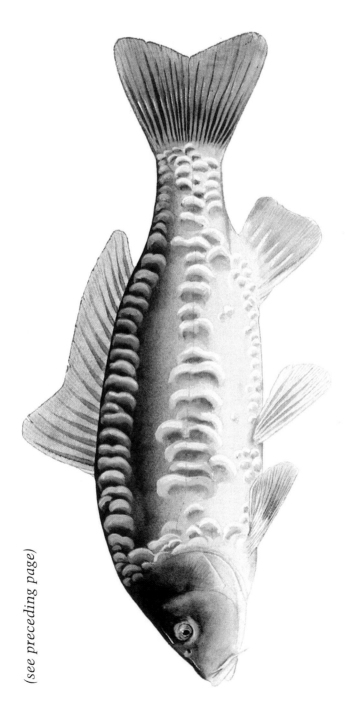

(see preceding page)

Mirror Carp
(Cyprinus carpio)

Leather Carp
(*Cyprinus carpio*)

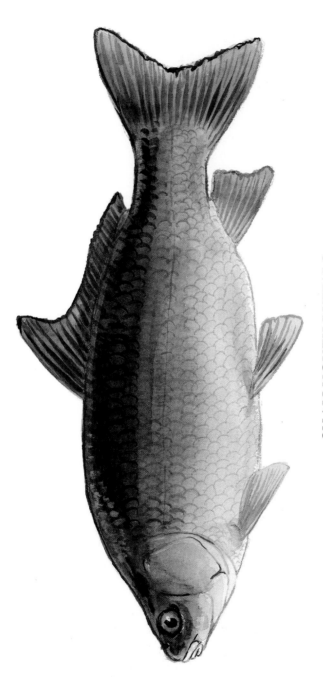

SMALLMOUTH BUFFALO
(Ictiobus bubalus)

DESCRIPTION: The smallmouth buffalo is a member of the sucker family, Catostomidae. The mouth is small, although it is more terminal than is that of other suckers. The body is stocky and

REMARKS: Texas has 2 other buffalo species, the bigmouth buffalo (*Ictiobus cyprinellus*) and the black buffalo (*Ictiobus niger*). They have larger mouths than that of the smallmouth buffalo and

the head large. This fish resembles the carp, but unlike the carp, a buffalo has no barbels (whiskers) around the mouth, and the body is somewhat more compressed, with a higher arch in the back. Coloration is olive-brown. Typical weight often exceeds 10 pounds.

HABITS/HABITAT: Buffalo may be found in every river system in the state and in most of the reservoirs, except those in the Panhandle, but it is not nearly as plentiful as the carp. Smallmouth buffalo can flourish in either clear or turbid water. Not much is known about the buffalo except that it seems to be most active in cooler water and can be caught with the same techniques and baits as used for carp. No one knows exactly where these fish go when the water gets warm, perhaps into deeper areas where they can't be readily reached by fishermen. Buffalo spawn in the spring when the water temperature reaches about 60° to 65°F. Spawning takes place randomly over weed beds and mud bottoms. Eggs hatch in 7 to 14 days. Food consists primarily of plankton, insect larvae and vegetation. Growth is rapid.

they are virtually identical in appearance—slate-blue in color, although the black buffalo tends to be darker. They prefer clear water and are found primarily in the far eastern part of the state. Although a buffalo is bony, the white meat is quite tasty.

STATE RECORD: 78 pounds. Toledo Bend Lake. June 23, 1992. Travis Thornton, Pineland.

WORLD RECORD: 68 pounds, 8 ounces. Lake Hamilton, Arkansas. May 16, 1984. Jerry L. Dolezal.

State record bigmouth buffalo: 41.50 pounds. Lake Texoma. June 30, 1990. Walter M. Cole, Sherman.

World record bigmouth buffalo: 70 pounds, 5 ounces. Bussey Brake, Louisiana. April 21, 1980. Delbert Sisk.

World record black buffalo: 55 pounds, 8 ounces. Cherokee Lake, Tennessee. May 3, 1984. Edward H. McLain. (No state record.)

Bigmouth Buffalo
(Ictiobus cyprinellus)

(see preceding page)

Black Buffalo
(Ictiobus niger)

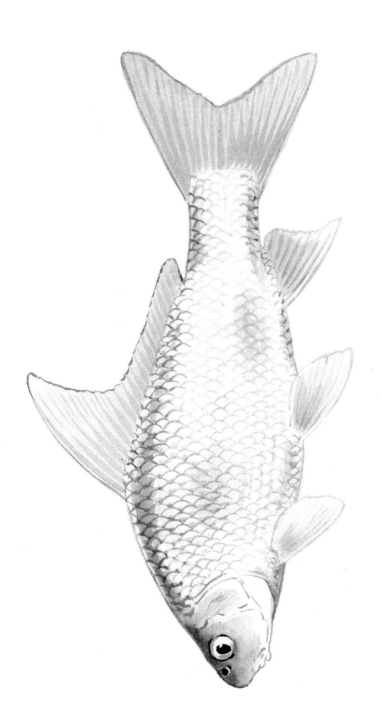

NORTHERN CARPSUCKER
(*Carpiodes carpio*)

DESCRIPTION: Also called the river sucker, the nothern carpsucker belongs to the family Catostomidae, which includes the buffalo. In shape it resembles a minnow, a close relative. Coloration is dull silver, sometimes brassy. The mouth is inferior, or slightly turned down, making it convenient for rooting along the bottom to find food, which consists mainly of insect larvae and plants. The tail is deeply forked. Average size is 12 to 14 inches and less than 2 pounds in weight.

HABITS/HABITAT: The carpsucker is found statewide. It is a river fish that has adapted to reservoirs, although you are more apt to catch one in a stream. A carpsucker is not often taken on rod and reel. If one does hit, the bait most likely will have been something small, such as an earthworm, still-fished on bottom. The carpsucker spawns in the spring and is prolific, a female capable of laying up to 50,000 eggs. It prefers running water for spawning but is an adaptable fish that can spawn in a river slough or along the shore of a lake. Otherwise, not much is known of its life history.

REMARKS: A cousin of the carpsucker you might encounter in the eastern half of the state is the spotted sucker (*Minytrema melanops*). Not as plentiful or widespread, it has the same minnow-like shape but is more slender than the carpsucker, and it has a shorter dorsal fin. The tail is deeply forked. Grayish-brown above and white below, the spotted sucker displays a pattern of black spots, one on each scale, forming rows. It weighs about a pound or less and is more prevalent in rivers than reservoirs. Both the carpsucker and spotted sucker are edible, but their bodies have numerous small bones.

STATE RECORD: None.

WORLD RECORD: 7 pounds, 11 ounces. Canadian County, Oklahoma. April 18, 1990. W. C. (Bill) Kenyon.

If you use a hook advertised as extra sharp or ultra sharp, check it regularly while you fish to see if the fine-tapered point has become bent.

BOWFIN
(Amia calva)

DESCRIPTION: The bowfin, commonly called the grinnel, is the last survivor of Amiidae, an ancient, primitive family of fishes. The body is stout and cylindrical in shape, and the mouth is large and filled with strong, sharp teeth. The dorsal fin runs more than half the length of the body. Coloration is olive or dark green along the back, lighter green on the sides, and cream on the belly. Near the tail of the male is a large, black the first year. They feed on insects, frogs, crayfish, and fish. The adult bowfin is primarily carnivorous and feeds mostly on other fishes.

REMARKS: Since the bowfin is not considered edible, it generally is not sought by fishermen. It is, however, a vicious striker and strong fighter. When handling a bowfin, you want to be careful. Those teeth are sharp.

spot bordered in orange. The skin feels smooth and leatherlike to the touch, but the bowfin actually is covered with round, hard scales. Average size is 4 to 8 pounds, but larger specimens are not uncommon.

HABITS/HABITAT: The bowfin is mostly confined to the far eastern portion of the state. It likes sluggish streams and reservoirs with lots of aquatic vegetation. The catching of a bowfin is almost always incidental to casting lures for bass or fishing on the bottom with minnows and crayfish, usually in spring and fall. Bowfins are also taken regularly on trotlines. They spawn in late spring in the coves of lakes and backwaters of sluggish streams, usually among vegetation. The male clears a crude nest, a circular area, brushing away loose material with his tail and fin, providing a place where the female deposits her eggs. Two or more females might use the same nest. The male guards the nest until the eggs hatch, in about 8 to 10 days, and then he tends the young, which roam about in a large, compact school until they reach a size of about 4 inches. The young grow rapidly, attaining a size from 12 to 14 inches

STATE RECORD: 17.65 pounds. Lake Fork. February 21, 1993. Brenda Walsh, Dallas.

WORLD RECORD: 21 pounds, 8 ounces. Florence, South Carolina. January 29, 1980. Robert L. Harmon.

Many fishermen use too large a hook when fishing for carp. A No. 10 treble is about right. And keep the bait small—doughbait molded into a ball about the size of a grape. Even a big carp has a small mouth.

Whole-kernel corn makes a good carp bait. Put four or five kernels on a small but strong single or treble hook. You also can pitch small amounts of corn into the water to attract carp to the area you are fishing.

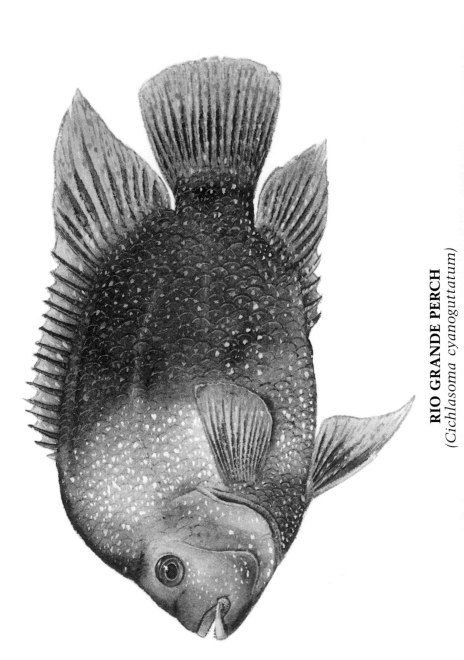

RIO GRANDE PERCH
(*Cichlasoma cyanoguttatum*)

part might hatch no more than 5,000 offspring in one spawn, almost all the young survive. Both parents remain with the young until they grow to about a half-inch in length, and the parents will aggressively challenge any threat, including bass more than twice their size.

REMARKS: Cichlids, a family of about 600 species found worldwide, are among our earliest known fish, dating back to biblical times, and various species are popular with aquarium owners. The Rio Grande perch is edible. There is no state or world record for this species.

> Most fish are attracted to a moving bait. One exception is the carp. The scavenger roots along bottom and picks up food with its suctionlike mouth. If the bait moves, it will alarm the fish. Keep the bait motionless until a carp wanders by and finds it. You can attract carp to your bait by using cottonseed cake or range cubes, available at a feedstore. Scatter some pieces of cake or cubes in the water where you intend to fish.

cichlid, belonging to the family Cichlidae. Smaller Rio Grandes vary in color from a bluish-black dotted with tiny white specks to a grayish coloration with conspicuous bars on the sides. The most notable characteristics are a humped back and a black spot on either side of the tail. On larger adults the coloration turns almost black, the hump behind the head is more pronounced, and often the black spots on the tail are barely discernible, if at all. Average size is a half-pound, although fish weighing more than 2 pounds are caught.

HABITS/HABITAT: The fish is tropical in nature and cannot survive temperatures below 48°F, which greatly restricts its range. It is found primarily in spring-fed areas of the Rio Grande, San Marcos, Guadalupe and San Antonio river basins. Town Lake in downtown Austin is at the northernmost edge of its range. Because it occurs in spring-fed areas where water temperature fluctuations are not great, it is active throughout most of the year, feeding on insects, crayfish and small fish. A small crayfish is probably the best bait for catching it. The Rio Grande perch preys on the eggs of other fish. The adults will mate and reproduce several times annually, and although a

A Guide to the Saltwater Fish

TEXAS has the longest tidewater coastline of any of the 48 contiguous states, an expanse of some 624 miles that includes a vast system of bays and estuaries. The fertile marine reaches of the Gulf of Mexico support a variety of fish species that range from the little "bay stealers" such as hardhead catfish and pinfish to brutes like blue marlin, jewfish and tiger shark, which can weigh more than 500 pounds.

These are fish of varied habits, too. Some are year-round residents of limited range, such as sheepshead and snappers, which can be found in about the same places at any time of year. Others live in one type of habitat most of the time, moving any significant distance only when they are spawning. Thus, we have the "croaker run" or the "black drum run." In the fall, for instance, Atlantic croakers move out of the bays into the Gulf to spawn; for big black drum in late winter it is the reverse, fish coming from the Gulf into the bays to spawn, following the deep cuts and channels.

Pelagic species, those which live in the open sea, are more generally nomadic, living in one place in the winter, another place in the summer. Consider the king mackerel. One king was tagged one February off Fort Pierce on Florida's east coast and 163 days later was caught off Port Aransas, a distance of some 1,110 miles. Another tagged at Port Aransas was later caught off Mexico.

Consequently, the saltwater fisherman has to know something about the seasonal habits of his quarry, where the fish likely will be and when. King mackerel show up in ever-increasing numbers when the water temperature reaches about 70°F, which means they won't be "out there" from late fall to spring.

I can remember when charter boats brought in tremendous

numbers of kingfish. These were ego trips more than anything, since most of the kings went to waste. And no one thought much about it. As mentioned in the discussion of minimum legal lengths and daily creel limits, the mass of the Gulf of Mexico along with the various bay systems gave us fishermen a false sense of security. The supply of fish seemed inexhaustible.

Researchers knew better. A combination of factors such as overfishing and loss of nursery grounds was depleting the seafood resource at an alarming rate. But political interests kept anyone from doing much about the trend. This led to the formation of the Gulf Coast Conservation Association and a bitter fight to take the popular redfish and spotted seatrout out of the commercial marketplace. On the federal level, the Gulf of Mexico Fishery Management Council, working through the National Marine Fisheries Service, became more active. The catches of both commercial and recreational fishermen were sharply curtailed in both state and federal waters. Biologists learned how to make redfish and some other fish spawn in captivity and in recent years millions of hatchery-raised redfish have been stocked in various bay systems by the Texas Parks and Wildlife Department. And as technology and facilities expand, other fish might be spawned and reared in hatcheries and released in coastal waters to give nature a helping hand.

At the same time, research of saltwater species is getting an urgent emphasis, mainly through the use of tagging studies to learn something about the history of any given fish, its migratory patterns, life expectancy and growth rates.

Because of the state's lengthy coastline, the prime fishing periods can vary from place to place for various fish. The general fishing seasons for different species have been provided by biologist Mike Weixelman of the Texas Parks and Wildlife Department, based on landings (catches) compiled by the department over a 12-year period.

Saltwater Fish

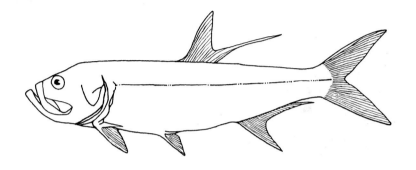

INSHORE SPECIES
(in bays and close to shore)

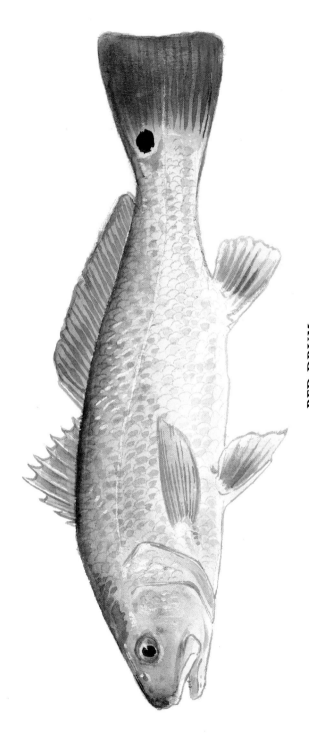

RED DRUM
(*Sciaenops ocellatus*)

DESCRIPTION: Known as the redfish, the red drum is a member of the croaker family, Sciaenidae. It is similar in shape to its close relative the black drum, but it has a more streamlined appearance and displays more color: silver to bronze, but most often a reddish-bronze. The most no-

Along the rest of the coast, the shallow reefs and grass flats are most productive during the warm months, while deeper holes and tributaries pay off in the winter, especially when cold fronts drop the temperature to near or below freezing. The bigger reds are normally caught in September and

table characteristic is a prominent round or oval black spot on the top posterior portion of the tail. Occasionally, a specimen will have multiple spots, but rarely will you find one without this identifiable feature. The first dorsal fin normally numbers 10 spines, about 25 rays are in the second dorsal, and there are 7 or 8 in the anal fin. Average size is 3 to 8 pounds, although fish over 10 are not unusual.

HABITS/HABITAT: Adult red drum at least 4 years old seem to spend most of their time in the Gulf, while the more abundant smaller specimens stay in the bays year-round. They prefer oyster reefs and grass flats where food is most available, and they are caught on both artificial and natural baits. Redfish will readily forage in muddy or sandy water. Even on large shallow flats, more fish are caught along the shoreline areas, sometimes in water no more than 6 inches deep, than in the more open areas. They like shallows near deeper water, which provides a convenient escape route. Red drum in shallow water are very easily spooked. The popular redfish can be caught year-round. Along the lower coast, from Port Mansfield to Port Isabel, the fish seldom leave the flats.

October in the surf, and in and near passes, from jetties and piers. Fall also is a prime time to catch redfish on the grass flats. It is often necessary to wade to get into the better areas without alarming the fish, which travel in small, compact schools, sometimes numbering only 2 or 3 fish. The so-called "bull reds" (larger than 12 pounds) spawn each fall in the Gulf. Eggs hatch in 1 or 2 days and the tiny fish immediately move into the bays to find food and shelter. Smaller fish, which remain in fairly shallow water unless cold weather drives them to deeper open water, are typically called "rat reds" if they are smaller than the legal minimum. A redfish will grow about 12 inches its first year, and will be about 20 inches on its second birthday.

REMARKS: Redfish longer than the legal maximum length are sometimes called bull reds. The fish is excellent to eat.

STATE RECORD: 51 pounds, 8 ounces. Padre Island surf. January 1967. Johnny (Shorty) Cizmar.

WORLD RECORD: 94 pounds, 2 ounces. Avon, North Carolina. November 7, 1984. Ferdie Van Nooten.

BLACK DRUM
(Pogonias cromis)

DESCRIPTION: Although closely akin to the red drum, the black drum has a more humped back and a more blocky appearance. The snout when the bigger fish are migrating into the Gulf to spawn. Most of the spawning activity is in and around passes and ship channels. They congregate

is blunt, the tail squarish, and the scales large. Younger specimens are silvery-gray with 4 or 5 broad, dark vertical bars. Adults are dark gray ranging to silvery-black or bronze with no bars. Barbels are always present on the lower jaw. Dorsal fins are contiguous, the forward portion with 10 slender spines, the second with 22 to 25 rays. Three large plates in the throat allow the black drum to crush shells. Average size is 5 to 6 pounds, although fish better than 25 pounds are not unusual.

HABITS/HABITAT: One of the world's largest croakers, the black drum, like other members of the Sciaenidae family, is primarily an inshore fish that stays mostly on the bottom. The fish can be found throughout the bay systems, but it prefers areas with shell substrate (a base on which an organism exists), and areas around jetties, piers, dock pilings and rock piles. Juveniles are frequently abundant in muddy sloughs in the bays but are not restricted to these. They roam in large schools. The black drum feeds primarily on small clams and crabs. The fish can be caught year-round, a prime time being late February to April

in the deeper cuts and channels as they migrate. The average size of drum caught during the spawn has gotten progressively smaller over the years, probably due to overfishing. It is estimated that a 25-pound drum is at least 12 years old. Growth is relatively slow, about 10 inches the first year, and only about 5 inches more in the second. Larger fish are often parasitized with "spaghetti worms," which are unsightly but harmless to humans.

REMARKS: The black drum, noted for its ability to make a loud croaking sound, especially during the spawning run, is a strong but unspectacular fighter. Smaller specimens are edible, but the big ones are coarse and not much good. Consequently, large drum should be released, especially since a big female is capable of laying up to 5 million eggs. Upon release, the exhausted fish might appear dead, but it eventually will recover.

STATE RECORD: 81 pounds. Gulf of Mexico. June 19, 1998. Wally Escobar, Jr., Bay City.

WORLD RECORD: 113 pounds, 1 ounce. Lewes, Delaware. September 15, 1975. Gerald M. Townsend.

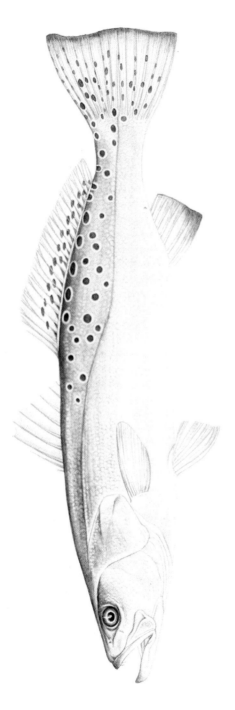

SPOTTED SEATROUT
(*Cynoscion nebulosus*)

DESCRIPTION: Called the speckled trout or simply "speck," the spotted seatrout is a member of the family Sciaenidae. It has a distinctive, streamlined shape with silvery sides, a grayish back with a metallic blue sheen, and numerous black spots on the upper sides and on the dorsal and tail fins. These spots distinguish it from its cousin, the sand trout. The mouth is large and the surf in April and May. Baitfish such as small croakers, piggy perch or mullet, or artificials that imitate baitfish, are the best bet for larger trout. Most of the fish weighing about 3 pounds or less, though, are taken on live shrimp or shrimp imitations. The fish spawn mostly in April and May, but some spawning activity continues through the summer into fall, on shallow, grassy bay flats.

colored yellow-orange inside, and 1 or 2 prominent canine teeth are usually found on the tip of the upper jaw. The mouth membrane is thin and tears easily. Average size is 1 to 2 pounds, with some specimens growing to 8 pounds or better.

HABITS/HABITAT: The speckled trout is widely distributed throughout the year in all the bay systems, around jetties and passes, and in the surf. Being democratic in its choice of habitats, plus being readily available to fishermen, makes this fish universally popular. Speckled trout are in shallower water from spring through fall, but they go into deep water during the winter to avoid abrupt temperature fluctuations. They don't have much tolerance for very cold water. Small trout feed primarily on shrimp and small fish. At 2 or 3 years of age, adults tend to feed mostly on other fish such as mullet. Speckled trout can be caught year-round. During the summer months they are around oyster reefs (including man-made ones near oil platforms in the bays) or in shallow water or in deeper cuts near the shallows. In the winter, they are found in deep holes, boat basins and channels. Some of the bigger trout are caught in

Growth rate is slow. At age 1, a speckled trout will measure 8 to 10 inches, and on its second birthday, 10 to 12. A 14-inch trout will weigh about a pound, or slightly more, while a 16-inch trout will weigh about a pound and a half.

REMARKS: Speckled trout come close to the shore in bays and are readily caught off lighted piers and docks, especially in the warm-weather months. The fish is good to eat, but the flesh tends to get soft unless the fish are put on ice immediately after they are caught.

STATE RECORD: 13 pounds, 9 ounces. Upper Laguna Madre. March 16, 1975. P.M. (Mike) Blackwood, Corpus Christi.

WORLD RECORD: 19 pounds, 2 ounces. Jones Beach Inlet, Long Island, New York. October 11, 1984. Dennis Roger Rooney.

When wading out in the surf to fish the troughs between breakers, wear a life jacket. The undertow from the surf can be strong in places, especially near passes.

SAND SEATROUT
(Cynoscion arenarius)

DESCRIPTION: The body configuration and fin arrangement of the sand trout, as this fish is commonly known, are similar to its more popular cousin, the speckled trout, although the sand trout is a smaller fish. The sand trout has a pink-sand trout is the fish's main drawback, but because of minimum size and creel limits on speckled trout, fishing for sand trout has become more popular. There is no minimum length or daily limit for sand trout. The fish is edible, although it

ish sheen along its upper sides and there are no black spots. It also is often confused with another cousin, the silver seatrout, a fish with similar shape but without spots. The best way to distinguish between them is to count the rays in the anal fin. The sand trout has 11, the silver seatrout 8 or 9. Average size is less than a pound.

HABITS/HABITAT: Sand seatrout spend most of the year in the bay systems and do not take part in extensive migrations except to move into the Gulf upon the arrival of cold weather. They are school fish, and a good number of them can be caught from a small area, one reason they are popular with party boats that fish the bays. Although sand trout can be caught year-round, the prime periods are spring and fall. They can be found in open areas of the bays in spring and summer months; and in the surf, in ship channels around jetties, and in deeper water near passes in colder weather. They feed on small fish, shrimp and crustaceans, and the best baits are small pieces of cut bait or a shrimp fished on or near the bottom. Spawning is in the spring. Not much else is known about this abundant species.

REMARKS: The generally small size of most

has numerous featherlike bones. It should be put on ice immediately after it is caught, to preserve the flavor.

STATE RECORD: 6 pounds, 4 ounces. Texas City. February 26, 1972. Dennis C. Herrick, Houston.

WORLD RECORD: None.

> One piece of equipment the saltwater fisherman shouldn't leave home without is rain gear. Squalls can pop up suddenly and unexpectedly. The best protection is a storm suit. It includes a waterproof top with a hood and a drawstring that snugs it around the hips, and trousers. The top can also be used with chest-high waders when wade-fishing. Storm suits are available in economy vinyl or more expensive water-proofed fabric. Vinyl is hot to wear and tears more easily. Your best bet is to invest in the more expensive suit. It will pay off in the long run.

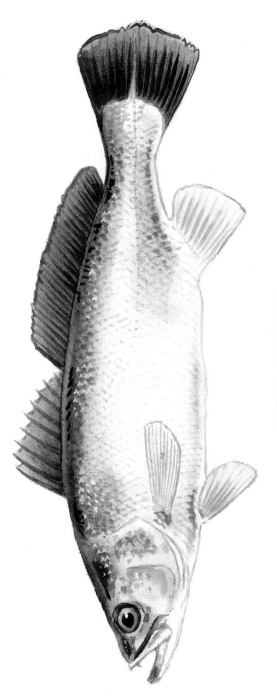

SILVER SEATROUT
(Cynoscion nothus)

DESCRIPTION: The silver seatrout, better known as the Gulf trout or Gulf sand trout, is a member of the croaker or drum family, Sciaenidae. The fish has a pale coloration, with silvery sides and sometimes with a faint impression of an irregular row of dots. The silver seatrout has 8 or 9 rays in the anal fin while the sand trout has 11.

June to August in the Gulf, and that is where most of them are caught, quite a few around oil platforms. The staple diet consists of shrimp, fish and small crustaceans. The best bait is a small piece of cut bait or a shrimp fished near or on bottom. The best fishing months are July, August and September.

Average size is a pound or less, although fish weighing twice that much are caught occasionally.

HABITS/HABITAT: The silver seatrout is primarily a Gulf species, the preferred habitat being water 3 to 20 fathoms deep, but the fish is also caught in the bays. Silver seatrout spawn from

REMARKS: The silver seatrout is a hard striker, but doesn't put up much resistance.

STATE RECORD: 6.91 pounds. Gulf of Mexico. February 28, 1992. Gerry L. Tompkins, San Antonio.

WORLD RECORD: None.

Many fishermen are hesitant to wade in salt water because they fear getting hit by a stingray. But there is not much of a stingray threat if the angler shuffles his feet, moving slowly, and watches where he is going. A stingray normally will flee when he hears or sees a fisherman approaching. Also, Walk 'N' Wade leggings, available at many tackle stores, can provide protection. Similar to snake leggings, they are made for wading. Just strap them on your legs below the knees for peace of mind.

When buying a landing net, check to be sure you are getting nylon netting. Cotton mesh is less expensive, but it will rot and weaken in salt water. Most landing nets have a frame with a handle made of aluminum, and they come in various sizes. Get one that is large enough to handle the fish you are after. There also is a special hoop net designed to be lowered with a rope that is made for fishing off higher piers and docks where even a long-handled net won't reach the water. Coastal tackle stores carry both kinds.

ATLANTIC CROAKER
(Micropogon undulatus)

DESCRIPTION: The Atlantic, or golden, croaker belongs to the family Sciaenidae. An adult Atlantic croaker is brownish-bronze and has a row of small barbels on each side of the lower jaw. The called "panfish" in the bay systems. It is especially popular along the upper coast in the vast Galveston Bay system.

STATE RECORD: 5 pounds, 2 ounces. East

WORLD RECORD: None.

body shape is similar to that of a juvenile redfish, to which it is closely related. It also is sometimes confused with the spot croaker since both have the blunt heads common to the bottom-feeding croakers. The Atlantic croaker does not have a spot, however. Another way to tell the two apart is by the number of rays on the dorsal fins, which are contiguous on both. The Atlantic croaker has 28 or 29 rays in the second dorsal, the spot has 30 to 34. Average size is about a half-pound or less, with a maximum size of about 5 pounds.

HABITS/HABITAT: Abundant in the bay systems year-round, Atlantic croakers prefer to eat small crustaceans, shellfish and worms. The best bait is a small piece of peeled shrimp fished on bottom. The best time for catching this prolific fish is October and November during the fall spawning run, in ship channels, passes and cuts.

REMARKS: A croaker is one of the few fish capable of making a sound. The Atlantic croaker has a tough mouth, and any small hook needs to be very sharp to penetrate. Delicious to eat, this fish is possibly the most-sought of the smaller so-

A jig is one lure you want to have in your tackle box if you fish in salt water. It is one of the best shrimp imitations. Speckled trout, redfish and flounder, along with other species, really go for it. Use a bright-colored plastic grub on it.

Larger red drum and spotted seatrout often are found on shallow flats, in water less than 2 feet deep, sometimes much less, because this is where the food is. But fish in shallow water are extremely spooky. The best approach is to wade and fish. A boat creates too much commotion. Also, the wader can do a better job of fishing.

SPOT CROAKER
(*Leiostomus xanthurus*)

DESCRIPTION: The spot croaker, or simply "spot," as it is commonly called, has the blunt and around passes. Spot croakers are highly prolific. The fish is primarily a bottom feeder and its

snout typical of the croaker family. Coloration is silvery to whitish with darker vertical stripes along the upper half of the body. Its common name comes from the dark spot just above and behind the gill slit. A spot about 12 inches long and weighing a pound is near maximum size.

HABITS/HABITAT: Spot croakers are caught in the bay systems throughout the warm-weather months, although the prime time is in spring and fall when they are migrating to and from the bays. The larger adult specimens are generally caught in the fall, during spawning activity, in the surf diet includes small shrimp, worms, small shellfish and baitfish. The best bait is a portion of a peeled shrimp fished on bottom, using a small hook because the fish has a small mouth.

REMARKS: The spot croaker, because of its size, is not actively sought for sport or food. Its flesh is edible but bony. The preferred cooking method is to fry the fish whole. Small spot croakers also are used for bait to take species like the spotted seatrout. There is no state or world record for the spot.

Larger spotted seatrout (speckled trout), those weighing about 4 pounds or more, feed almost exclusively on baitfish. The ticket is a plug that resembles a baitfish, or use the real thing. One of the best natural baits is a small croaker. Its distressed croaking noise attracts big trout. Also good is a small pinfish, which grunts.

Sheepshead and black drum, especially the larger specimens, are not widely utilized for food because they are difficult to clean. The scales are coarse and tough. Instead of scaling the fish, try this: Cut the skin along the top and bottom of the fillets, pull the skin away with pliers, and slice off the fillets. This can be done without removing the head or entrails.

SOUTHERN KING WHITING
(Menticirrhus americanus)

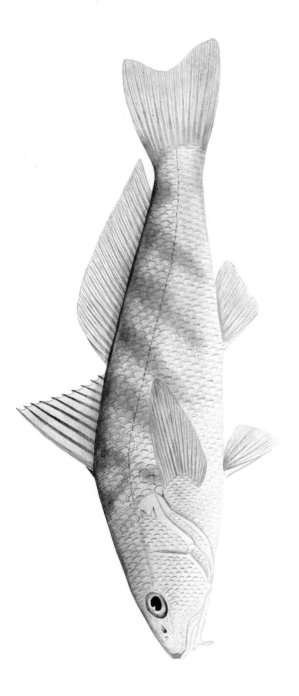

DESCRIPTION: Sometimes called the southern kingfish, the southern king whiting belongs to the croaker family, Sciaenidae. Coloration is silver-gray to brown, with darker bars on the shrimp fished on bottom. A small bait should be presented on a small hook. Whitings are most active in the summer, with the best fishing months being July, August and September.

sides—a pattern often more mottled than regular. The belly is white. A typical fish measures less than 12 inches and weighs less than 1 pound. Maximum weight is about 2 pounds.

HABITS/HABITAT: Southern king whitings are normally found in small schools in the Gulf surf and in the bays near passes. The fish feed primarily on bottom-dwelling organisms such as worms and crustaceans. The best bait is a peeled

REMARKS: Because of its size, the southern king whiting is most sporty to catch on light tackle. In the surf it will sometimes hit a tiny artificial bait such as a spoon or bucktail jig. Although smallish, it is good to eat.

STATE RECORD: 3.62 pounds. Gulf of Mexico. March 7, 1992. Gilbert Perez, Alice.

WORLD RECORD: None.

A productive bait for catching speckled trout is the so-called "speck rig," which is available at any coastal tackle outlet. Two small jigs are tied on separate monofilament leaders, one longer than the other to prevent tangling. Favored colors are white and yellow. The speck rig can be fished as is, but normally the jigs are fished below a popping cork. The speck rig is one of the better producers when night fishing off a lighted dock or pier.

Sometimes the saltwater fisherman needs to go deep when jetty fishing, since speckled trout and redfish tend to swim deep along the rocks. Any tide current makes it necessary to use a sinker, normally about a half-ounce or larger in weight, to get a bait deep. Use the slip-sinker rig described under "Hooks and Sinkers" in the chapter on Equipment. Either a shrimp fished on a treble hook or a baitfish on a single hook can be used.

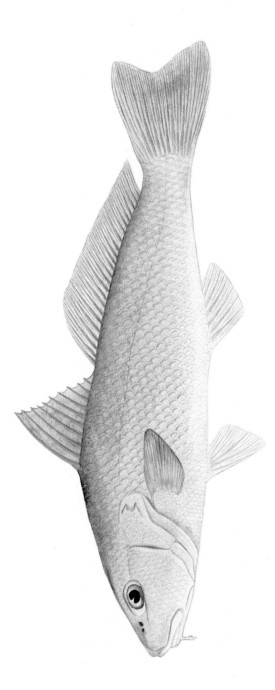

GULF KING WHITING
(Menticirrhus littoralis)

DESCRIPTION: The Gulf king whiting, usually known simply as the whiting, belongs to the croaker family. Although it is similar in shape and fin arrangement to the southern king whiting, the Gulf king whiting is generally lighter in color—silvery gray on the back shading to bright silver the warm-weather months. Gulf king whiting are mostly bottom feeders and the best bait is a peeled shrimp fished on a small hook on bottom. The prime fishing months are July, August and September. Not much else is known about the fish's life history, except that it is believed spawning oc-

on the sides and almost white along the belly. It has no colored bars or mottlings along the sides. The typical fish is only about 10 inches long and weighs a half-pound, if that.

HABITS/HABITAT: Of the 2 whiting species, the Gulf king whiting is much more abundant and is found primarily in the surf. The fish are numerous almost anywhere in the surf during curs in the Gulf. Some young show up in the bays, however.

REMARKS: Because of its diminutive size, the Gulf king whiting is not actively sought.

STATE RECORD: 2.13 pounds. Gulf of Mexico. November 18, 1991. Alan G. Butt, South Padre Island.

WORLD RECORD: None.

When wading the saltwater flats, wear Polaroid glasses to cut the surface glare. This way you can spot prowling fish and cast to them. It saves a lot of effort.

After a few minutes without a bite, there is a temptation to change baits. Many fishermen don't give a bait a chance to produce before they switch to something else. Pick out two or three lures you think will work and stay with them all day. You'll catch more fish that way.

When wading a shallow flat and the warm surface is calm, you can often locate redfish by watching for "tailing" activity. As a fish roots head down along the bottom, its flipping tail rises above the surface, and you can see the tail or the water swirls it creates.

When fishing a popping cork, you should balance the float to your rod and reel. It takes a rather long and stiff popping rod to bring a jumbo model through the water.

SHEEPSHEAD
(*Archosargus probatocephalus*)

DESCRIPTION: Also called the convict fish, the sheepshead is a member of the porgy family, Sparidae. It has the same profile as other porgies: deep body and slim through the shoulders. But the sheepshead can be differentiated from other family members by its tail, which is not deeply forked and has rounded instead of pointed ends. With the rounded tail, the sheepshead somewhat resembles a small black drum, since both have blunt heads. Look at the dental work, though, and you can tell the difference. Those sheeplike, close-fitted buck teeth are a dead giveaway. In color, the sheepshead is a tarnished silver with seven broad, vertical dark bands on its body. These bands stand out prominently on juvenile sheepshead but are faded and much less distinct on larger specimens. The dorsal fin is large and has very sharp spines. Average size is about a pound or slightly more, although the fish will grow to about 10 pounds.

HABITS/HABITAT: Sheepshead are resident fish. They will be in the same area, almost in the identical spot, day after day. They particularly like to hang around pilings, piers, jetties and reefs but also may be found along channel edges. Sheepshead use those strong incisor teeth to graze barnacles and small shellfish off pilings and rocks. They can be caught year-round, but the bigger ones are most plentiful in December, January, February and March. The best baits are shrimp and small fiddler and hermit crabs. Like other members of the porgy family, the sheepshead is a very efficient bait stealer. The angler had best pay attention to what he is doing, fishing a tight line with a bait on a small treble hook, jerking hard when he feels the first nibble. It is not unusual for the viselike jaws to bend a hook flat, and it must be reshaped before further use. Spawning occurs in February and March in the Gulf near jetties, rock piles and reefs. Smaller fish live in shallow, grassy areas where food is abundant, while adult fish prefer deeper water.

REMARKS: The fish gets its name from the sheeplike teeth. It is not a flashy fighter but uses its broad body to good advantage and pulls hard in short, stubborn runs. Although the sharp fins and tough scales make the fish difficult to clean, sheepshead are good to eat.

STATE RECORD: 12 pounds, 14.72 ounces. Galveston West Bay. December 4, 1983. Gary R. Davis, Galveston.

WORLD RECORD: 21 pounds, 4 ounces. Bayou St. John, New Orleans, Louisiana. April 16, 1982. Wayne Desselle.

GAFFTOPSAIL CATFISH
(*Bagre marinus*)

DESCRIPTION: Better known as the gafftop, the gafftopsail catfish is a member of the sea-catfish family, Ariidae. It has the familiar catfish shape, although the back has more of a hump. The gafftopsail name comes from the extended rays on the dorsal spine, the most distinguishing feature. Coloration is darkish blue-gray along the back, shading to whitish on the sides and belly. The dorsal and pectoral fins have extremely sharp spines covered by a toxic slime. Average size is about 2 pounds, although fish weighing more than 5 are caught.

HABITS/HABITAT: Gafftop prefer open water over mud or sand bottom and they swim actively in channel currents. They are found in Texas waters year-round. Although gafftop can be caught during all the warm months, the prime period is April through June. The larger fish, though, are normally taken in the fall. Live shrimp, small crabs and small live pinfish are productive baits. Gafftop will feed from the bottom to the surface, but most of them are caught deep, near or on bottom. Spawning occurs in the spring. The eggs are large and are carried in the mouth of the male after fertilization until they hatch and the fry can feed on their own. During this period, which may extend up to 65 days, the male does not eat.

REMARKS: Gafftop will occasionally hit artificials such as plastic-tailed jigs. When handling a gafftop, beware of the sharp fin spines. They can hurt. While the body slime makes the fish slippery and hard to clean, the gafftop is good to eat.

STATE RECORD: 13 pounds, 5.33 ounces. Mouth of Brazos River. December 13, 1981. Herman Frank Koehne, Jr., Houston.

WORLD RECORD: 8 pounds, 12 ounces. Indian River, Florida. March 30, 1991. Jack Leadbeater.

One fishing accessory that is almost indispensable for the serious saltwater angler is a pair of fisherman's pliers carried in a belt sheath for quick access. These pliers, featuring squared, wrench-grip jaws and a side-cutter, perform myriad jobs, from cutting leader wire and monofilament to tightening reel nuts, clipping fish fins, and straightening hooks.

SEA CATFISH
(*Arius felis*)

DESCRIPTION: The sea catfish, called the hardhead or hardhead catfish, is the other member of the family Ariidae in Texas waters. Its shape and silvery coloration are very similar to the freshwater channel catfish, including the weapons: dorsal and pectoral fins supported by sharp, barbed spines coated with a toxic slime. Average

But what you catch might be a blue catfish (see catfish in freshwater section), which can tolerate brackish water. The blue catfish is delicious to eat, but the hardhead is not considered edible.

STATE RECORD: 3.17 pounds. Gulf of Mexico. October 1, 1987. Mike Lombardl, Galveston. WORLD RECORD: 2 pounds, 6 ounces. Fort

Lauderdale, Florida. February 17, 1991. Kevin McKinnon.

size is about 10 inches in length and a half-pound in weight, although adults may reach 2 pounds or more.

HABITS/HABITAT: Hardheads are abundant in the bays, passes and channels, and in open waters close to shore. The voracious bait stealer will eat most anything, and consequently will attack almost any natural bait. It slows down only in the wintertime. Hardhead catfish spawn in the spring, and like the gafftopsail catfish, the male carries the fertilized eggs in his mouth until they hatch and the fry are able to care for themselves.

REMARKS: Because hardheads are so eager to gobble a bait and are caught in such great numbers, they are often referred to as "tourist trout." But those sharp fin spines are no joking matter. A puncture wound is very painful, and a hardhead always is poised to fight back, since the dorsal spine normally is held erect when the fish is excited. It is a good idea to grasp the lower jaw with a pair of pliers to immobilize the fish while the hook is worked free. And don't try to pin the fish down with a foot; a spine can easily penetrate the sole of a shoe. Hardheads can sometimes be caught in the brackish water of a tributary river.

The sharp fin spine of a catfish has a toxic substance and is capable of inflicting a painful injury on the fisherman who gets careless. If you get wounded, you can get some quick relief by scraping a little of the slime off the fish's body and rubbing it into the puncture. The slime is a natural antidote.

Many fish species have bony mouths that are hard to penetrate with a hook. A sharp hook is much more effective than a dull one. Carry a small file or whetstone in your tacklebox and periodically use it to touch up the hook point. Also, examine the point to be sure it hasn't become bent or broken.

SOUTHERN FLOUNDER
(*Paralichthys lethostigma*)

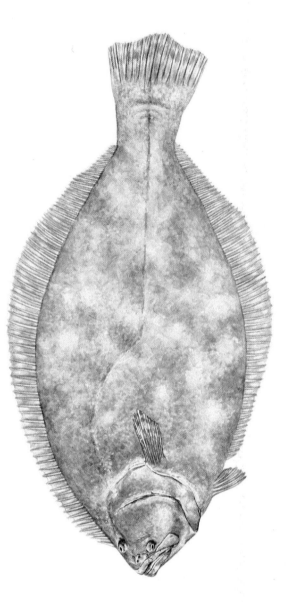

DESCRIPTION: The southern flounder (family Bothidae), commonly called the flounder, has, like its close relative the Gulf flounder, a body that is laterally compressed, and the fish lies on its side rather than on the abdomen, always looking up. The flounder is salt water's answer to the

REMARKS: A flounder is an ambush feeder. On a grassy flat, it will fan out a spot in the vegetation not far from shore and snuggle down on the mud or sand bottom in a motionless state, keeping its vision trained for any unsuspecting marsh minnow or shrimp that might swim by and be

chameleon; it is capable of changing its color pattern to match the bottom type, a natural camouflage. The topside color ranges from a blackish-brown to a light gray or mottled coloring if the bottom is as varied as an oyster reef. The downside is a pure white. Average weight is about 1 to 3 pounds, but the fish can attain more than 8 pounds, with a length of up to 3 feet.

HABITS/HABITAT: The southern flounder is, by far, the most abundant member of the flatfish family in Texas waters. Flounder stay mostly in shallow water along the shores of bays during the warm months, from April to October. Juvenile fish feed on crustaceans but switch to fish as they grow older. The general fishing season is April through November. A prime time is October and November during the "flounder run," as the fish migrate through channels and cuts toward the Gulf to spawn. The best baits are cut mullet, shrimp and artificials like a jig with a bright plastic tail, or what is called a worm-jig. After flounder spawn in the Gulf, the small fish enter the bay systems in the spring and grow rapidly, reaching 12 inches by the end of their first year. Females grow more rapidly than males.

converted into a meal. Lying still on its side in shallow water, the fish can be seen at night in the beam of a bright light. Many flounder are taken by gigging (spear-fishing) at night. The best season is April to November, and the best hunting is on a high tide, which brings fish up onto the flats, and during a light wind that allows the water to clear. Giggers either wade, using gasoline lanterns, or hunt from special-rigged boats, with bright 12-volt quartz lights on the bow, that can navigate in water only inches deep. A flatbottom boat like this is usually propelled by what looks like a miniature airplane motor with a prop mounted on a steel frame above the outboard motor, which is tilted up when the air propulsion device is being used. Flounder are delicious to eat and normally are baked.

STATE RECORD: 13 pounds. Sabine Lake. February 18, 1976. Herbert L. Endicott, Groves.

WORLD RECORD: 20 pounds, 9 ounces. Nassau Sound, Florida. September 5, 1975. Larenza W. Mungin.

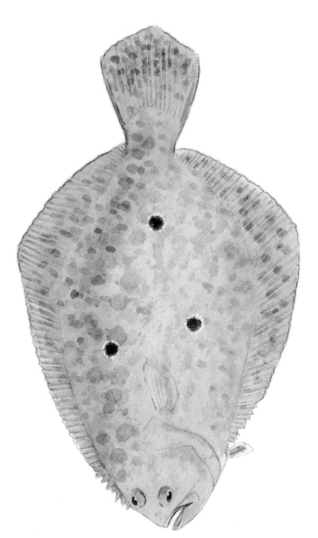

GULF FLOUNDER
(Paralichthys albigutta)

DESCRIPTION: In color, the Gulf flounder is similar to that of the more-common southern flounder, since these fish adapt to the color of the bottom, where they partially bury themselves and wait for unsuspecting prey to wander within range. Most often, the topside of the Gulf flounder is tannish or brown with numerous blotches and with three ocellated spots arranged in a triangular pattern. This feature distinguishes it from the southern flounder, although the pattern might be faint on some specimens. The underside is white. The typical Gulf flounder is smallish, averaging about a pound or less in weight.

HABITS/HABITAT: The Gulf flounder lives mostly on shallow grass flats, the same place where the southern flounder is found, another reason for confusing the pair. Giggers take Gulf flounder right along with southern flounder. Gulf flounder are in the bays from spring into the fall, migrating to the Gulf as the temperature drops.

REMARKS: The Gulf flounder is not nearly as large or as abundant as the southern flounder.

STATE RECORD: None.

WORLD RECORD: 2 pounds, 15 ounces. Cayo Costa Island, Florida. March 24, 1991. Alan Rubin.

Shrimp seem to be just looking for an excuse to die, particularly in the summer when warm air and water temperatures put more stress on them. An ice chest, which keeps the water inside from warming rapidly, makes a good bait bucket. It should be fitted with a pump or aerator, powered by the boat battery or an auxiliary battery, to provide plenty of oxygen in the water. At the same time, change some of the water at frequent intervals. Keep the water shaded and add a small amount of ice when needed to cool it. But don't put in too much ice; that results in a sharp drop in temperature. You might also carry some O-Tabs, commercial tablets that release oxygen into the water, and add them if necessary.

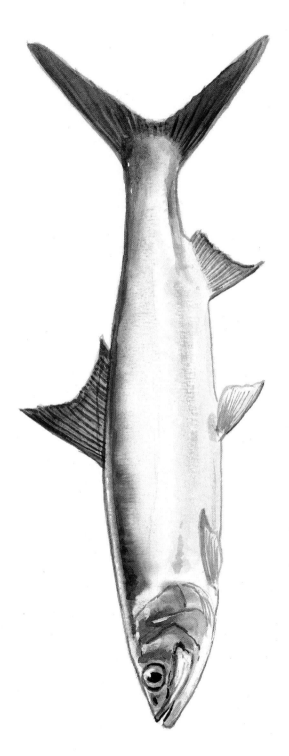

LADYFISH
(*Elops saurus*)

DESCRIPTION: Best known as the skipjack and sometimes called the tenpounder, the ladyfish belongs to the family Elopidae, which includes the tarpon. Long, slender and almost cylinder-shaped, it is not as compressed in body shape as is the tar-tened, transparent larvae. These larvae feed and grow and finally change into juveniles. Some of these juveniles, which resemble adults in shape and appearance, are actually shorter than late larvae.

pon. Its color shades from a greenish hue on the back to bright silver along the sides and abdomen. The large mouth, sheathed fins, elliptical eye socket and small scales distinguish it from other fish. Average weight is about 2 pounds or less, with 5 pounds being about maximum.

HABITS/HABITAT: The ladyfish is common along Gulf beaches and in passes and inner bays. It is a voracious predator, feeding on shrimp and small fish. Skipjacks will hit both natural and artificial baits. Spawning occurs in the open Gulf and eggs hatch not into fry but instead into flat-

REMARKS: The common nickname comes from the fish's fighting style, skipping repeatedly out of the water in spectacular leaps. The name tenpounder also derives from its fighting ability, a fish that is stronger than its size suggests. Although edible, the ladyfish is not normally consumed.

STATE RECORD: 4 pounds, 8 ounces. Port Isabel. July 22, 1978. Neely Johnson II, McAllen.
WORLD RECORD: 4 pounds, 10 ounces. Jupiter, Florida. March 27, 1991. Joshua L. Becker.

One way saltwater fishermen locate schools of feeding fish such as Spanish mackerel and speckled trout in the summer is to watch for feeding birds. When the predators rush baitfish to the surface, the frantic little fish jump out of the water and the dive-bombing gulls get their share. The idea is to stay back from the activity and fish with long casts. Otherwise, you will drive the fish down and they will move someplace else.

Any channel or pass connecting a bay with the Gulf is a natural place for fish to move into periodically to feed, especially if there is a tide coming in or going out. Sometimes the fish are present on the bay side of the channel while at others they will be out toward the Gulf or actually in the channel somewhere between the two ends. Try all the different places.

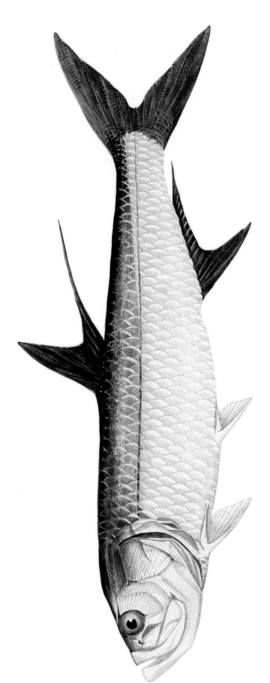

TARPON
(*Megalops atlantica*)

DESCRIPTION: The tarpon, nicknamed the silver king, belongs to the family Elopidae. It is silver in color and has a large, uptilted mouth. There is a large bony plate at the center of the lower jaw. The tarpon's body resembles that of a giant herring. Scales are extremely large and heavy. with a jump and wild shakes of the head. Because of its acrobatics and size, it is highly prized as a game fish.

STATE RECORD: 210 pounds. South Padre Island. November 13, 1973. Thomas F. Gibson, Jr., Houston.

Average size is 35 to 50 pounds, although the fish grows larger.

HABITS/HABITAT: An occasional tarpon will be hooked along the upper coast, from Port Aransas to Sabine Pass, but most are found at the southern tip, around South Padre Island and Port Isabel, since the fish prefers a tropical or sub-tropical climate. It ranges close to shore, going into passes and mouths of rivers. Its food consists of mullet, pinfish, crabs, shrimp, menhaden, and other small fish. A live baitfish or an artificial that imitates one is the best bait, whether drift-fishing or casting. The bony mouth makes it ex-tremely difficult to hook. Little is known about the tarpon's spawning activity or growth.

REMARKS: Tarpon are increasing in number, albeit slowly. Once plentiful along parts of the Texas coast, the tarpon went into a drastic de-cline, attributed to the damming of rivers, droughts, pesticides, and overfishing—or a com-bination of all. The tarpon is a spectacular leaper and, more often than not, will throw the hook

WORLD RECORD: 283 pounds, 4 ounces. Sherbro Island. April 16, 1991. Goo Vogt.

Saltwater wade-fishing is thought of as shallow-water fishing, in water no more than knee deep. But wade-fishing is equally effective in water waist deep or slightly deeper. The wade fisherman can move slowly and fish all the water thor-oughly in front of him, either with lures or with live bait under a popping cork. He also is making less noise than he would in a boat. If he gets into a school of fish, he can stop right there and fish until action ceases. A boat can drift out of range of the fish, or, when an anchor is put down, the fish get spooked. When down in the water like this, the fisherman needs to use a long rod, 7 feet or longer, preferably longer. The long rod makes it easier to cast and work a bait.

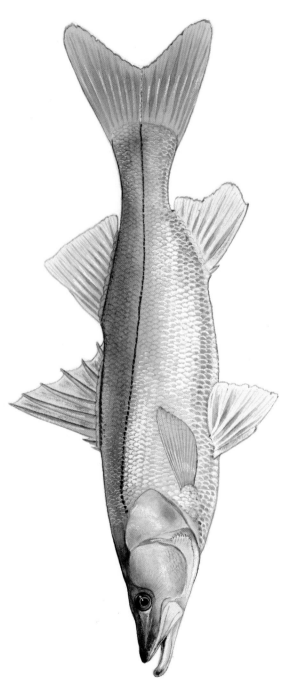

SNOOK
(Centropomus undecimalis)

DESCRIPTION: The snook, also called the robalo or pike, is a member of the family Centropomidae. The fish has a long, concave snout with a jutting underjaw. It has a high back, 2 dorsal fins that are well separated, and a deeply forked tail.

STATE RECORD: 57 pounds, 4 ounces. Padre Island. 1937. Louis Rawalt, Corpus Christi.

WORLD RECORD: 53 pounds, 10 ounces. Rio de Parismina, Costa Rica. October 18, 1978. Gibert Ponzi.

Sides are silvery, the belly white. A dark, conspicuous lateral line extends the entire length of the body onto the tail. Average size is about 5 to 8 pounds, although the fish grows to larger sizes.

HABITS/HABITAT: The snook, a tropical species, is primarily found in South Bay, the southern tip of the Texas bay system that has the state's only mangroves, and in the southernmost part of the Lower Laguna Madre, places where waters remain warmer throughout the year. It also is equally at home in the brackish water of a tributary river. Its diet consists of other fish, shrimp and crabs. Snook can be caught year-round. Fall is one of the better fishing times. Adults tend to hang around Gulf passes and around pilings, mangrove roots and other types of underwater structure. The fish will hit both natural and artificial baits. Not much is known about the fish's life cycle along the Texas coast.

REMARKS: The snook strikes hard and is a strong fighter, often jumping repeatedly, similar in style to a freshwater largemouth bass. But a fisherman should beware when landing a snook or when attempting to unhook it. The gill-cover edges are razor-sharp.

The difference between freshwater artificial plugs and those made for salt water is the action. Redfish and speckled trout generally prefer plugs that come fairly smoothly through the water without a lot of wiggle, or those that dart slowly back and forth; freshwater plugs have a much stronger wobble. Saltwater lures are supposed to imitate small baitfish like finger mullet. The most productive colors in salt water are often the brightest: orange, red, yellow or fluorescent, although white can pay off when the bright colors won't.

When fishing a popping cork, jerk back the instant you see the float disappear into the water. Trout particularly have the knack of hitting a bait, then immediately rejecting it if the fish feels any resistance or doesn't catch the bait properly for swallowing.

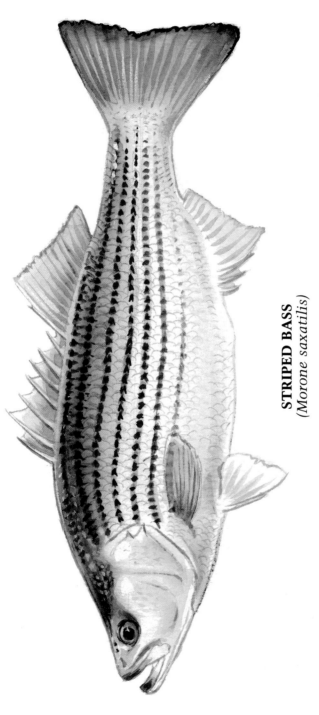

STRIPED BASS
(Morone saxatilis)

DESCRIPTION: The striped bass, or striper, belongs to the temperate bass family, Percichthyidae. It is a long and fairly heavy-bodied fish. Coloration is olive-green on the back, shading to silvery on the sides and white on the abdomen. eat. Any red meat on a fillet is strong-tasting and should be trimmed away before cooking.

STATE RECORD: 46 pounds, 8 ounces. Below Lake Amistad. May 12, 1993. Johnny Freeman, Del Rio.

The most prominent characteristic is the stripe pattern, 7 or 8 uninterrupted black stripes along the sides. Average size is 8 to 12 pounds, although the fish grows much larger.

HABITS/HABITAT: Striped bass are school fish that like to roam close to shore, and they can be caught in cold weather as well as warm. The primary diet is small fish, and stripers are taken on both natural and artificial baits. Striped bass in the spring run up rivers to spawn, since running water is necessary for reproduction. The growth rate is rapid, up to 12 inches the first year.

REMARKS: The striped bass, which has been stocked in many inland lakes, is a saltwater fish that has adapted to fresh water, not the other way around. The Texas Parks and Wildlife Department, in conjunction with the U.S. Fish and Wildlife Service, continues to stock this fish to reestablish striped bass in the Trinity and Galveston bay systems. Commercial fishing records indicate the species was found in this area around the turn of the century but eventually disappeared, for reasons unknown. Any striper caught should be examined closely to see if it is carrying a tag. The striper is a fine game fish and good to

WORLD RECORD: 67 pounds, 8 ounces. San Luis, California. May 7, 1992. Hank Ferguson.

A popular method for fishing deeper water is what is called "free shrimping." A No. 8 treble hook is tied directly to the monofilament line. No other weight such as a sinker or swivel is included, since it will take the bait down too rapidly. A live shrimp is hooked through the bony horn on top of its head. When hooked this way the shrimp is uninjured and remains lively. Cast out and let the shrimp sink slowly and naturally, struggling where it can be seen by any roving predator. Once it sinks to the level where feeding fish are, it likely will be attacked. This method also will work with a small baitfish like a pinfish or piggy perch. But with a fish, use a larger hook, about a No. 3/o single hook.

CREVALLE JACK
(Caranx hippos)

DESCRIPTION: The crevalle jack, commonly called the jackfish, is a member of the family Carangidae. The head is sharply rounded and there are strong bony scutes on the tail, which is deeply forked. There is a conspicuous dark spot on the gill cover. Coloration is bluish-green along the back, shading to silvery along the sides. Sometimes the lower part of the body will have a yellowish tinge. Average size is 3 to 6 pounds, but fish exceeding 25 are not unusual.

HABITS/HABITAT: Crevalle jack are common in Texas waters. Bigger specimens tend to hang around the mouths of passes and rivers, but some go into the bays in the fall. A prime time to catch larger crevalle jack is September and October, when it is not uncommon for big ones to tear up the tackle of surf fishermen. For numbers, however, the best angling season is warm weather, May through August. Crevalle jack eat mullet, other small fish, and crabs. Spawning occurs in the Gulf and juveniles are abundant in the surf, often moving into bays and roaming in schools around pilings, reefs and other structure.

REMARKS: Crevalle jack can be caught on almost any bait or lure. Incredibly strong, the fish is a bulldog-like battler. Most fishermen despise the crevalle jack because it is an unspectacular fighter and is worthless for food.

STATE RECORD: 50 pounds, 4 ounces. Port Aransas. June 26, 1986. Francis Lyon, Leander.

WORLD RECORD: 57 pounds, 5 . ounces. Barra do Kwanza, Angola. October 10, 1992. Cam Nicolson.

When fishing an artificial lure in a bay, some anglers tend to retrieve too rapidly. The slower the retrieve, the better, under most conditions. Retrieve just fast enough to keep the bait off bottom or out of bottom grass. With some plugs, like the MirrOlure, the angler has to improvise, since this popular bait has less built-in action. This calls for little jerks of the rod tip while you are reeling, or stopping and starting the retrieve to make the plug dart erratically to imitate a mullet or some other baitfish.

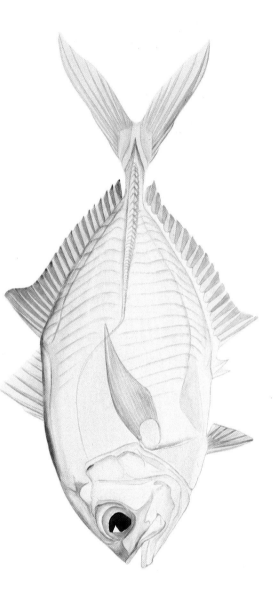

HORSE-EYE JACK
(Caranx latus)

DESCRIPTION: The horse-eye jack, also called the goggle-eye jack, belongs to the jackfish family, Carangidae. The head is not as angular as that of the more-common crevalle jack. The back is bluish-gray, the sides silvery, the underside yel- channels and passes or in them, but it also is not unusual to catch them much farther out in the Gulf. The primary diet is small fish and shrimp. Little is known about the life history other than that spawning occurs in the Gulf.

lowish-silver. All fins except the pectoral are yellowish or dusky. Juvenile horse-eye jacks typically will have dark vertical bars, but the markings fade or even disappear as the jacks grow older. In shape the fish somehow resembles the Florida pompano, but it has the bony scutes along the side and tail that are typical of jacks. Average size is about 2 pounds, with anything larger than 10 being unusual.

HABITS/HABITAT: The bigger horse-eye jacks normally will be caught near the mouths of

REMARKS: Like its cousin the crevalle jack, the horse-eye jack is not much good for anything except to make a nuisance of itself, getting hooked when an angler is fishing for something else. It fights in unspectacular, strong, steady pulls down deep. The fish is undesirable for food.

STATE RECORD: 18 pounds, 15.68 ounces. West Flower Gardens off Galveston. July 17, 1986. Adolph Schulz, Galveston.

WORLD RECORD: 24 pounds, 8 ounces. Miami, Florida. December 20, 1982. Tito Schnau.

A cast net is one piece of equipment that will pay for itself; use it to catch your bait instead of buying bait. Learning to toss a cast net just takes a little practice. At daybreak, when the water is calm, schools of small fish such as finger mullet and mud minnows can be seen working, dimpling the surface. A few tosses of the net will put you in business.

One of the favorite lures for fishing the shallow grass flats for redfish and speckled trout is a thin-metal Johnson Sprite gold spoon. With rod tip held high, you can retrieve it slowly above the vegetation. If the water is abnormally clear, use a tarnished spoon; if it is slightly off-color, try a shiny new spoon. The idea is to match the flash to the water conditions.

FLORIDA POMPANO
(*Trachinotus carolinus*)

DESCRIPTION: The Florida pompano, better known simply as the pompano, belongs to the jackfish family, Carangidae. It is a deep-bodied fish, grayish-blue on the back shading to silver on jumping in the wakes of boats. The pompano is considered to be one of the finest eating fish, particularly when broiled with butter.

the sides with yellow underneath. There is a bluish tint above and in front of the eyes. It is sometimes mistaken for the crevalle jack, but it is easy to tell the difference. The sides of the deeply forked tail and the caudal peduncle are smooth, while a crevalle jack has rough or bony scales called scutes. Average size is 2 to 4 pounds, occasionally larger.

HABITS/HABITAT: Florida pompano are shore fish that inhabit waters along sandy beaches. The diet is composed of mollusks, beach fleas, shrimp, small fish and various burrowing crustaceans. The general fishing season is late spring through early fall, along beaches and around the mouths of passes. Pompano are usually found just inside the breakers, where they work in the troughs between sandbars. Since the mouth of the pompano is small, appropriate-sized baits and hooks should be used. Baits include small shrimp, crustaceans and junior-sized artificial lures. Spawning activity is in the Gulf in the summer, and the young are in the surf in great numbers in warm weather.

REMARKS: In September and October, adults move far into the bays and sometimes are sighted

STATE RECORD: 6.25 pounds. Gulf of Mexico. January 1, 1989. Wilbert Hettinger, Winamac. WORLD RECORD: 8 pounds, 1 ounce. Flagler Beach, Florida. March 19, 1984. Chester E. Dietrick.

Night fishing off lighted piers and docks is normally more productive than fishing the same location during the day. The bright lights trained on the water create a food chain. Swarms of insects are drawn to the illumination. Those that fall into the water are gobbled by small fish. Predatory species such as speckled trout prey on the small fish. Anglers prey on the trout. Often the best fish are caught after midnight, when things have quietened and the more suspicious larger fish move in. A speck rig with two jigs is an effective lure under the lights. But bigger trout are often taken on a live baitfish such as a pinfish or piggy perch.

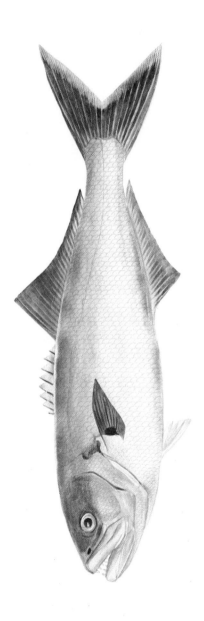

BLUEFISH
(Pomatomus saltatrix)

DESCRIPTION: The bluefish is the only member of the family Pomatomidae. It is dark greenish-blue along the back, shading to a bluish-silver on the sides, white on the belly. The tail is deeply forked. The large mouth, with its projected lower jaw, is brimming with caninelike teeth. Average size is about 1 to 2 pounds, but the fish grows much larger.

with a variety of plugs and spoons. Not much is known about the bluefish's migratory habits or other life history.

REMARKS: Since bluefish often school with other offshore fish such as small dorados (dolphin), they tend to get confused with other fish. Some fishermen call the small specimens snapper, while larger fish are referred to as skipjack. A

HABITS/HABITAT: The bluefish is a migratory species that comes close to shore in Texas waters from about April through August. The fish are aggressive, cannibalistic predators, often going on frenzied feeding sprees, killing more fish, squid and shrimp than they eat. Most are caught offshore as they prowl around in dense schools, but they sometimes are taken from piers and around jetties and oil rigs that are close to shore. Prime fishing months are April, May and June. They can be taken on live shrimp and finger mullet along bluefish strikes very hard. When handling one, the angler should beware of the sharp teeth. Bluefish have been known to attack humans. Their flesh is edible but not highly desired.

STATE RECORD: 16 pounds, 9.92 ounces. Offshore 45 miles out of Freeport. January 11, 1987. Alex Koumonduros, Houston.

WORLD RECORD: 31 pounds, 12 ounces. Hatteras, North Carolina. January 30, 1972. James M. Hussey.

A prime time to go fishing, especially in the fall, is right before a front arrives. Fish are most active shortly before a front hits, then soon after it passes, although the early period normally is best, when the water is calm before the wind switches to the north. But once the weather becomes threatening, get off the water. Fronts can become violent.

One accessory every saltwater angler should have in his boat is a pair of heavy-duty cotton gloves. Wear the gloves when grasping a leader, either wire or monofilament, as you lead a fish in for gaffing. Otherwise, a sudden run by the fish could burn your palms. It is not a bad idea either to wear gloves when handling fish with teeth, sharp dorsal spines or gill covers.

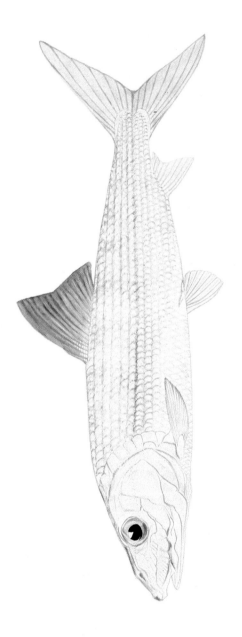

BONEFISH
(*Albula vulpes*)

DESCRIPTION: The bonefish, belonging to the family Albulidae, has a rather torpedo-shaped body, silverish-green in color, with a small turned-down mouth useful for bottom feeding. The head has bony plates, hence the name. In Texas waters, the bonefish does not grow as large as in warmer areas.

unless it is to be mounted or submitted as a new state record.

STATE RECORD: 3 pounds, 12 ounces. Port Aransas North Jetty. November 19, 1977. C.W. Morris, Dallas.

WORLD RECORD: 19 pounds. Zululand, South Africa. May 26, 1962. Brian W. Batchelor.

HABITS/HABITAT: The odds of catching a bonefish are slim, but an occasional one is taken in Texas waters. It stays mostly in shallow water and is not migratory, residing in one general area. It is a tropical species, and most Texas waters, including those at the far southern part, probably are too cool to sustain bonefish in any numbers. Bonefish cruise in small compact schools. Like red drum, bonefish look for food on shallow grassy flats, feeding on tiny grass shrimp and bottom-dwelling invertebrates. Because it has a small mouth, the bonefish can only be taken on a small bait, such as a mud minnow or shrimp. The fish is very easily spooked.

REMARKS: The bonefish is known for its speed. Once hooked, it streaks across a flat, making a reel drag screech. It is a light-tackle species. It is possible to see these fish on the shallow flats, but fishermen often confuse them with mullet, since any bonefish found in Texas waters is small-ish and because the shape of a small bonefish and a large mullet are pretty much alike. Any bonefish caught should be reported to the Texas Parks and Wildlife Department. The bonefish is not considered edible and should always be released,

Whether fishing in salt water or fresh, the angler can improve his chances by keeping records—nothing elaborate, only a few basic facts: Where he was fishing, what he caught, what day of what month, what bait he was using, water depth, water temperature, what time of day or night, moon phase, and anything else that comes to mind such as water conditions or tides. After two or three years and many fishing trips, the angler can compare information from different trips. Usually, a pattern will emerge. Fish will be at a certain place at a certain time of year and bite on certain baits. The "profile" drawn by the accumulation of information will tell the angler where to fish when certain conditions are met. Thus, if he caught fish in mid-June in a particular place the past two years, he can return to the same place about the same time in June this year and probably catch fish.

PINFISH
(*Lagodon rhomboides*)

DESCRIPTION: The pinfish, also called the pin perch, is a member of the porgy family, Sparidae. Upper-body coloration is greenish with blue and yellow tinges and spots. The belly is white. A dark spot on the shoulder might be prominent or blurred. The dorsal fin spines are slender and sharp, or pinlike, hence the name. Average size is about 5 inches. Few adults exceed 8 inches in length.

HABITS/HABITAT: Pinfish are widespread and plentiful in the bays and passes, and also are common in the Gulf. They like to hang around jetties, piers and wharves. Small mollusks, crustaceans, fish and vegetation comprise the basic diet. Small bits of shrimp or cut fish are good baits for catching pinfish. The fish spawn in the Gulf, but not much else is known about the life history. Growth rate is slow. A year-old fish is about 3 inches in length, while a 2-year specimen is only about 5 inches.

REMARKS: The pinfish provides amusement to youngsters fishing from docks and piers since it is so plentiful and eager to hit a baited hook. With more serious anglers, though, it is despised as a bait stealer, a trait members of the porgy family are noted for. A pinfish has to be handled carefully because of the sharp fin spines. While the fish is edible, its size and numerous bones discourage the practice. It is more commonly used as live bait to fish for larger species like speckled trout.

STATE RECORD: 2.46 pounds. Galveston Bay. January 4, 1992. Mark Duncan, Houston.

WORLD RECORD: 3 pounds, 5 ounces. Horn Island, Mississippi. September 4, 1992. William Davis Fountain.

Wade fishermen know that getting a fish off the hook and onto a stringer can be a tedious operation. A redfish or speckled trout is slippery and difficult to grasp with one hand. A solution is to take a landing net with a cord that ties to your belt. The aluminum net will float along behind as you wade, but it is there when you need it.

KNOBBED PORGY
(*Calamus nodosus*)

DESCRIPTION: The knobbed porgy is a member of the family Sparidae. It has a deep, compressed body with a sloping forehead and a small mouth with incisorlike front teeth. Coloration is silvery. The preopercle, or "cheek bone," is dark purple with yellowish spots and dark stripes. There is usually a dark splotch on the pectoral fin near where it attaches to the body. Above the rear of the nostril is a knoblike protrusion, hence the name. Maximum size is about 2 feet in length and about 4 pounds in weight.

HABITS/HABITAT: The knobbed porgy lives primarily on deep-water banks and around oil platforms, where it uses its sharp teeth to browse barnacles and vegetation. The strong jaws are also used to crush invertebrates. Porgies are occasionally caught by anglers fishing for snapper. Because of its small mouth and tough jaws, the knobbed porgy is difficult to hook, making it more of a pesky bait stealer than anything. Little is known of the life history of the knobbed porgy, other than that it is probably resident year-round.

REMARKS: A porgy species found offshore is the whitebone porgy (*Calamus leucosteus*), whose body is silvery-white with faint vertical bars. There are dark blotches on the dorsal and anal fins. It also prefers deep water, but the fish is not abundant along Texas shores. Average size is about 1 pound. Porgies are edible, but the sharp fin spines make them difficult to clean.

STATE RECORD: 4 pounds, 2.8 ounces. Flower Gardens off Galveston. June 20, 1986. Adolph Schulz, Galveston.

WORLD RECORD: None.

State record whitebone porgy: 2.63 pounds. Gulf of Mexico. July 15, 1989. G. A. Landry, Rio Hondo. (No world record.)

Fishing reports make interesting reading, but they are not always reliable. The main problem is timing. There is generally a lag of two days or more between the time the report is compiled and the time it hits print. A fish's habits can change a lot over this period of time. In fact, the habits can change over a matter of hours.

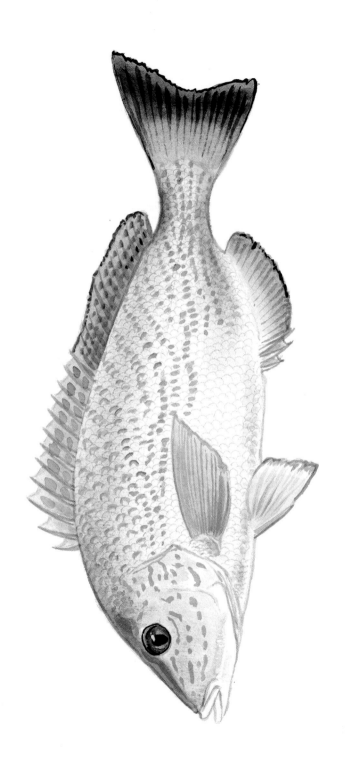

PIGFISH
(*Orthopristis chrysoptera*)

DESCRIPTION: Best known as the piggy perch, the pigfish is a member of the grunt family, Pomadasyidae. Grunts closely resemble the snappers but, unlike the snappers, they do not have teeth in the roof of the mouth. The fish has a deep body and pointed snout. Coloration is bluish on the back shading to silvery or white below. Each scale has a blue center and a bronze spot on the edge, and this produces an irregular barring effect, particularly on the cheeks. Often mistaken for the pinfish, the pigfish has shorter dorsal fin spines, the eye is smaller, and the distance from eye to mouth is greater. Average size is 6 inches or less, with 12 inches being about maximum length.

HABITS/HABITAT: Pigfish are not as abundant as pinfish. Adults spawn in the Gulf, and the young grow up in the bays, feeding primarily on small crustaceans and mollusks. Pigfish are most active in the warm-weather months. The best bait for catching them is a tiny piece of peeled shrimp fished on a small hook on bottom. They like to hang along the edges of channels.

REMARKS: The name grunt comes from the grunting sound the piggy perch and other mem-bers of this family are capable of producing. It isn't unusual for a pigfish to become vocal after being caught. The diminutive fish is rarely sought for sport or food. Its normal role is to be used as bait for taking larger species.

STATE RECORD: 13.75 ounces. Galveston Bay. July 5, 1987. Ronald W. Mache, Houston. WORLD RECORD: None.

Saltwater fishes relate to structure, or breaks in the topography, just as freshwater species do. Examples are the natural channels, commonly called "guts," in the bay and surf, along with the reefs and sandbars in between. Unlike man-made navigational channels, these are created by wind and tide action. At times fish will feed along the edge of a channel, and at other times right in the guts. Although some channels are better producers than others, any "break" like this in the topography is worth fishing.

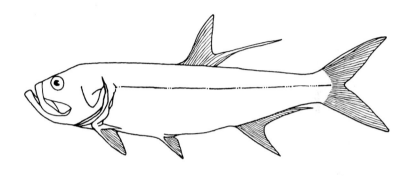

OPEN-WATER SPECIES

KING MACKEREL
(*Scomberomorus cavalla*)

DESCRIPTION: Better known as the king-fish, the king mackerel is the largest of the mackerels (family Scombridae). The body is long and slim, javelin-shaped. Young kings possess yellow spots, but adults are readily identified because, unlike the Spanish and cero mackerels, they lack eral fishing season is May through October, with the prime months being June through September. The earliest arrivals are usually larger fish. Primary food is other fish. Most kings are caught by trolling or drift-fishing, using natural baits like cigar minnows (ice fish) imported from Florida,

markings of any kind. Coloration is drab: iron-gray along the back shading to drab silver along the sides to white along the belly. But perhaps the most unusual characteristic is the lateral line. It is angulate and curves down abruptly, then back, in the region below the second dorsal fin. Tiny finlets, or miniature fins, are on the back of the body between the dorsal and tail; there are 9 dorsal finlets and 8 or 9 anal finlets. There are 15 to 16 spines in the first dorsal fin. The mouth is full of sharp canine teeth. Average size is 8 to 12 pounds, although fish of more than 20 pounds are regularly caught.

HABITS/HABITAT: The king mackerel is a pelagic species that roams in schools. Adults tend to be in smaller groups than juvenile fish. Kings can be close to shore or many miles out. One place to find them is along a tide-line where the greenish inshore water meets blue offshore water. Debris and seaweed collect along this distinct line, attracting smaller fish that king mackerels feed on. King mackerel also relate to oil platforms, reefs and anchored shrimpboats. The gen-ribbonfish (cutlassfish) and mullet, although kings will hit artificials. The ribbonfish is typically presented on a 2-hook rig with the second hook near the tail of the bait, to keep a short-hitting king from chomping the bait in half without getting hooked. King mackerel show up along the Texas coast only in warm weather, with most of the fish thought to migrate from the waters off Florida, although the fish's life history still remains something of a mystery.

REMARKS: The kingfish's slim, streamlined body suggests speed, which it has. The fish is continually on the move. A king mackerel hits a bait at fast speed and fights in extremely fast runs. Because it fights in open water, it can be caught on lighter tackle, which makes its fast-running style even more spectacular. The flesh is edible but oily.

STATE RECORD: 71 pounds, 8 ounces. Three miles south of Buccaneer Field off Galveston. May 27, 1977. L.F. Higdon, Spring.
WORLD RECORD: 90 pounds. Key West, Florida. February 16, 1976. Norton I. Thornton.

SPANISH MACKEREL
(*Scomberomorus maculatus*)

DESCRIPTION: The Spanish mackerel, smallest member of the mackerel family, has the same javelin-shaped body and sharp teeth of the other two mackerels. It is more colorful, though, with golden-yellow spots. The pectoral fins are smooth, without any scales, while those of the goes by the generic name "hootie," which is sparse pieces of white nylon tied around 2 hooks in tandem on a wire leader. (When fishing for any of the mackerels, use a wire leader because of their sharp teeth.) Trollers often find active fish around the end of a rock jetty. There is an "apron" area of

cero and king mackerels are scaled. Average size is about 15 to 18 inches and weight 2 pounds or less.

HABITS/HABITAT: Spanish mackerel are a migratory species. They range in large schools that move fast and far. They stay relatively close to shore and congregate around the mouths of channels and passes, but they rarely go into bays. Shrimp is a principal food, but Spanish mackerel also prey on squid and small fish. Anglers after Spanish mackerel watch for "bird works." When a ravenous school of Spanish mackerel push frantic baitfish to the surface, gulls hover overhead to ambush any fish that clears the surface as it tries to escape the Spanish mackerel. A school normally stays up only briefly before sounding and reappearing nearby shortly, as the Spanish mackerel pursue their prey. Spanish mackerel come into Texas waters during the warm months, May through September. August is the prime fishing month, as both the fish and seagulls are most active at this time. Trolling is a popular way of taking Spanish mackerel. One of the favorite baits large rocks out from the end of a jetty, and since this is where food can be found, it is where predators like Spanish mackerel prowl. If the fish are not working the surface, try trolling deeper, using a trolling sinker to get the bait down. Spanish mackerel will also take small plugs, jigs and spoons.

REMARKS: Fishermen standing on rock jetties protecting Gulf passes and channels often catch Spanish mackerel, although most of these fish are caught from boats not far from land. Rarely will a king mackerel be caught that is as small as an adult Spanish mackerel. The fish is a determined fighter, strong for its size, that pulls in fast runs. The flesh, not as oily as that of a king mackerel, is delicious to eat.

STATE RECORD: 8 pounds, 11.8 ounces. Sabine Pass. August 15, 1976. Bobby Tarter, Bridge City.

WORLD RECORD: 13 pounds. Ocracoke Inlet, North Carolina. November 4, 1987. Robert Cranton.

CERO MACKEREL
(Scomberomorus regalis)

DESCRIPTION: The cero mackerel, sometimes called the cero, belongs to the family Scombridae, which includes the king and Spanish mackerels. The fish has a javelin-shaped body and a mouth full of sharp teeth. The cero has elongated yellow markings, while the Spanish mackerel has

mackerel. The cero will readily hit the same baits, natural and artificial, used for king mackerel. Cero mackerel are common in the Florida Straits and off Cuba; any cero caught in Texas waters is considered a stray, which suggests that cero mackerel do not migrate as far north as king and Span-

spots and the king has no markings. The cero mackerel also usually possesses a yellowish horizontal stripe running from the gill cover to the tail. The cero and Spanish mackerels have 17 to 18 spines in the front dorsal fin, while the king mackerel has 15 to 16. Cero are smaller than kings but larger than most Spanish mackerel. The average weight is about 3 to 5 pounds.

HABITS/HABITAT: The occasional cero taken is usually running with a school of king ish mackerel. This mackerel is present in Texas waters only during the warm-weather months.

REMARKS: Cero and other mackerels are kin to the bonitos and tunas, all being wide-ranging school fish of the open Gulf. The fish is edible, but oily.

STATE RECORD: None.

WORLD RECORD: 17 pounds, 2 ounces. Islamorada, Florida. April 5, 1986. G. Michael Mills.

Most shrimp fishermen use a treble hook, hooking the bait through the bony horn atop its head to keep from injuring it. Treble hook sizes vary greatly, but a No. 8 is popular. For live baitfish, some anglers prefer a single hook, about a No. 3/0 or 4/0. The hook should be light in order that the bait can swim around. The more active the bait, the more appeal it has.

If you are trolling in the Gulf for an offshore species such as the king mackerel (kingfish) and you are getting no takers, try drift fishing; allow a bait such as a ribbonfish to sink near bottom and be pulled along slowly by wind action. A trolled bait doesn't always get down to where the fish are.

COBIA
(*Rachycentron canadum*)

DESCRIPTION: Better known to Texas fishermen as the ling, the cobia belongs to the family Rachycentridae. Coloration is brownish, darker along the back, and a young specimen often has a black lateral band from the snout to the base of the caudal. The fish is long and fairly round with a hook one of the others. Ling are also taken by trolling near oil platforms, shrimpboats, buoys and floating debris. Shrimp, squid and live fish are good baits, as are large artificials such as spoons, plugs and jigs. Heavy line, more than 30-pound test, is needed since a cobia is incredibly strong,

long, flat head. The smooth-appearing skin of the cobia is actually covered with very small scales. The first dorsal has 8 or 9 spikelike spines, while the second dorsal fin contains 26 soft rays and the anal fin 23 to 26. The average fish is 20 to 25 pounds, although specimens exceeding 50 are not uncommon.

HABITS/HABITAT: Cobia dislike direct sunlight. When fishing for ling, look for anything that provides shade. The fish like to hide under buoys, oil platforms, anchored shrimpboats, and even floating debris. They feed on 2 types of food: crabs, flounder, shrimp and squid on or near the bottom, and small fish like menhaden closer to the surface. The general fishing season is April through September, with the prime months being July and August. When approaching a shady area, be quiet and watch. Often a ling or even several will swim out. Cobia are curious. Hook one and the others sometimes try to take the bait from its mouth. Drop another bait close by and it is not unusual to

and typically it will try to return to its sanctuary under a platform, shrimpboat or buoy. A wire leader is also normally used to prevent the fish from rubbing the monofilament on barnacles and severing it. These migratory fish show up off Texas as the weather warms. Earlier spring migrations along the Florida Panhandle and Alabama suggest the fish probably winter in the tropical waters off Florida.

REMARKS: Almost without exception, Texas anglers know this fish as the ling. It grows to a large size and is one of the most prized catches in Texas waters. The firm, white meat has been compared to that of a freshwater catfish, and it is highly sought for both sport and food.

STATE RECORD: 105 pounds. Galveston Bay. May 28, 1989. John W. Lodge III, Houston.

WORLD RECORD: 135 pounds, 9 ounces. Shark Bay, Western Australia. July 9, 1985. Peter William Goulding.

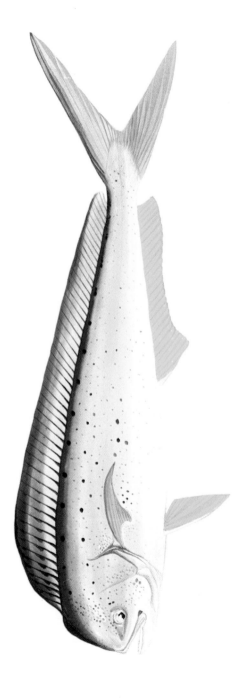

DOLPHIN
(Coryphaena hippurus)

DESCRIPTION: Also called the dorado, the dolphin belongs to the family Coryphaenidae. The dolphin's beautiful coloration is brilliant and changeable. Basic colors range from yellowish to metallic green to green-gold to dark blue with are migratory and prefer water of 7o°F or warmer. Thus, they come into Texas waters only during warm weather.

REMARKS: Dolphin, the fish, is not to be confused with the mammal of the same name. Texans

silvery markings. When seen darting about in clear water, the fish appears to be almost vivid blue. The brilliant coloration, which perhaps is brought on by excitement, quickly fades after the fish is removed from the water and dies. The elongated body has flattened sides. The male has a high, blunt forehead while the female has a more rounded head. The dorsal fin runs almost the entire body length. The anal fin also is unusually long, the tail deeply forked. Average size is 4 to 10 pounds, although fish weighing more than 40 are sometimes caught.

HABITS/HABITAT: Dolphin roam the blue offshore water, all the way from the 100-fathom curve, to closer in over snapper banks, around oil rigs, shrimpboats and masses of floating seaweed. The general fishing season is from late April through September, with the prime months being May and August. Dolphin, which feed near the surface, will strike most any trolled bait, the favored method of taking the fish. The primary diet is small fish, and dolphin will readily hit artificial lures, a feathered jig being one of the better producers. The dolphin is a spectacular fighter, jumping repeatedly between long, hard runs. Dolphins know the mammal dolphin as the porpoise. There is one other dolphin fish in Texas waters, the pompano dolphin (Coryphaena equisetis). While it looks like the common dolphin, the difference is size. If the fish is more than 30 inches long, and in most instances longer than 24, it is the common dolphin. A quick way to identify the fish is to count the rays in the fins. Common dolphin: dorsal fin, 55 to 65; anal fin, 26 to 30. Pompano dolphin: dorsal, 51 to 55; anal, 24 to 26. The pompano dolphin is typically called the "school dolphin" because it roams in large schools. Common or "bull dolphins" tend to be loners or in small groups. The flesh is delicious, but since the dolphin is a very bloody fish, it should be cleaned and put on ice immediately to preserve the flavor.

STATE RECORD: 65.60 pounds. Gulf of Mexico. July 4, 1989. Robby DeLeon, Corpus Christi.

WORLD RECORD: 87 pounds. Papagallo Gulf, Costa Rica. September 25, 1986. Manuel Salazar.

State record pompano dolphin: 4.10 pounds. Gulf of Mexico. August 3, 1990. Tommy Gueldner, Port Aransas. (No world record.)

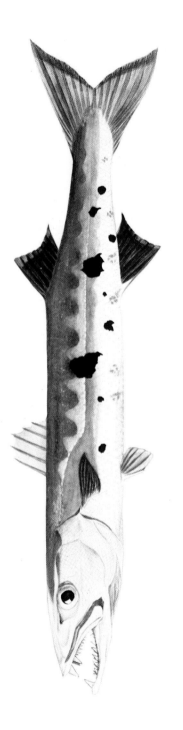

GREAT BARRACUDA
(Sphyraena barracuda)

DESCRIPTION: The great barracuda is a member of the family Sphyraenidae. It is a fearsome-looking specimen, with a pikelike, elongated body and a large mouth filled with sharp teeth. The 2 dorsal fins are well-separated, and the eye is small in relation to the jaw. Coloration var-

lives off other fish, the best bait. The general fishing season is May through October, with the prime months being July and August. Great barracuda spawn in the Gulf.

REMARKS: A barracuda is a strong, slashing-type fighter. The flesh is edible, but not highly

ies from sea-green to almost black along the back, with silvery sides and white belly. There usually are irregular black spots on the side. Average size is 5 to 25 pounds, but the fish grows larger.

HABITS/HABITAT: A great barracuda normally swims alone near the surface over a reef or around an oil platform. Smaller specimens roam in schools inshore. It is a voracious predator that sought. Specimens over 15 pounds are not normally eaten because of claims that the flesh could be toxic.

STATE RECORD: 50.25 pounds. Gulf of Mexico. September 2, 1989. David R. Lindsay, Austin.

WORLD RECORD: 85 pounds. Republic of Kiribati. April 11, 1992. John W. Helfrich.

When trying to gaff a fish, don't jab at it with the gaff hook. Simply lower the hook below the fish as it is brought alongside the boat, then bring the hook up into the fish, and with a smooth, uninterrupted motion, hoist it out of the water, and deposit it into the boat. If it is a fish with sharp teeth such as a king mackerel that you don't want to bring aboard while it is still active, hold it over the gunwale, more over the boat than over the water, to club it over the head to subdue it. This way, if the fish tears off the gaff, it will flop into the boat and not into the water.

If you come upon an anchored shrimp trawler in the Gulf, try fishing around it. When the crew culls the catch, they discard the unwanted fish. This creates a chum line that attracts predators like kingfish (king mackerel) and even ling (cobia). One way to fish is to drift with the prevailing breeze, passing on either side of the trawler. But don't try to tie to the trawler or get too close and bump it. Shrimpers frown on both practices. And if the wind is brisk, you could damage your boat and wake up the sleeping crew on the shrimpboat.

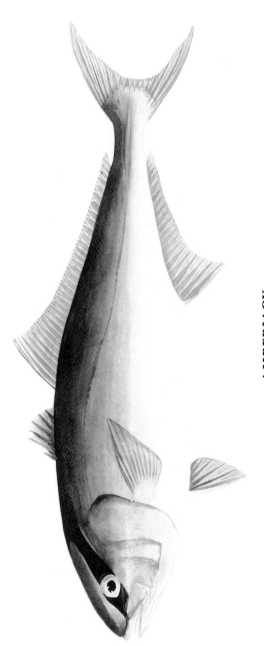

AMBERJACK
(*Seriola dumerili*)

DESCRIPTION: The amberjack, a member of the family Carangidae, is kin to the crevalle jack and pompano, although it is more slender in body configuration than other jackfish. The fin arrangement includes an insignificant first dorsal, a long ever, from October to April, and those that come to Texas waters in the summer might possibly have migrated here from that region.

REMARKS: Some fishermen on headboats drift baits for amberjack while at the same time

second dorsal, and a forked or moon-shaped tail. Coloration is a light bluish-purple on the back, yellowish on the sides, and silver underneath. Sometimes the yellow along the side appears as a light stripe, but it fades rapidly after the fish is caught. A dark band runs from the mouth through the eye to just in front of the first dorsal fin. Average weight is 15 to 20 pounds, but fish weighing more than 50 are not unusual.

HABITS/HABITAT: Amberjacks like deep water offshore around some sort of structure such as oil platforms and snapper banks. The fish are found in Texas waters during the warm months and the prime fishing season is May through September. Smaller amberjacks may congregate, but big specimens are normally solitary. They swim above bottom-feeding fish like snappers probably to escape the fierce competition for food. The most productive fishing method is to drift a small live fish such as a grunt, mullet or pigfish. Also good is squid or a chunk of cut bait. Virtually nothing is known of the amberjack's life history, except that it is migratory and appears off Texas shores after the water temperature warms to about 70°F. Amberjacks are abundant off Bermuda, how-fishing the bottom for snappers. Because of its size and strength, an amberjack is a hard-pulling but rather unspectacular fighter. The fish is edible but not highly prized as food.

STATE RECORD: 107 pounds, 8 ounces. Freeport, 68 miles out. June 6, 1987. Fred Carter, Streetman.

WORLD RECORD: 155 pounds, 10 ounces. Challenger Bank, Bermuda. June 24, 1981. Joseph Dawson.

The best time to fish is during the week because of less activity on the water. But, by necessity, most of us must fish on the weekend. One way to get the first shot at a choice place is to be there at first light. It is one of the most rewarding times to fish. That first hour is one of relative calm. Dawn is a peaceful time and the beauty and serenity of a sunrise is one of nature's masterpieces. And the fishing can be great. Fish, undisturbed through the night, are often active.

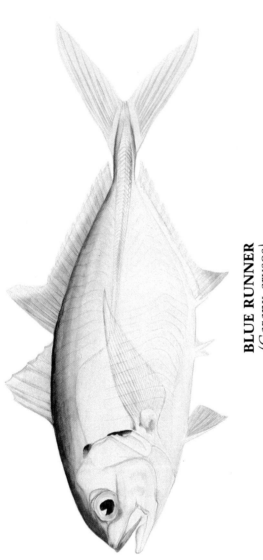

BLUE RUNNER
(Caranx crysos)

DESCRIPTION: The blue runner, sometimes called the hardtail jack, is a member of the family Carangidae, which includes the crevalle jack, horse-eye jack, amberjack and pompano. A small jack, the blue runner seems misnamed because it is more green than blue. Back and upper sides are small fish, shrimp and crabs. Like all jacks, it is migratory and spawns in the Gulf in the summer. Little blue runners often mingle with other juvenile jacks in the surf. The fish will readily hit a bait, natural or artificial, and it is a strong but unspectacular fighter.

greenish shading to yellowish-silver below. Fins are almost colorless. In shape the fish resembles the crevalle jack, but there are no black spots on the gill covers. The blue runner does, however, have hard bony scutes along the tail and sides, typical for jacks. Average size is 2 or 3 pounds, occasionally reaching 4.

HABITS/HABITAT: Blue runners tend to school around reefs and jetties. Food consists of

REMARKS: The blue runner is not actively pursued by sport fishermen. The fish is edible but not sought for food. It is occasionally caught inshore in spring and summer.

STATE RECORD: None.

WORLD RECORD: 8 pounds, 4 ounces. Bimini, Bahamas. September 9, 1990. Brent C. Rowland.

When fishing with a popping cork, many anglers exhibit a tendency to fling the line way out. With a long cast, it is difficult to control slack, and with slack in the line, it is harder to pull the float and make it pop and also to set the hook when a fish hits. A long cast is not necessary if you are not making any noise. A cast of about 35 feet is sufficient. Also, if the water surface is calm or only slightly rippled, the cork does not have to be pulled so vigorously to create enough sound to attract fish.

When redfish are cruising about on a shallow grass flat, they are just naturally suspicious. But during a weekend, when boating activity in the bays increases, they become even more skitterish and more difficult to catch. In most instances, the weekend fisherman who succeeds works a bit harder. In a shallow bay, he anchors his boat and gets out and wades a long way, to fish shallow flats undisturbed by boat traffic. Or maybe he has a jet-powered scooter or some other shallow-running boat to go into areas that are off-limits to conventional boats. He gets away from the crowd.

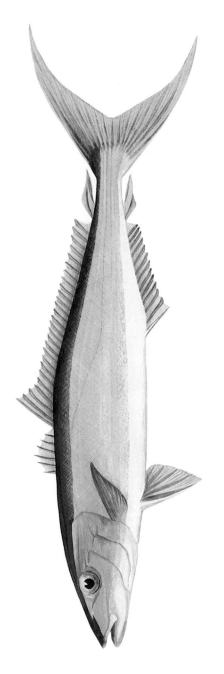

RAINBOW RUNNER
(Elagatis bipinnulata)

DESCRIPTION: A member of the jackfish family, the brightly colorful rainbow runner is bluish above, changing to green, reddish and blue streaks along the side. The bright blue streak is quite prominent, starting at the snout and running below the eye along the entire length of the

HABITS/HABITAT: The rainbow runner is a tropical fish, and only rarely is one caught in Texas waters. It is a pelagic species that prowls far out in the Gulf and is typically caught by fishermen trolling for billfish. Food consists of small fish and crustaceans.

body to the anterior part of the tail. The belly is light yellowish or silvery. Fins are yellowish. Even though it belongs to the family Carangidae, it does not look like any of the other jacks, even the blue runner. The colors and its elongate shape set it apart. Like family-members amberjack and pompano, it does not have bony scutes along the lateral line near the tail. Average weight is about 5 to 10 pounds. It can grow as long as 4 feet.

REMARKS: The rainbow runner is present in Texas waters only during warm weather, and even then it is rare. It is both a fine sport and food fish.

STATE RECORD: 20.35 pounds. Gulf of Mexico. July 20, 1991. Sergio A. Flores, San Antonio.

WORLD RECORD: 37 pounds, 9 ounces. Isla Clarion, Mexico. November 21, 1991. Tom Pfleger.

The Texas Parks and Wildlife Department has two in-state, toll-free telephone numbers, one for general information, the other to report illegal fishing activity. The information service is available only during regular business hours, but the number to report fishing violations is answered around the clock. Have you noticed, though, that you never seem to have the numbers when you need them? Look on your fishing license. You'll find them printed there.

A pair of old-fashioned overalls can make wade-fishing easier. The shoulder straps carry the weight, rather than a belt around the waist. This is more comfortable, with the weight of the soaked fabric distributed across the shoulders. Also, the pockets on the bib are handy for carrying extra tackle such as lures, hooks and sinkers. If you want to drag a live-bait bucket, cinch a belt lightly around your waist and tie the bucket to it with a short piece of cord.

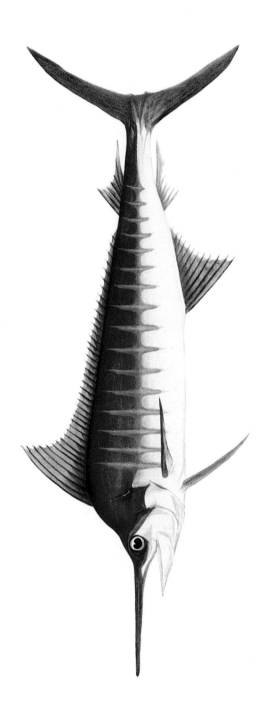

BLUE MARLIN
(Makaira nigricans)

DESCRIPTION: The blue marlin is a member of the billfish family, Istiophoridae. Coloration is almost cobalt blue along the back, shading to silvery-white on the lower body. Vertical, narrow skip baits along the surface. Fish and cephalopods, such as squid, comprise the basic diet. A favored bait is a cylinder-shaped plastic artificial that has a 3-inch flat-nosed head and a 12-inch

row dark bars are normally present. Soon after the fish dies, the back part of the body turns much darker and the bars or vertical stripes fade away quite rapidly. The bill is shorter and heavier in comparison to the body than is true of the white marlin. A small blue marlin is sometimes mistaken for a white marlin, but the blue has more sharply pointed anal fins, and its dorsal fins do not have spots. Blue marlins typically weigh 200 to 250 pounds, with a specimen over 500 being a real trophy. The larger blue marlins are females, since males seldom exceed 300 pounds.

HABITS/HABITAT: Blue marlins move into Texas waters during the warm-weather months. They primarily roam the 100-fathom curve, where Gulf currents wash food to the surface. This curve comes closest to Texas shores about 40 miles out of Port Isabel. It gets progressively farther out on up the coast and is about 95 miles off Galveston. The general fishing season is June through September. Blue marlin are normally taken by trolling with boats of 31-feet-plus, using outriggers, long poles on either side resembling wings, which bright plastic tail. The lure leaves a stream of bubbles as it is trolled. Natural baits such as ballyhoo (imported from Florida), mullet and squid are also used, but it takes an angler or deck hand with expertise to rig one of these so that it looks natural swimming through the water. Most marlin fishermen use 80-pound-plus line.

REMARKS: A big blue marlin possibly is the most prized of all catches along the Texas coast. It ranges far out in open water, where it is hard to find; it is the largest billfish in the Gulf; and it is difficult to fool. Unfortunately, however, blue marlins have become scarce. Commercial fishermen using longlines, which are trotlines several miles in length, have depleted the blue marlin population drastically. Unless it is to be mounted, a blue marlin should always be released.

STATE RECORD: 876.50 pounds. Gulf of Mexico. August 20, 1988. James H. Farrow, Dallas.

WORLD RECORD: 1,402 pounds. Vitoria, Brazil. February 29, 1992. Paulo Roberto A. Amorim.

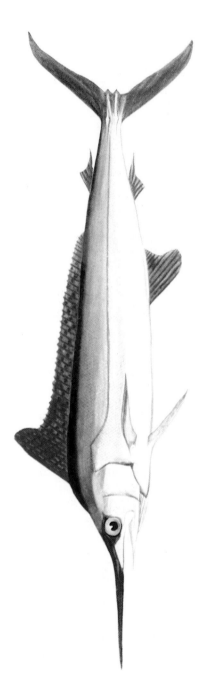

WHITE MARLIN
(Tetrapturus albidus)

DESCRIPTION: The white marlin is the smallest of the marlins. Coloration is greenish-blue above, silvery-white below. Light blue stripes may be present. The dorsal and anal fin tips are rounded and the lateral line is conspicuous, while on a small blue marlin, the fin tips are pointed and the lateral line can't be seen. The white's bill lins, are sought. Anglers use the same baits and methods for both species. The general fishing season is June through September.

REMARKS: The white marlin is a fine game fish, mixing spectacular jumps with fast runs. Because it is smaller than the blue marlin, it probably is not quite as prized a catch. Although more

is smooth on top and raspy on the sides and ventral surface. Average size of white marlin is 50 to 100 pounds, but it can grow to 10 feet and weigh 150 pounds or more.

HABITS/HABITAT: White marlins are migratory fish that move into Texas waters in warmer weather. They roam along the same 100-fathom curve where their bigger cousins, the blue marplentiful than the blue, this species is not common in the Gulf; any caught should be released unless it is to be mounted.

STATE RECORD: 111 pounds, 8 ounces. Hospital Rock. August 5, 1979. Geo Taggart, Rockport.

WORLD RECORD: 181 pounds, 14 ounces. Vitoria, Brazil. December 8, 1979. Evandro Luiz Coser.

If you are heading offshore where there is the chance of hooking into a fish of some substance and you are inexperienced in this type of fishing, ask the boat captain or a veteran of saltwater fishing to coach you on the proper technique for playing a big fish. The procedure really is simple, a smooth up-and-down pumping action. You drop the rod tip, taking quick turns on the reel to gather slack, then bring it up again, pulling the fish toward you. Repeat this procedure in a steady rhythm.

If you are going to release a fish such as an undersized ling (cobia) or a king mackerel that puts you over your limit of 2 fish, a helpful aid is a release gaff, which originally was designed for tarpon release. This is a small gaff hook with a handle just long enough to grip with one hand. Be sure the fish is completely played out, then lead it close and shove the gaff in the mouth and hook straight down through the lower jaw. This way you can hold the fish safely while you remove the hook or cut the leader, and maybe tag the fish. Running the point through the lower jaw won't cause the fish any lasting harm.

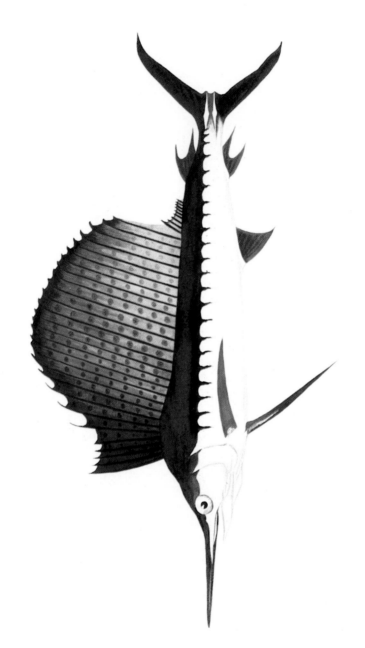

SAILFISH
(*Istiophorus platypterus*)

DESCRIPTION: The sailfish, which belongs to the billfish family, is easy to identify because of its huge, saillike dorsal fin, commonly called the sail, which extends almost the entire length of the body. This high-standing, prominent fin is dark blue with black dots in rows between the spines. It is sometimes folded down into a depression in the back, where it can't be seen. The fish has a spearlike upper jaw, a torpedo-shaped slender body and a forked tail. The back is a dark bluish-green or bluish-purple shading to white on the abdomen. Pectoral, anal and tail fins are also dark bluish. Average weight is about 35 to 45 pounds, seldom more than 60.

HABITS/HABITAT: Sailfish are migratory, and although they are found in the same places where blue and white marlin spend the summer, an occasional sailfish will stray in closer to shore than will marlin. The general fishing season is May through September, with the prime months being May, June and July. Sailfish are caught by trolling along the same 100-fathom curve where blue and white marlin are sought. While not abundant, there are more sailfish than there are marlin. The sailfish is one of, if not the most spectacular of all fighters. It jumps time and again, its entire body coming out of the water. Sailfish can often be seen traveling in small groups when migrating, but when feeding, they travel singly or in pairs. Tagged fish indicate a south to north migratory pattern as the water warms. Fish wintering off southern Florida move to Texas for the summer. Studies also indicate a lifespan of only 3 years or so. But the fish compensates for this with a rapid growth rate during its first 2 years. Spawning probably takes place in the open Gulf in early summer. Periodically, someone will catch a tiny specimen less than 5 or 6 inches long in the summer.

REMARKS: Many sailfish are kept rather than released because they make such strikingly beautiful wall mounts. The average length of a sailfish, which is the criterion for trophy status, is about 7 feet or less. Even though a sailfish is edible, it should not be eaten. If it is not to be mounted, release it.

STATE RECORD: 95 pounds. East Breaks off Port Aransas. July 12, 1972. Morton Cohn, Houston.

WORLD RECORD: 135 pounds, 5 ounces. Lagos, Nigeria. November 10, 1991. Ron King.

BLACKFIN TUNA
(*Thunnus atlanticus*)

DESCRIPTION: The blackfin tuna is a member of the family Scombridae, a group of wide-ranging, open-water fish. Its stout body distinguishes it from the slender mackerels. Although it has finlets similar to those of the mackerels, common of all the tunas, roam in fast-moving schools in the open Gulf and feed mostly on small fish. In the Atlantic they range from Massachusetts to Brazil and are known to frequent deep waters. The blackfin can be caught either trolling

bonitos and wahoo, the blackfin tuna lacks any pronounced markings, which most other finlet fish have. All tunas typically have dark-colored backs and silvery sides. The blackfin tuna has light vertical bars and dots along the lower sides. Unlike other tunas, its finlets are not yellow but rather are uniformly dark. Finlets number 7 to 9 on the top, 7 to 8 on the bottom. The long pectoral fin reaches almost to the second dorsal. Average size is 10 to 20 pounds, but the fish grows to weights exceeding 30.

HABITS/HABITAT: Blackfin tunas, the most

or casting, using small fish, strip bait, or various artificials such as jigs, spoons and plugs.

REMARKS: The blackfin is a true tuna (*Thunnus* spp.); skipjack tuna and little tunny are bonitos (*Euthynnus* spp.). The bonitos are much more common. A blackfin tuna is a hard fighter, pulling in swift, surging runs. The flesh is of good quality and desired for food.

STATE RECORD: 38.89 pounds. Gulf of Mexico. June 23, 1988. John Alvarez, Port Mansfield.
WORLD RECORD: 42 pounds. Bermuda. June 2, 1978. Alan J. Card.

For fishing around offshore oil platforms, one of the more productive artificial baits is a half-ounce white bucktail jig fished on 20-pound-test line. The lure should be tied directly to the line without using a wire leader. Although you will lose hooks to the sharp teeth of some fish like king and Spanish mackerel, and also by pulling the line against sharp barnacles on pilings, you also will get more strikes without the wire.

If you are going to a strange lake or a part of the coast you are unfamiliar with, it might be wise to hire the services of a guide. He knows where fish are and what they are hitting on. With him, the odds of catching fish are much better. Call the chamber of commerce in the town nearest to the fishing spot and you probably can get a name or two.

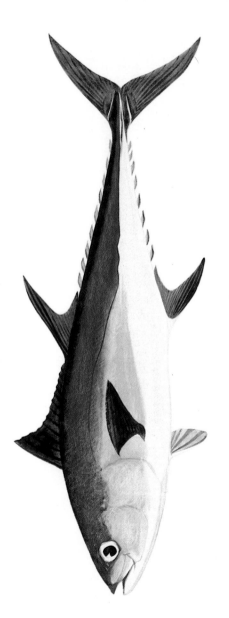

BLUEFIN TUNA
(Thunnus thynnus)

DESCRIPTION: The bluefin tuna, the heavyweight member of the family Scombridae, has a blocky body that tapers to a slender caudal peduncle. The tail is forked. Coloration is dark blue above, shading to silvery-white on the sides. The first and second dorsal fins are dark, with the topside finlets being yellowish with dark edges. The vice. Any bluefin caught should be released, first being tagged if equipment is aboard, to help in a study of the fish.

STATE RECORD: 808 pounds. Offshore at Port Isabel. May 4, 1985. Trina Isaacs, Port Isabel. WORLD RECORD: 1,496 pounds, Aulds Cove, Nova Scotia, Canada. October 26, 1979. Ken Fraser.

anal fin and bottomside finlets vary from silvery-gray to yellowish. Average weight is large, 300 to 400 pounds, but the fish is capable of growing much larger.

HABITS/HABITAT: Bluefin tuna, among the fastest swimming fish known, range far and wide in the oceans of the world. In the Gulf of Mexico, they are most likely to be found in blue water far offshore in the spring and early summer. Food is primarily fish, particularly those that range in schools. The occasional bluefin tuna caught is taken by trolling.

REMARKS: The bluefin tuna, growing to weights of more than 1,000 pounds, is one of the great sport fish of the world. But because of intense commercial fishing pressure in other regions, this migratory species is considered rare or endangered by the National Marine Fisheries Ser-

---

A tendency among many saltwater fishermen is to buy a gaff that is too large. One with a 4-inch hook (measured from the point straight across to the shaft) is made for big fish like sharks and billfish. It is difficult to hook a king mackerel or school dolphin with a gaff this size. More practical is a gaff with a 2-inch hook. It is made for smaller offshore fish, yet it will do the job on much bigger fish. Some fishermen carry two gaffs, a 4-inch and 2-inch, to take care of all needs. A gaff with a 3- or 4-foot handle is sufficient for most smaller boats, but a 6-foot gaff or even an 8-footer might be needed if the boat has a high transom.

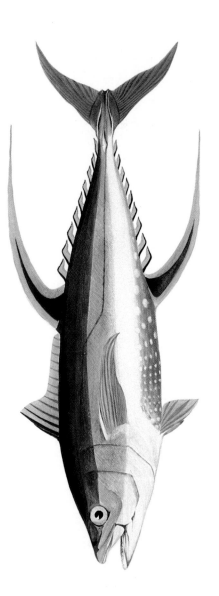

YELLOWFIN TUNA
(*Thunnus albacares*)

DESCRIPTION: The yellowfin tuna gets its name from the yellowish tint on the breast and fins. It is the most colorful of the tuna members of the family Scombridae. Other than the yellowish color, the fish's most prominent features include greatly elongated second dorsal and anal fins that

ior is typically tunalike, ranging in fast-moving schools far offshore, although yellowfins have been known to come closer to shore than other tunas. They eat flying fish, small school fish, squid and crustaceans. Like all tunas, the yellowfin can be caught on a variety of baits, natural and

sweep back almost to the tail on older specimens; young yellowfins, which do not possess these exaggerated fins, may be confused with other tunas. Bright finlets separate the yellowfin from the bluefin tuna, and the longer pectoral, about the length of the head and reaching to the second dorsal, distinguishes it from the blackfin, which has a pectoral that is about three-quarters of the head length. The body is fully scaled. The fish grows to weights of more than 100 pounds.

HABITS/HABITAT: The yellowfin's behav-

Catch and release makes good sense. Take along a compact 35mm camera, and if you or your buddy catches a good fish, take several photos of it before releasing it. An enlargement of the photo, framed and hung on the wall, makes a nice trophy. Cheaper than taxidermy, too.

artificial, either by trolling or chumming and drift fishing. Most are caught in the summer.

REMARKS: The yellowfin is commercially the most valuable of tunas. It is a hard, determined fighter and a popular game fish. The flesh is good to eat.

STATE RECORD: 210 pounds. Gulf of Mexico. May 7, 1989. Alex Koumonduros, Houston.

WORLD RECORD: 388 pounds, 12 ounces. Mexico. April 1, 1977. Curt Wiesenhutter.

One of the better live baits for enticing a ling (cobia) to hit is a common sea catfish, or hardhead. It is a good idea, though, to clip the sharp fin spines off the catfish you are keeping alive for bait. Otherwise, you could get stabbed while handling the bait and putting it on the hook.

LITTLE TUNNY
(Euthynnus alletteratus)

DESCRIPTION: The little tunny belongs to the family Scombridae. It is called the bonito, and it is indeed a bonito and not a tuna, although it has a stocky tunalike body. Coloration varies

WORLD RECORD: 35 pounds, 2 ounces. Cap de Garde, Algeria. December 14, 1988. Jean Yves Chatard.

from dark blue or green above shading to silver below. The most distinguishing feature, though, is the scattering of large black spots below the midline between the short pectorals and ventral fins. Average size is 5 to 10 pounds, but specimens exceeding 15 are not unusual.

HABITS/HABITAT: Little tunny, or bonito, are common to Texas waters. This is an open-water species that roams in large schools, sometimes prowling close to shore. The food is primarily other smaller fish. Most little tunny are taken by random trolling with subsurface lures like feathered jigs. The fish is hard-hitting and very fast. Once a fish is hooked, it is usually possible to cast around with light tackle in the same area and take others. Little tunny is migratory and found in Texas waters during the warm months.

REMARKS: The little tunny's oily taste makes it undesirable for food. But because of its tough skin and flesh, it is often cut into strip bait to be used in trolling for other species.

STATE RECORD: 27 pounds. Freeport. July 1969. Eddie Groth, Lake Jackson.

Artificial plugs made for freshwater fishing have a place in saltwater fishing, too. A jointed minnow-shaped lure like the Red Fin is good for taking speckled trout and redfish on shallow grass flats. Just swim the lure slowly along the surface. For deeper-water fishing, maybe along the edge of a channel, use a top-water lure such as the Zara Spook or Heddon Chuggar in conjunction with a small shrimptail jig. Remove the back hook and tie about a 15-inch leader in the eye. Put the jig at the end of the leader. As you chug the plug slowly along the surface, making a disturbance to attract attention, the jig will come trailing erratically behind, swimming a foot or more beneath the surface, depending on the leader length. The jig will account for the most strikes, but occasionally a larger specimen will attack the plug.

SKIPJACK TUNA
(Euthynnus pelamis)

DESCRIPTION: The skipjack tuna, also known as the oceanic bonito, belongs to the family Scombridae. It is a colorful fish with a greenish-blue back shading to silvery sides, with dark stripes running lengthwise along the bottom half Aransas. June 20, 1981. Jimmy Welder, Corpus Christi.

WORLD RECORD: 41 pounds, 14 ounces. Pearl Beach, Mauritius. November 12, 1985. Edmund K. R. Heinzen.

of the body from behind the pectoral fins to the tail. The chunky body tapers to a slender caudal peduncle, giving a sort of bullet-shaped appearance. The dorsals are close together but not contiguous, with the first having a high anterior lobe. Average weight is 3 to 6 pounds, although fish weighing more than 20 are caught.

HABITS/HABITAT: Skipjack tuna are a wide-ranging school fish of warm waters that might be encountered almost anywhere in the Gulf during the warm-weather months, although they are not common. Most skipjack tuna are hooked by fishermen trolling at a fairly brisk rate, using a subsurface lure such as a feathered jig or a whole small fish or strip bait.

REMARKS: The name skipjack comes from the tendency of the fish to skip out of the water while in pursuit of prey, like flying fish, at the surface. The fish is a strong and determined fighter, but it is not sought as food by sport fishermen.

STATE RECORD: 28 pounds, 4 ounces. Port

A fisherman normally can find some kind of action in the surf, in the troughs or "guts" between breakers. Many different species come into the surf to feed. Both natural and artificial baits can be used, but you generally will catch more fish in greater variety with natural baits. Shrimp is the most popular, but it is expensive and difficult to keep alive. Dead shrimp and cut bait are two other favorites, although in the summer these baits are preyed upon by blue crabs, which are abundant in the surf. Also good are live piggy perch, mudfish and mullet. Smaller bait-stealing fish species and blue crabs are not as much of a problem with these baits, and a small live fish bait generally appeals more to larger specimens than does shrimp.

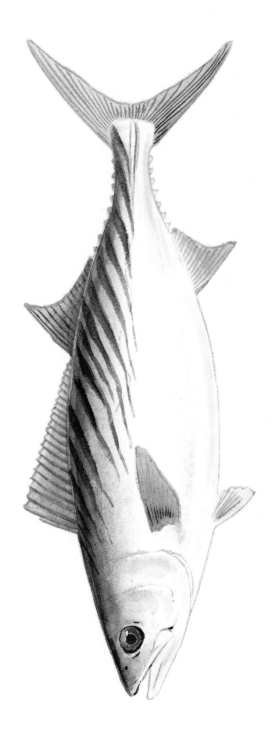

ATLANTIC BONITO
(*Sarda sarda*)

DESCRIPTION: The Atlantic bonito belongs to the family Scombridae, which includes the mackerels. Its shape is somewhat like that of the tunas, but it is not as stocky through the body. It has a large mouth and is fully scaled. Coloration is dark bluish above shading to silvery below. A distinguishing feature is the series of dark stripes running obliquely from near the lateral line to the back. Average size is 1 to 3 pounds.

HABITS/HABITAT: The Atlantic bonito, an offshore open-water species, is rare to Texas waters, but one occasionally is caught during the warm-weather months. Primary food is small fish. Although this fish is plentiful in the Atlantic Ocean, not much is known about its migratory travels in the Gulf.

REMARKS: The Atlantic bonito can be confused with the more-common little tunny, also called bonito. It is a hard fighter for its size. The fish is edible, but the flesh is soft and extremely oily.

STATE RECORD: 4 pounds, 13.6 ounces. Eighty-five miles southeast of Galveston. March 29, 1986. Patrick Maass, Katy.

Fly tackle is an effective and challenging fishing tool in salt water, especially on shallow grass flats with reasonably clear water, such as those in the lower Laguna Madre, where a fly fisherman can actually see cruising or feeding fish and cast to them. There is not much difference between freshwater and saltwater fly fishing, with the following exceptions: Because redfish, speckled trout and other fish on the flats are easily spooked, casts have to be longer to keep from alarming them; and the presence of prevailing winds on the coast makes for more difficult casting. The best combination for this fishing is a 9-weight rod with No. 9 line: weight forward, floating regular or floating-shooting taper line.

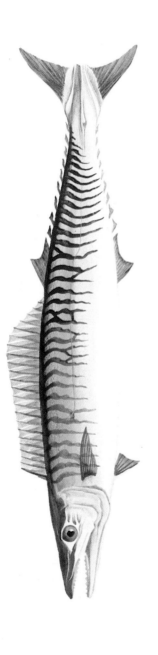

WAHOO
(*Acanthocybium solanderi*)

DESCRIPTION: The wahoo is a member of the family Scombridae. It is a slim, streamlined fish. The small tail is not deeply forked and the snout is pointed. The large mouth brims with teeth. The long first dorsal is of fairly uniform height and contains 24 to 26 spines. Coloration can vary, but the back typically is golden-greenish typical mackerel fast-run style. It is highly prized as a sport fish and is delicious to eat.

STATE RECORD: 124 pounds. Gulf of Mexico. July 5, 1987, Terry Crider, Denton.

WORLD RECORD: 155 pounds, 8 ounces. San Salvador, Bahamas. April 3, 1990. William Bourne.

with a touch of blue, shading to silvery-blue on the sides with dark, vertical bars. Average weight is not known, but the few fish caught normally weigh more than 50 pounds.

HABITS/HABITAT: Wahoo are migratory and prefer warm seas. In the Gulf, they range in blue water far offshore during the warm-weather months. The prime fishing season is July and August, although few are caught. Unlike its close relative the king mackerel, the wahoo travels alone instead of in schools. But like a king mackerel, it has a habit of hitting short, and this is why a hook, on a wire leader, should be placed well back in a bait when fishing for wahoo. They feed on squid and small fish.

REMARKS: A wahoo is a hard fighter, in

A marker comes in handy if you locate fish and want to mark the spot. It is easy to make your own. Use a sealed half-gallon plastic household bleach jug and enough cord or fishing line to go deeper than the water you normally fish. Tie one end of the line to the finger grip on the jug, wrap the line around the jug, and to the other end tie a heavy sinker. When you toss the marker overboard, the plummeting sinker will spin the jug, releasing line. When the sinker hits bottom the marker float is anchored in place. After you've finished fishing the spot, retrieve the jug and rewrap the line. It is ready to use again.

SWORDFISH
(Xiphias gladius)

DESCRIPTION: The swordfish is the only member of the family Xiphiidae. It is not related to the marlins or sailfish (billfish), although it resembles them somewhat. The bill is longer and wider than that of any of the billfish family. Color-

catching a swordfish, or a broadbill, is the ultimate achievement because the fish is so scarce and so large. Furthermore, it is difficult to get the fish to hit. A very finicky feeder that is easily frightened by a moving boat, a swordfish will

ation on adults is bronze or a dark metallic purple on the back, shading lighter along the sides, and dull whitish on the belly. Younger specimens normally are blue along the back. The dorsal fin is nonretractable. A swordfish has no ventral fins. The fish grows extremely large, to lengths of more than 15 feet and weights of more than 1,000 pounds.

HABITS/HABITAT: The swordfish is rare in Texas waters, if indeed it is present at all. It is a free-roaming fish of the open sea. Very large swordfish are always females.

REMARKS: For many big-game fishermen,

rarely strike blindly. Finally, the hook can easily tear out of the soft mouth, and the slashing bill can rip through the line or leader. Since the swordfish is a deep feeder in warmer Gulf currents, about the only way to get it is to drift-fish a bait like a large bonito down deep. A big swordfish normally travels alone. The fish is highly prized as food.

STATE RECORD: 317 pounds. West Flower Gardens. July 21, 1979. J.P. Bryan, Jr., Houston.
WORLD RECORD: 1,182 pounds. Iquique, Chile. May 7, 1953. L. Marron.

If you hear someone on the coast talking about "butterfly drum," he is not referring to some exotic species. The reference is to smaller black drum (big drum are sometimes called bull drum). There are a lot of butterfly drum weighing about 4 to 6 pounds in the bays in the winter. That is a good time to fish for them.

If your casting reel has a dry pawl or the bail of your spinning reel is balky, not opening and closing smoothly, a drop or two of lubricant will help. If you have none in your tacklebox, use the dip stick of your vehicle in an emergency. A little oil will do the job.

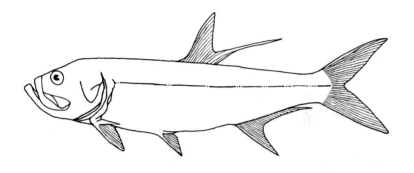

OUTER REEF SPECIES

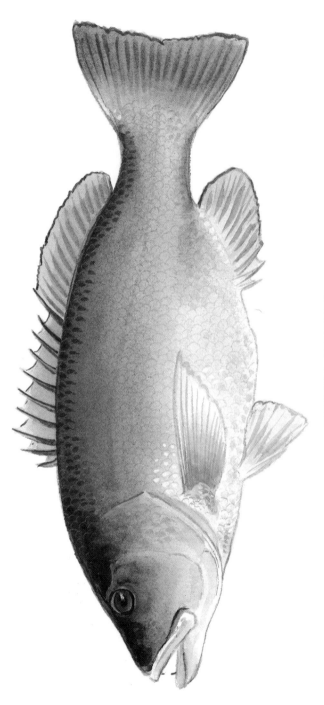

CUBERA SNAPPER
(*Lutjanus cyanopterus*)

DESCRIPTION: The cubera snapper, nick-named the Cuban snapper, belongs to the family Lutjanidae, as do all the other snappers found

REMARKS: Since various snappers inter-mingle on the reefs and snapper banks, and since snappers are capable of producing different color

in Texas waters. Coloration is generally grayish, with faint bars present on small fish. Fins are grayish with the exception of the reddish anal fin. Both jaws have large canine teeth. While the average size is not known, cubera snapper weighing 25 to 75 pounds are not unusual.

HABITS/HABITAT: The cubera snapper, a tropical species, is a deep-water reef fish and is fairly rare in Texas waters. Very little is known about its habits, but it is believed that this snapper does not migrate any significant distances, staying pretty much in the same places. Tagging studies have shown this is true of red snappers.

> If you locate fish at a certain depth with your depth-sounder, getting a bait to them is relatively simple. If they are at the 10-foot depth, strip line off your reel in pulls about a foot long each. With 10 pulls, you know you have your bait at about the right depth.

phases, it is sometimes difficult for an angler to know exactly what species he has caught. The cubera is often confused with the dog snapper and the gray (mangrove) snapper, since all three are large members of the snapper family. The fish is edible.

STATE RECORD: 131 pounds. Fifteen miles off Port Mansfield. August 8, 1983. Ricky H. Preddy, Port Mansfield.

WORLD RECORD: 121 pounds, 8 ounces. Cameron, Louisiana. July 5, 1982. Mike Hebert.

> An effective bait around an offshore oil platform is a live fish such as a croaker or pinfish. The bait is fished without a sinker. It is lobbed up next to the platform and allowed to sink and drift, struggling against the line. Fish such as king mackerel, amberjacks and ling (cobia) can't resist it.

DOG SNAPPER
(Lutjanus jocu)

DESCRIPTION: The dog snapper is a member of the large and widespread snapper family, whose members living in the Gulf of Mexico are generally called Atlantic snappers. The fish's most small numbers on outer Gulf reefs during the summer. As with most snappers that reside in deep water, which makes them difficult to study, not much is known about the dog snapper's life

notable characteristic is a large mouth with big canine teeth. Coloration is dark coppery-red with faint vertical bars on the sides. Sometimes a blue bar or blue spots appear beneath the eye. Since the dog snapper can change color to conform to its environment, its background color can range from dark to a light, silvery-gray. Because the blue markings below the eye are not present on all fish, the dog snapper is often confused with the gray snapper and cubera snapper. Although the average size is not known, dog snapper grow to large sizes. HABITS/HABITAT: Dog snapper are found in

> October and November are prime months to find larger redfish on the shallow flats. But the water can be on the cool side. Wear a pair of lightweight chest-high waders.

history. Any catch is usually incidental to fishing for red snapper.

REMARKS: The dog snapper, like all snappers, is edible, but in some parts of the world it has the reputation of being unsuitable for human consumption. This myth probably originated in the warm tropical areas, the dog snapper's principal range, where lack of refrigeration or ice simply caused the fish to spoil.

STATE RECORD: 128 pounds. Offshore of Port Aransas. 1962. Chris Page, Port Aransas. WORLD RECORD: None.

> When heating lard or oil to fry fish, drop a wooden kitchen match in the oil and let it float about. When the match flames, the oil is at the right temperature for cooking.

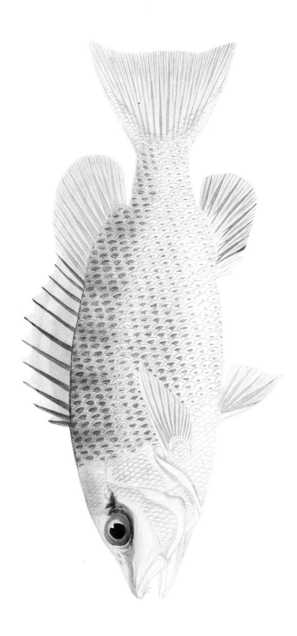

GRAY SNAPPER
(Lutjanus griseus)

DESCRIPTION: The gray snapper, widely known as the mangrove snapper, is one of the more plentiful members of the snapper family found in Texas waters. Like other snappers, the

STATE RECORD: 14 pounds. Gulf of Mexico. June 21, 1992. Jerry W. Sims, Houston.

WORLD RECORD: 17 pounds. Port Canaveral, Florida. June 14, 1992. Steve Maddox.

fish has varying color phases depending on the habitat. It can range from a deep brownish red, dark or light, to almost grayish white. There are faint vertical bars extending down part-way along the back. The canine teeth in the upper jaw are larger than those in the lower. Average size is 1 to 2 pounds.

HABITS/HABITAT: Gray snapper are typically caught around offshore oil platforms and reefs, and infrequently one will be taken around the mouth of a Gulf pass or channel, using small baits fished on bottom. The diet includes small fishes, blue crabs, shrimp and squid. They feed at night but will bite during the day. They are most active in warm weather.

REMARKS: The gray snapper is often confused with the dog snapper and cubera snapper, both close relatives. The fish is good to eat.

When fishing for redfish or trout, try combining natural and artificial baits. This combination generally is used in conjunction with a popping cork. To rig, tie the leader below the cork to one eye of a three-way swivel (the distance from the float to the bottom bait will depend on water depth). To another eye is attached a short leader with a No. 10 or No. 8 treble hook and live shrimp. To the third is tied a longer leader with a plastic shrimptail jig, about a quarter-ounce, or some other imitation of a shrimp. When a fish hits the live shrimp and begins jerking and pulling, the artificial dancing around draws the attention of other trout. It isn't uncommon to catch fish two at a time, especially when speckled trout are schooled to feed.

LANE SNAPPER
(Lutjanus synagris)

DESCRIPTION: The lane snapper, also called the spot snapper, is a smallish member of the snapper clan. The fish is fairly slender in shape

STATE RECORD: 5.81 pounds. Gulf of Mexico. July 14, 1990. Timothy Walden, Lake Jackson.

WORLD RECORD: 7 pounds. Perdido Pass, Alabama. June 23, 1991. Suzanne Ridgon.

when compared with most other snappers. Coloration varies from rosy-red to olivaceous. There are horizontal yellow stripes along the sides, often masked by vertical blotching. The most distinguishing characteristic is a dark spot between the lateral line and the beginning of the rear soft dorsal fin; hence the nickname "spot snapper." The tail is tinged in black. Other fins are red and yellow. Average size of adults is 1 pound or less, with a few reaching 3 or 4.

• HABITS/HABITAT: Lane snapper inhabit the outer banks and are caught regularly in Texas waters, although not in great numbers. They are most active during the summer months.

REMARKS: Lane snapper are normally caught while fishing for red snapper. The diminutive size of the typical lane snapper is probably the main reason that no more are caught. Hooks and baits are too large. The fish is good to eat.

In fishing for species where a wire or cable leader is not required, it still is a good idea to add a so-called shock leader to the end of your line. A shock leader is a length of monofilament that is stronger than your line. Lighter line makes for casting ease; the shock leader is more abrasion-proof, providing some protection against fish teeth and rough bottom such as a rock jetty. The strength of the leader will vary with line size and the protection needed. Doubling the strength of your line is a pretty good rule of thumb for general inshore fishing. Thus, with 15-pound line, you use a 30-pound leader.

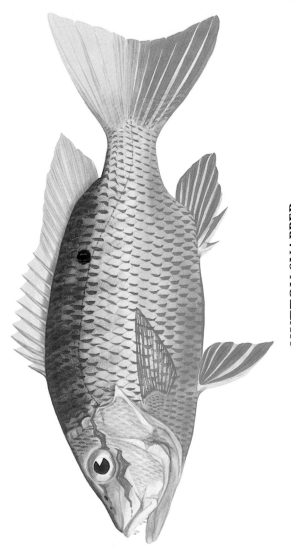

MUTTON SNAPPER
(Lutjanus analis)

DESCRIPTION: The mutton snapper, better known as the muttonfish, is a member of the snapper family that resembles the red snapper in shape, and the two are sometimes confused, particularly when the mutton snapper is in a dark-red phase. But mutton snapper can vary greatly in color, as can all snappers. Coloration is usually dark olive on the back, shading to pink below, with dark vertical bars or indistinct blotches. A small black spot is located on, or just above, the lateral line, slightly back from the middle of the body. On a red snapper, the splotch is on the base of the pectoral fin. Average size is about 3 to 5 pounds, although the fish grows much larger.

HABITS/HABITAT: Muttonfish are found on the deep outer snapper banks, usually in water up to 200 feet. This species is not one of the more common snappers.

STATE RECORD: None.
WORLD RECORD: 27 pounds, 6 ounces.

Johns Pass, Florida. September 16, 1989. Roger McCrady.

Fishing a bait under a float in either salt water or fresh is thought to be a shallow-water method. But a float can be used in deeper water, too. Use a sliding-type float. Some type of stop, such as a piece of rubberband wrapped around the line, goes on the main line where you want the float to stop. Thus, if you want to fish at a 10-feet depth, you position the stop 10 feet from the hook. The float slides against the sinker on the cast, but once on the water, the weighted line and hook slide down until the float hits the stop, putting your bait at the 10-foot level, right where you want it. Most tackle stores have sliding floats.

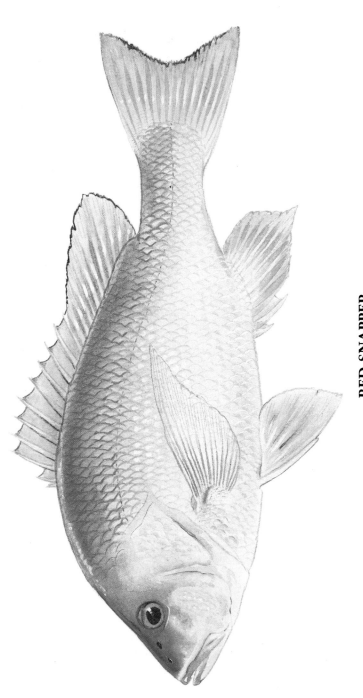

RED SNAPPER
(Lutjanus campechanus)

DESCRIPTION: The red snapper, belonging to the family Lutjanidae, has a distinctive coloration that is most frequently vivid red with dark during the summer, due to the presence of bait-stealing triggerfish, which are thickest during warm weather. Red snapper will feed at night, but

fringe around the dorsal and caudal fins. The red is a deeper shade along the back, shading lighter on the underside. The dorsal fin is united with 10 spines in the forward part, with 14 to 15 rays in the second. Average size is 1 to 2 pounds, but the fish grows much larger.

HABITS/HABITAT: Red snapper prefer hard bottom in deep Gulf water, 20 to 100 fathoms. They swim in schools around reefs, old wrecks, offshore banks and oil platforms. The diet consists mostly of shellfish, small fish, shrimp and crabs. Tagging studies have shown that when red snappers become recruited to a particular reef habitat, the fish tend to become faithful to the habitat. Since they do not move, they are prey to fishermen, and even a massive school can eventually be decimated. This is why snapper fishing at a certain place might be good early, but slacks off as the fishing season progresses. Although red snapper can be caught year-round, they are taken in largest numbers during the warm-weather months. The bigger specimens, called sow snapper, are usually taken in the winter, when there is not as much fishing pressure. Headboats that operate out of the various ports often fish at night

triggerfish are sight feeders and eat in the daytime. Cut squid is a popular bait because red snapper like it and it is tough, making it difficult for other small fish to pull it off the hook. Larger snappers, which are much more wary, are sometimes caught in the warm-weather months by drifting a bait deep, near bottom but above the smallish snappers, which gather in defensive schools. Anglers drift-fishing for sow snapper often use a whole fish for bait. Spawning occurs from June through September. Juveniles are widely distributed over muddy or sandy bottom and are caught in great numbers by shrimpers. Growth is fairly fast, about 8 inches the first year, 3 to 4 inches every year thereafter.

REMARKS: The red snapper is highly sought because of its delicious flavor. Many people consider it the finest eating of all saltwater fish.

STATE RECORD: 35 pounds. Claypiles off Galveston. March 13, 1985. Randy G. Bellamy, Galveston.

WORLD RECORD: 46 pounds, 8 ounces. Destin, Florida. October 1, 1985. E. Lane Nichols III.

VERMILION SNAPPER
(Rhomboplites aurorubens)

DESCRIPTION: The vermilion snapper, or bastard snapper, as it is sometimes called, is a colorful junior-sized member of the snapper family. Its color is vermilion or reddish-pink, with faint oblique lines on the sides. The pectoral fin is yellow months. It is believed the fish is found in Texas waters in only limited numbers.

REMARKS: Perhaps one reason more vermilion snapper are not caught is the fish's diminutive size. It only nibbles at instead of taking a fisher-

lowish, while the caudal fin and iris of the eye are vermilion. The tail has a black edge. There are 12 spines in the first dorsal fin. Average size is less than a pound, with a maximum length of about 15 inches.

HABITS/HABITAT: The vermilion snapper is one of several snappers a fisherman might encounter while fishing a deep-water reef or around an oil platform, particularly in the warm-weather man's bait. On the snapper banks, most anglers would catch more fish, and a wider variety of fish, by using smaller hooks and baits. The fish is good to eat.

STATE RECORD: 4.31 pounds. Gulf of Mexico. September 4, 1991. Stanley Cernik III, DeSoto.

WORLD RECORD: 4 pounds, 3 ounces. Dauphin Island, Alabama. July 20, 1991. Marcus R. Kennedy.

If you have some freezer-burned fish or fresh fish that are fatty, one way to eliminate most of the strong taste is to sprinkle the fillets liberally with Louisiana red-hot sauce and rub it in. Use enough to turn the fillets lightly red. When you fry the fish, the flavor of the Louisiana red disappears. You'll never know it has been put on the fish, but the overall flavor will be much improved.

Most of the bigger flounders, or "saddle blankets," as some anglers call them, are caught during the second half of the fall run, starting in mid-October. The fish are moving in large schools. Look for them in and along channels, cuts and passes connecting bays with the Gulf. A prime time is right after a cool front when the barometer is rising. Instead of live shrimp, try a mud minnow or finger mullet for bait. Larger flounders feed on small fish.

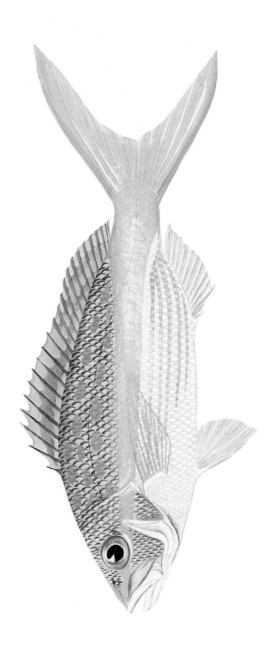

YELLOWTAIL SNAPPER
(Ocyurus chrysurus)

DESCRIPTION: The yellowtail snapper, one of the smaller representatives of the snapper family, is a colorful fish with a distinctive shape: its

WORLD RECORD: 8 pounds, 8 ounces. Fort Myers, Florida. July 24, 1992. Suzanne Axel.

slim body tapers to an elongated and narrow caudal peduncle, and the bright yellow tail is oversized for the body and deeply forked. A bright yellow streak extends across the midbody from one end to the other. The underside is white and all fins are yellow. Average size is about 1 pound or less, with maximum size being about 5 pounds.

HABITS/HABITAT: Yellowtail snapper are school fish, found on the deep-water outer reefs and snapper banks. These areas provide only marginal habitat for the yellowtail snapper, since it is a tropical species. Unlike most snappers, the yellowtails swim a few feet off the bottom and feed on small fish, crabs and shrimp.

REMARKS: This fish is rarely confused with other snappers because its body shape is more streamlined and the tail is always a vivid yellow, hence the name. The yellowtail snapper is delicious to eat.

STATE RECORD: 9.87 pounds. Gulf of Mexico. October 10, 1992. Steve Kinzel, St. Peters.

When fishing the surf with natural baits, you have to fish the bottom, using a sinker to keep the wave action from washing your bait to shore. The most basic bottom rig is fashioned off a three-way swivel. One swivel eye ties to the main line. To another eye tie about an 18-inch leader with a pyramid-shaped sinker, the size depending on how much weight you need to hold your bait stationary in the surf. To the other eye attach a shorter leader, about 12 to 15 inches, with the appropriate-size hook for the bait you are using. No. 3/0 is one of the more popular sizes when using a live baitfish. With the sinker on bottom and the main line relatively taut, the bait will be suspended right off the bottom and will sway back and forth with wave action.

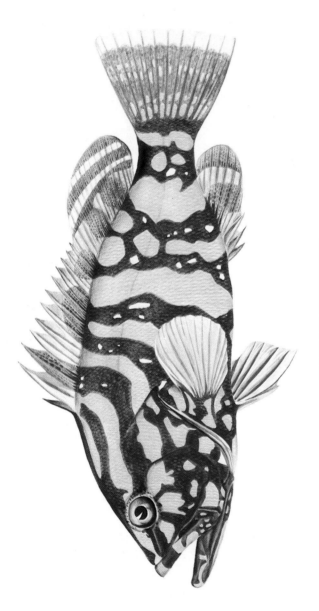

NASSAU GROUPER
(Epinephelus striatus)

DESCRIPTION: The Nassau grouper belongs to what is called the grouper section of the far-flung and diverse family Serranidae. Coloration of platforms. If one is caught it is usually incidental to fishing the snapper banks. The species is rare to Texas waters. Little is known about its life history.

the basslike body is usually pale olive-gray and much paler on the underside, but it can vary since the fish has the ability to change to a solid grayish-white. The color pattern can be with or without irregular dark bars on the sides. There is usually a saddle-shaped black blotch on the caudal peduncle. The inside of the large mouth has an orange cast. Average weight is 5 to 10 pounds, but the Nassau grouper grows larger.

HABITS/HABITAT: Nassau groupers reside on deep-water reefs or on rough bottom around oil

REMARKS: Nassau groupers, along with other groupers, are basslike fish not prone to school, but instead live in small groups.

STATE RECORD: None.

WORLD RECORD: 27 pounds, 8 ounces. Bimini, Bahamas. April 22, 1989. Richard L. Sullivan.

Frozen shrimp is a much better bait in the winter than it is during warmer weather. There are a couple of reasons. First, many small fish like pinfish and piggy perch have left the bays in winter, so species such as speckled trout and redfish have less available food and are more likely to go for the shrimp. Also, the little fish are bait stealers, and when they leave, a lot of an angler's problems leave. During warm weather, these plentiful bait stealers will rob the hook of a choice bite of shrimp before a game fish has a chance to get to the bait.

Piano wire leader material is stronger per diameter than is stainless steel. For example, the breaking strength of No. 9 piano wire is 114 pounds, while for No. 9 stainless, it is 104 pounds. The trouble with piano wire is, it rusts quickly, which weakens it. For this reason, a piano wire leader should be used the day it is rigged, then discarded.

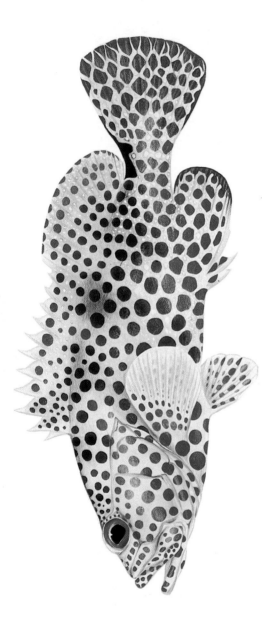

ROCK HIND
(Epinephelus adscensionis)

DESCRIPTION: Also called the "calico grouper," the rock hind is a member of the grouper section of the sea-bass family, Serranidae. Although coloration can vary, it is typically an olive

WORLD RECORD: 6 pounds, 8 ounces. Ascension Island, United Kingdom. November 22, 1991. DeWayne Kunkel.

background with pale white blotches and—the most notable characteristic—small red or reddish-brown spots all over the body, including the fins. The forward part of the dorsal has 11 spines, the second part 16 soft rays. The mouth is large. Average size is a pound or less, with a maximum length of about 15 inches.

HABITS/HABITAT: The rock hind is a deep-water fish that lives on reefs and other rough bottoms. It is sometimes found inshore where bottoms are rocky. Its diet includes crabs and small fish. Rock hinds are wary of taking a bait.

REMARKS: The rock hind is one of many unusual and colorful specimens a person might catch on the snapper banks. The basslike body resembles other groupers, but the numerous measleslike spots give the fish a distinctive appearance. The rock hind is edible.

STATE RECORD: 3.70 pounds. Gulf of Mexico. August 10, 1991. Juan DeLeon IV, Port O'Connor.

To bake fish that will bring everyone back for seconds, all you need is a gallon-sized plastic bag, 2 cups of milk, 1 egg, a lemon or two, a stick of margarine or butter, and two sacks of Ritz crackers.

Take the crackers and roll them into crumbs, the finer the better, and poor into the plastic bag. Add the egg to the milk in a bowl and mix thoroughly. Dip fish fillets into the liquid, then put them into the bag and, holding the mouth shut, shake until the fillets are coated.

Cut the lemon into circular pieces 1/4-inch thick. Spread the lemon slices on a baking dish, then lay a fillet on each lemon slice. Add crumbs to cover places where your fingers removed the coating. Pour a tablespoon of butter or margarine on each fillet. Bake at 350°, up to 25 minutes depending on the thickness of the fillet, or until done. Don't burn the crackers.

WARSAW GROUPER
(*Epinephelus nigritus*)

DESCRIPTION: The warsaw grouper, a member of the large family Serranidae, is sometimes called the black grouper or black jewfish. Coloration is uniformly brown or bluish-black, with or without a few light spots. The mouth is large. The anterior part of the dorsal fin is as high as the posterior part. The tail is squarish. Average size is large, 50 pounds or more.

HABITS/HABITAT: Warsaw groupers live on deep-water snapper banks. The big fish are caught primarily from December through February on the banks, where they mingle with red snapper. Favored food includes the Gulf blue crab and squid. Little is known about the fish's life history, although it is believed that during the warm-weather months warsaw groupers move far out into the Gulf beyond the range of most fishermen. In the winter, an occasional juvenile warsaw grouper might be found inshore near a Gulf pass, but the big specimens will always be out in deep water.

REMARKS: Because of its size and strength, a large warsaw grouper is almost impossible to pull off the bottom with a rod and reel. Most of those weighing 100 pounds or more are caught on a handline, typically strong nylon like parachute cord, with a length of chain or cable above the hook to prevent the fish from severing the cord on rough rock. The flesh is edible but that from bigger specimens tends to be very coarse.

STATE RECORD: 277 pounds. Gulf of Mexico. October 26, 1989. Aubrey Eastwood, Matagorda.

WORLD RECORD: 436 pounds, 12 ounces. Destin, Florida. December 22, 1985. Steve Haeusler.

Ever wonder how fast a red drum grows? A redfish was 23 inches long when tagged in Christmas Bay near Galveston, and when it was recovered 11 years later in the Gulf of Mexico, it was 40 inches in length, a growth rate of less than 2 inches per year. During that time span it went from 4.7 pounds to 30.8 pounds.

JEWFISH
(Epinephelus itajara)

DESCRIPTION: The jewfish is a giant-sized grouper. Coloration ranges from dark- to choco- hunt around oil platforms and shoot the fish with spearguns. It is one of the largest fish found in late-brown. Some fish have faint, pale blotches. Younger fish are mottled and have small black dots. Average size is 40 to 120 pounds, but some fish weigh in at 300 or more.

HABITS/HABITAT: The jewfish likes to hang around jetties, oil platforms and shipwrecks, where it can hide and ambush food, mostly Gulf blue crabs and other fish. Because of its size, strength and habitat, the fish is extremely difficult to catch on rod and reel. One might come out from under an oil platform, take a bait, and then turn and go back under the shelter again, and no amount of tugging is going to get it out. Those taken on rod and reel usually are caught from June to October. A productive bait is a large mullet or some other baitfish or a mashed-up stingray.

REMARKS: The jewfish often is confused with the warsaw grouper. One way to tell the difference is to compare their dorsal fins. That of the warsaw grouper is of uniform height, front and back, while on a jewfish the forward part of the dorsal is much lower than the back. Almost all the really big jewfish are taken by divers who

Texas waters. The jewfish is edible but tends to be coarse.

STATE RECORD: 551 pounds. Galveston. June 29, 1937. Gus Pangarakis, Magnolia.

WORLD RECORD: 680 pounds. Fernandina Beach, Florida. May 20, 1961. Lynn Joyner.

Putting a light oil on a hone while sharpening a knife has long been an accepted practice. But according to John Juranitch, president of Razor Edge Systems, an edge consulting company, you should keep oil off the hone. The greasy stuff will only cost you money, make a mess, and give you a bad edge. All you need to do is keep the hone washed free of particles with water. For sharpening, Juranitch recommends a coarse grit, about No. 100, for grinding, and a fine abrasive, about No. 500, to finish the edge.

GAG
(Mycteroperca microlepis)

DESCRIPTION: The gag is a grouper, of the family Serranidae. Like other groupers, it is ca-

REMARKS: Catching a gag is normally incidental to fishing for snapper. A hard fighter

pable of changing colors. Usually it is light brown with irregular chain markings, some of which resemble puckered lips. The anal fins and tail are dark with a whitish trim. The mouth is large, and on some specimens there is a dark bar resembling a moustache above it. Scales are small. Average size is about 3 pounds or less.

HABITS/HABITAT: The gag is a bottom-dwelling fish that lives in deep water on the outer banks. Its principal food is small fish. It is believed this fish is present on the banks year-round, although it is not plentiful at any time of year.

Ask your doctor or vet if he has a hemostat or forceps he no longer uses. Either of these surgical instruments makes a handy hook remover.

---

in deep water, the gag usually succumbs to the change in pressure as it is pulled to the surface. A hooked gag will try to retreat into a hole or crevice, where it is difficult to pull free without severing the line on sharp rock.

STATE RECORD: 20.19 pounds. Gulf of Mexico. May 26, 1991. Troy Shewmaker, Raymondville.

WORLD RECORD: None.

Never discard used monofilament on land or water. Sea birds, animals, fish, or outboard motor props could become tangled in it. The monofilament can damage the seal behind the motor prop. Wrap the line in a tight bundle and carry it home and dispose of it in the trash.

SCAMP
(*Mycteroperca phenax*)

DESCRIPTION: Another grouper of the family Serranidae, the scamp is normally light tan with numerous spots on the body and also on the dorsal and ventral fins. The color can vary, and a miles off Port Aransas. December 31, 1980. Rudy Luna, Port Aransas.

WORLD RECORD: 28 pounds. Port Canaveral, Florida. December 30, 1991. Charles V. West.

scamp might be darker brown, with the dots not as prominent. The mouth is large. Average size is about 5 pounds or less, but fish weighing more than 10 pounds are caught.

HABITS/HABITAT: The scamp is a bottom-dwelling species that lives in deep water over snapper banks or around other structure such as an oil platform or a sunken ship. The basic diet includes small fish and crustaceans. It is present in Texas waters year-round but is not considered plentiful. Once hooked, it pulls hard for a time, until it leaves deep water and the change in pressure kills it.

REMARKS: When a scamp is pulled from deep water, it is not unusual to find its stomach protruding from its mouth, due to the abrupt change in water pressure. A scamp makes delicious eating.

STATE RECORD: 23 pounds. Thirty-four

If you hook a big ling (cobia), more than 50 pounds, and it comes on in without much resistance, don't be fooled into believing the fish is ready to give up. That ling has not begun to fight. Putting a gaff into a ling that is not yet exhausted, or pulling it into the boat, is asking for big trouble. If you stick it with the gaff while the fish is still frisky, it could yank you overboard. And get it into the boat, and its wild flounces and swinging tail hit like a sledgehammer, flattening everything it strikes, even fishermen. Be sure the strong fish is played down before attempting to land it. This might take an hour or more.

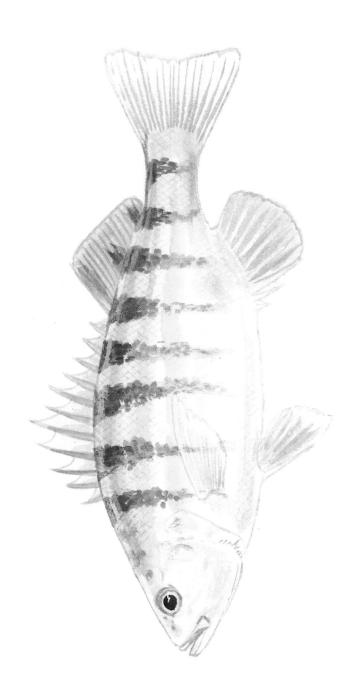

BARRED GRUNT
(Conodon nobilis)

DESCRIPTION: The barred grunt belongs to the grunt family, Pomadasyidae, and is a close relative of the pigfish, or piggy perch. Grunts closely resemble the snappers but they do not have teeth in the roof of the mouth. A grunt might also be confused with the croaker, since both species are capable of making sounds. The grunt, however, has a more deep-throated grunting sound, produced when the upper pharyngeal (throat) teeth grate against the lower teeth; the sound is amplified by a large air bladder. Coloration of the barred grunt is silverish with 8 broad vertical bars intermingled with lengthwise yellowish stripes on the sides. Anal and ventral fins and tail are yellow. The preopercle, or cheek bone, is serrated. The typical barred grunt is something less than a foot in length and less than a pound in weight.

HABITS/HABITAT: The barred grunt lives primarily on offshore snapper banks and deep water around oil platforms. It is common in spring and summer, particularly along the southern part of the coast.

REMARKS: Because of the diminutive size and small mouth, not many barred grunts are caught; instead, they only succeed in stealing baits intended for snapper. The fish is edible, but extremely bony.

STATE RECORD: 1 pound, 1 ounce. Port Aransas. July 14, 1984. Harry Hoffman, Corpus Christi.

WORLD RECORD: None.

Carrying extra tackle can be a problem, especially when wade-fishing or when you have to walk a long distance. One solution is to use a carpenter's nail apron. Stuff it with some plastic boxes filled with whatever you need. You can use 35MM film cannisters for extra hooks, sinkers and swivels. Another possibility is a fisherman's vest with its many pockets. Most larger tackle stores will have vests.

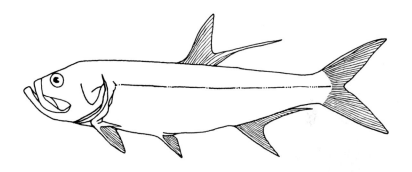

INSHORE AND OFFSHORE SPECIES
(not usually sought for sport or food)

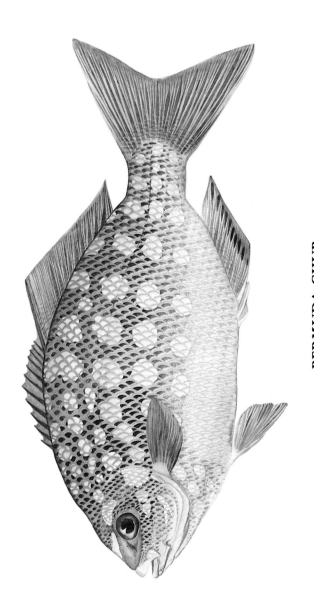

BERMUDA CHUB
(Kyphosus sectatrix)

DESCRIPTION: The Bermuda chub, belong-ing to the family Kyphosidae, is a deep-bodied, compressed fish with a small mouth containing

WORLD RECORD: 11 pounds, 2 ounces. Fort Pierce, Florida. January 18, 1993. Herman Cross.

short, strong teeth. The mouth is far out of proportion to the body. Coloration is brownish or bluish with yellow stripes lengthwise along the body. Some specimens have numerous white spots. Average weight is less than a pound.

HABITS/HABITAT: The Bermuda chub is normally found around pilings and rocks where its teeth enable it to nip food off the structure. It is more frequently seen inshore and moderately offshore, rarely far out in the Gulf over snapper banks or around oil platforms. Little is known about its life history.

REMARKS: The Bermuda chub is one of those ubiquitous "bait stealers" found in salt water. Because of its small mouth it can easily pilfer a bait off a hook without getting caught. More Bermuda chub probably are not caught because anglers do not use small hooks and baits. It is not desired for food.

STATE RECORD: 4.53 pounds. Gulf of Mexico. March 28, 1992. Frank Ramirez, San Antonio.

One item that every fisherman should have in his boat is a marker. A typical one is made of floating foam plastic with a cord wrapped around it and a weight tied to the end. When pitched into the water, the cord peels off the revolving marker until the weight hits bottom, anchoring the marker to stay in the spot where you tossed it. You can use it to mark a likely place to fish or a place where you've actually started catching fish. It is a reference point to prevent straying away from the spot.

If you have some smaller fish you wish to scale instead of skin, a tablespoon makes a good scaler. Use the rounded end of the spoon to quickly remove the scales.

ATLANTIC CUTLASSFISH
(*Trichiurus lepturus*)

DESCRIPTION: Commonly called the ribbonfish, the Atlantic cutlassfish belongs to the family Trichiuridae, and it is the only member of this family found in Texas waters. No other fish resembles it. The ribbonlike body is covered completely with a shimmering silver skin without scales. It is also tapered from the head to the pointed tail, cutlasslike, hence the name. The mouth is overloaded with large, arrow-shaped teeth. Average length is 18 to 20 inches, but adults will grow to 40 inches and weigh 2 pounds.

HABITS/HABITAT: Ribbonfish are abundant in the bays and in the Gulf close to shore during the warm-weather months. A voracious eater, the fish feeds in a tail-down position, hovering under the surface and rising to strike. Basic food is mostly small shrimp and fish. Not much is known about the fish's life cycle.

REMARKS: Ribbonfish will occasionally take a fisherman's bait, including an artificial lure. They are not utilized as food here as they are in some countries. Ribbonfish are much sought, though, as bait for catching king mackerel and some other open-water species.

STATE RECORD: 2 pounds, 10.24 ounces. Offatts Bayou. January 1, 1987. H. J. (Jeff) Smith, South Houston.

WORLD RECORD: 1 pound, 10 ounces. Port Canaveral, Florida. August 26, 1992. Doug Olander.

ATLANTIC NEEDLEFISH
(Strongylura marina)

DESCRIPTION: The Atlantic needlefish, also called the needle gar and saltwater gar, is not a gar, but a saltwater species belonging to the family Belonidae. It has an elongated, broomstick-like body and a long snout and mouth brimming with sharp teeth. Coloration is green on the back, shading to lighter green on the sides, white on the belly. Average length is about 2 feet or less.

HABITS/HABITAT: Atlantic needlefish are quite common in the inshore Gulf and the bays during the spring and summer. One often can be seen hovering just beneath the water surface, especially at night under a light, which makes the fish easier to see. It also can be found in brackish water in tributary rivers and often runs with freshwater in tributary rivers and often runs with fresh-water gars (see gars in the freshwater section). It is carnivorous and the main diet is small fish. A needlefish will hit a fisherman's bait, but it is very difficult to hook because of the bony mouth and its habit of holding prey in its jaws for some time before swallowing.

STATE RECORD: 9 pounds. Gulf of Mexico. August 3, 1990. Koy Kelley, Richmond.

WORLD RECORD: 3 pounds, 4 ounces. Brigantine, New Jersey. July 8, 1990. Charlie Trost.

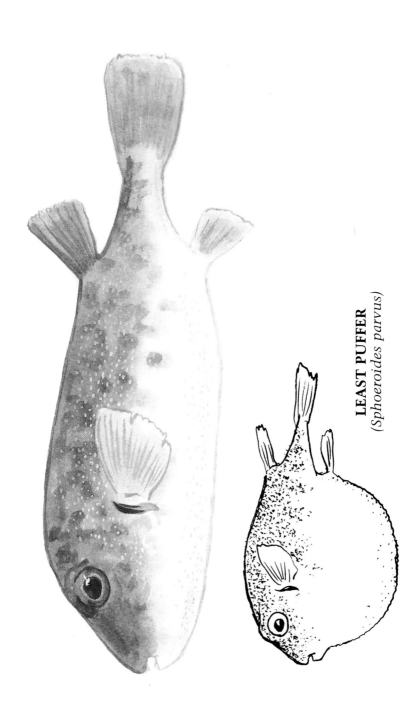

LEAST PUFFER
(*Sphoeroides parvus*)

DESCRIPTION: The least puffer belongs to the family Tetraodontidae. When excited, it puffs up, the body becoming bloated, hence the name. The body is a tan color with irregular dark and light markings on the sides and back. The body is also covered with prickles. The mouth is small. Average size is 4 inches or less.

HABITS/HABITAT: The least puffer is common in the bays and inshore, but little is known about its life history. Occasionally, one will be caught by an angler using a small bait, such as a piece of dead shrimp.

REMARKS: This is one of the real characters you will encounter in salt water. The puffer is capable of inflating its body by using air or water. The puffed-up body, along with the prickles, protects the small fish from larger predatory fish. Another member of the family is the bandtail puffer (*Sphoeroides spengleri*), a Gulf species generally found on reefs and around oil platforms. Coloration is a darker, brownish body with numerous black spots. There is a dark spot on the pectoral fin near where it attaches to the body. The tail has a distinct barred pattern, thus the name. It also is a small fish, 6 inches or less. A puffer has the reputation of being toxic and shouldn't be eaten.

STATE RECORD: 0.14 pound. Galveston Bay. January 30, 1990. Adolf Schulz, Galveston.

WORLD RECORD: None.

When keeping fish in a freezer, proper packaging and quick freezing are essential, but so is the thawing procedure. Fish should be thawed rapidly, not slow-thawed at room temperature or in a refrigerator. The slow thaw gives spoilage bacteria time to act, and also creates excessive drip loss from the ice crystals that locked in the flavor when the fish was quick-frozen. The two best ways of thawing are to put the fish under cold running water or in a microwave oven on the lowest setting. Quick freezing in conjunction with quick thawing will assure the best possible quality.

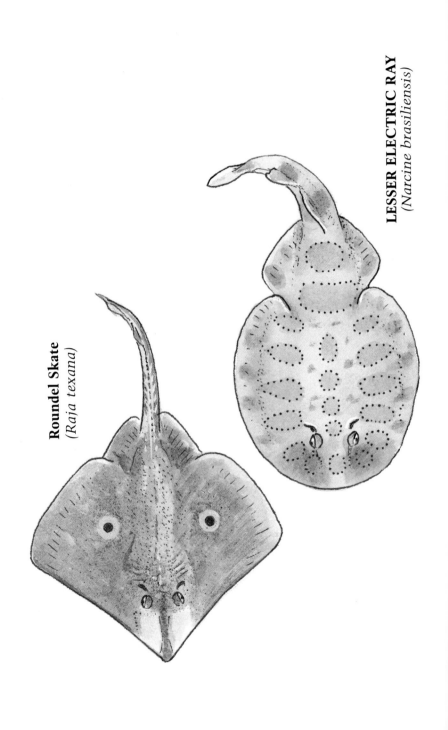

Roundel Skate
(*Raja texana*)

LESSER ELECTRIC RAY
(*Narcine brasiliensis*)

DESCRIPTION: The lesser electric ray belongs to the family Torpedinidae. It has the unusual ability to deliver an electric shock, hence the name. This feature, however, is rarely used. Voltage is produced through a pair of specialized organs occupying most of both sides of the disclike forward portion of the body. With the pelvic fins extended laterally, the flat body is almost teardrop-shaped. The tail is wide and thick. Color can vary, from light brown to a pattern of irregularly shaped blotches with a dark band forward of the eyes. There are no scales, thorns or spines. Length is about 12 to 15 inches.

HABITS/HABITAT: The lesser electric ray is present year-round in Texas waters, and it prefers shallow water where it can bury itself in the sand. Principal food is marine worms.

REMARKS: Resembling the lesser electric ray is the roundel skate (*Raja texana*) of the family Rajidae. The most conspicuous markings are 2 spots, each dark-centered and eyelike, bordered in yellow and located on each disc wing. The topsides of the wings are chocolate-colored. The snout has a translucent area on each side. There is a row of thorns on the middorsal line, continuing to the tail. The lesser electric ray and the roundel skate have no sport or food value. There are no state or world records.

A gadget called a "fish skinner" does a better job than pliers when you want to skin a fish. But when buying a fish skinner, get a heavy-duty or commercial model. Cheap skinners lack the proper bite, making it difficult to grasp slippery skin.

If you carry a camera aboard a boat, protect it from both salt water and direct sunlight, either of which can prove damaging. One solution is to carry photographic equipment and film in a Styrofoam ice chest (no ice), which keeps it dry and cool.

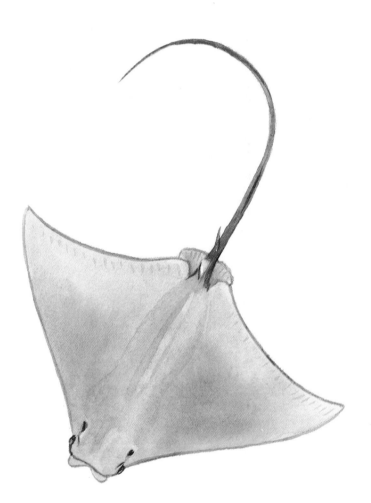

COWNOSE RAY
(Rhinoptera bonasus)

DESCRIPTION: The cownose ray belongs to the family Myliobatidae, the eagle rays. It is a large, free-swimming ray with wide, pointed pectorals (or "shoulders"). Eyes are on the side of the head. The unusual forehead projects partly over a deeply notched snout. One or more large spines are situated near the tail base. The smooth skin is brownish above, lighter below. Average width is about 3 feet, although it grows larger.

HABITS/HABITAT: The cownose ray is most abundant in shallow water where it cruises in search of food like snails, oysters and crabs, grinding and crushing them between large teeth.

REMARKS: Another member of the family is the spotted eagle ray (*Aetobatus narinari*). With pointed "wings," the spotted eagle ray is shaped similar to the cownose ray, but the bill-like snout is much more pointed, and the forehead angular instead of blunt. It is dark in color with regularly arranged spots, usually white or yellowish, all over the top of its body. The black tail is armed with 1 or more barbs that can be dangerous. The smooth butterfly ray (*Gymnura micrura*), fam-

ily Gymnuridae, is a small ray with a disc about twice as wide as long. Coloration is brown with dark blotches. The tail has no spine. Rays have no fishing or eating desirability.

STATE RECORD: 50 pounds, 8 ounces. Gilchrist Pier. May 27, 1986. Freeman E. Gage, Jr., Jasper.

WORLD RECORD: None.

State record smooth butterfly ray: 9 pounds. South Padre Island. August 2, 1986. Cameron Vere Wells, Port Isabel. (No world record.)

Don't make a drag of a seine to catch bait, pick out what you want, then dump the rest on the ground. If a warden sees you do that, it could prove expensive. State law specifies that a person commits an offense if he leaves edible fish or bait fish taken from the public waters of the state to die without the intent to retain the fish for consumption or bait.

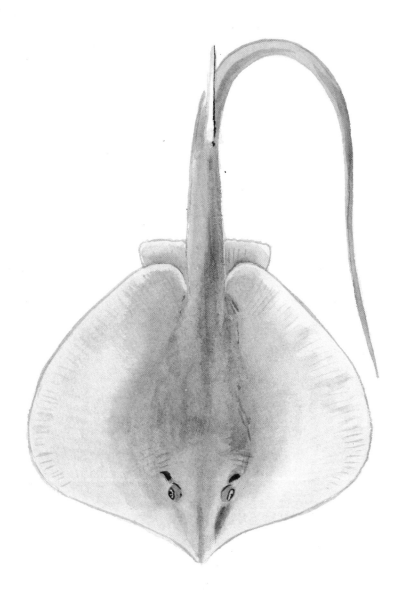

ATLANTIC STINGRAY
(Dasyatis sabrina)

DESCRIPTION: The Atlantic stingray belongs to the stingray family, Dasyatidae. This stingray, with its flat, almost round body and its eyes atop the head, is a brownish color above, lighter along the edges, and white underneath. The snout is triangularly pointed. The tail has one serrated spine. Average size is 6 to 8 inches wide; up to 2 feet.

HABITS/HABITAT: The Atlantic stingray is the smallest stingray, also the most common, and possibly the most dangerous, since it is abundant in shallow bays where fishermen wade. It is an ambush feeder, burying itself on the bottom with only eyes and spiracles showing. It preys on bottom worms, mollusks, crabs, shrimp and small fish. A stingray will occasionally bite a baited hook, and because of its flat body, it can put up determined resistance. When swimming, though, the stingray is a study of fluid motion, cruising along with casual flips of its "wings." The Atlantic stingray is in the bays most of the year but migrates into the Gulf for the winter.

REMARKS: Out in the open water of the Gulf it is not unusual to see a big stingray near the surface. This is the southern stingray (*Dasyatis*

americana), which essentially has the same shape—although the disc is more narrowly rounded—and coloration as the Atlantic stingray, but it comes in a larger package—much larger, up to 5 feet wide and 7 feet long. While it is an inshore species, it is often sighted farther out in the Gulf. The bluntnose stingray (*Dasyatis sayi*) is more broadly rounded than the others. Coloration is also darker, almost black on some specimens. The fold on either side of the tail is well-developed and dark in color. The bluntnose stingray is primarily an inshore species and does not go into the bays. The wings, particularly on smaller stingrays, are edible, similar to sea scallops. Soak the wings in salted cold water 24 hours before cooking.

STATE RECORD: 5.25 pounds. Galveston Bay. August 10, 1991. Justin Patterson, Hitchcock. WORLD RECORD: Same.

State record southern stingray: 214 pounds, 4 ounces. Bolivar Flats near Galveston. June 8, 1985. David Lee Anderson, Texas City. (No world record.)

ATLANTIC SPADEFISH
(*Chaetodipterus faber*)

DESCRIPTION: Also called the angelfish, the Atlantic spadefish is a member of the family Ephippidae. In shape it is more round than long, is thin through the body, and has two distinct dorsal fins. A pattern of vertical black and white bars may vary to nearly solid black or white. Average size is about a pound or less, although an adult might grow to 5 pounds or larger.

HABITS/HABITAT: The spadefish is an inshore Gulf fish and only infrequently will one be caught in a bay. Even then it will normally be near a Gulf pass or channel. The primary diet includes crustaceans and young fish, and it is known to eat large numbers of comb jellies and small jellyfish. Piers, reefs and jetties provide good fishing sites. Because it has a small mouth, little baits of peeled shrimp or cut fish and small hooks should be used. Spadefish spawn in the Gulf in the summer but little else is known about the fish's life history.

REMARKS: The spadefish is not a flashy fighter, but it uses its wide body for leverage to put up stubborn resistance. The fish is good to eat.

STATE RECORD: 10 pounds. Gulf of Mexico. November 24, 1990. Laramie Winczewski, Houston.

WORLD RECORD: 14 pounds. Chesapeake Bay, Virginia. May 23, 1986. George Brace.

Putting melted butter and lemon or lime juice on broiled fish is a proven winner. But for a different taste, try basting with Italian dressing. The oily dressing also helps to keep the fish moist.

When you buy your fishing license, it is a good practice to pick up your saltwater stamp at the same time. Both are needed to fish in salt water. And "I forgot" is no excuse.

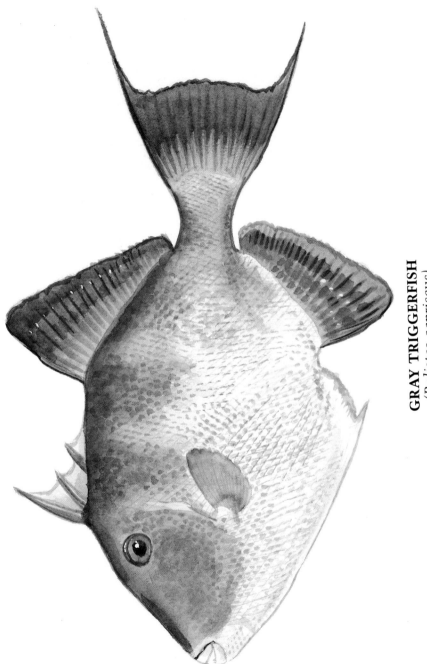

GRAY TRIGGERFISH
(*Balistes capriscus*)

DESCRIPTION: The gray triggerfish is a member of the family Balistidae. It is deep-bodied with a long dorsal spine. There is a projection on either end of the tail. The mouth, which is out of proportion to the body, is small and strong. The color is grayish with irregular dark markings, and small blue spots appear on the upper sides. Average size is 1 to 2 pounds.

HABITS/HABITAT: Triggerfish, which are most active in the warm-weather months, are a deep-water species, hanging around reefs and oil rigs and using their strong mouths to browse barnacles and other attached organisms. The small, tough mouth makes a triggerfish difficult to hook, which gives it the reputation of a pesty bait-stealer. Triggerfish are caught in the daytime, since they are sight-feeders. To catch triggerfish consistently, use a small, extra-sharp hook and a small bait such as a piece of squid. Most triggerfish caught are incidental to fishing for red snapper.

REMARKS: Although the gray triggerfish is the most abundant of this family, the queen trigerfish (*Balistes vetula*) is also common to Texas waters. The body profile of both is the same. The queen triggerfish is grayish to darkish in color with two broad blue bands on the cheek and a broad blue line on the caudal peduncle. A triggerfish is edible, but bony.

STATE RECORD: 11.12 pounds. Gulf of Mexico. April 25, 1982. Steven Griffith, Pasadena.

WORLD RECORD: 13 pounds, 9 ounces. Murrells Inlet, South Carolina. May 3, 1989. Jim Hilton.

State record queen triggerfish: 10.49 pounds. Gulf of Mexico. July 15, 1989. Bruce Goates, Groves. (World record: 12 pounds. Ponce Inlet, Florida.)

Saltwater fish, especially deep-reef fish, can vary widely in coloration. If you intend to have a fish mounted and you want it painted to look like the fish you caught, take a color photograph of it immediately after it is landed. When a fish dies the color fades rapidly. The taxidermist can use the photograph as a guide.

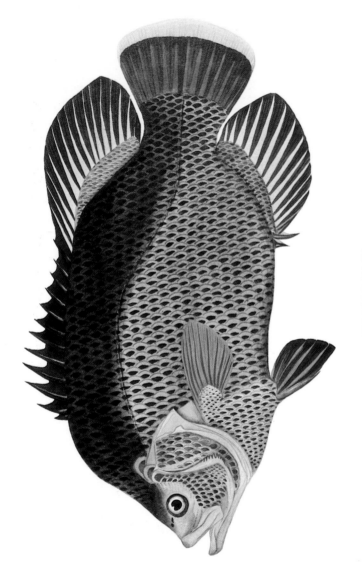

TRIPLETAIL
(*Lobotes surinamensis*)

DESCRIPTION: The tripletail, the only member of the family Lobotidae, is a deep-bodied fish. The dorsal and anal fins are set far back on the body near the tail. Coloration generally is blackish, although some specimens have a lighter yellowish or darkish tint, or are even mottled. Average weight is 5 pounds or less, but the fish grows to 25 pounds and larger.

HABITS/HABITAT: The tripletail inhabits different types of waters: near reefs not far offshore, and around buoys, oil platforms and jetties. The fish congregate in the mouths of rivers, passes and channels opening into the Gulf. They are sometimes caught in the bays, normally near a pass or channel. Food consists of shrimp, crabs and small fish. Since the mouth is small, a small hook should be used in conjunction with a small bait. Spawning occurs in the Gulf in spring or early summer, with the young drifting into bays to feed and grow.

REMARKS: When the tripletail's dorsal and anal fins are folded back, it creates the appearance of a triple tail, hence the name. The fish also has

the unusual habit of floating on its side on the surface, and the fish sometimes is mistaken for floating debris. Although bony, the fish is good to eat.

STATE RECORD: 33.50 pounds. Matagorda Bay. June 29, 1984. Mrs. Eddie Porter, Spring.

WORLD RECORD: 42 pounds, 5 ounces. Zululand, Republic of South Africa. June 7, 1989. Steve Hand.

Booze and boats don't mix. Alcohol reduces control, judgment and coordination, and can impair perception and reflexes. The age-old remedies for intoxication—black coffee, fresh air, or a quick dip in the water—will not sober anyone. All you have is a wide-awake drunk or a drowned one. Most people killed in fishing accidents fall out of boats for one reason or another, often because of alcohol consumption.

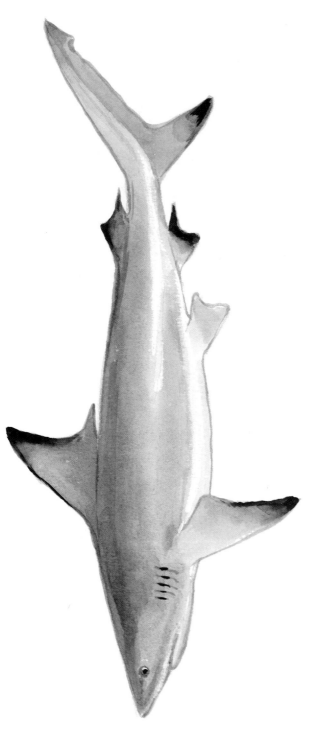

BLACKTIP SHARK
(Carcharhinus limbatus)

DESCRIPTION: The blacktip shark, belonging to the family Carcharhinidae, has conspicu-

STATE RECORD: 179 pounds. Gulf of Mexico. May 20, 1989. Gary Rooth, Bay City.

ous black-tipped fins, hence the name. It is sometimes mistaken for the larger spinner shark, which has similar marks on its fins. But the blacktip can be identified by its short gill openings, relatively larger eyes, and finely serrated teeth. Coloration is dark gray, bluish or dusky-bronze above, shading to white or yellowish below. Average length is 4 to 6 feet, maximum about 8.

HABITS/HABITAT: Blacktip sharks sometimes travel in schools, feeding on small fish of all kind. It is not unusual to catch a blacktip while fishing for other species, and it is one of the more prevalent shark species taken by fishermen on offshore party boats. Small blacktip sharks are also caught in the bays. The young are born alive in spring or early summer.

REMARKS: Anglers like the competitive spirit of the blacktip after it has been hooked. It puts up more resistance—even leaping out of the water occasionally—than do most other shark species of comparable size. The blacktip is good to eat.

WORLD RECORD: 270 pounds, 9 ounces. Malindi Bay, Kenya. September 21, 1984. Jurgen Oeder.

When fishing for many saltwater fish with sharp teeth, such as sharks and mackerels, use a wire leader. Long wire leaders are standard for trolling offshore for billfish. These are usually made in advance and coiled and stored. This way a leader can be replaced immediately without losing much fishing time. Wire leaders are referred to by numbers, which indicate diameters and breaking strengths.

Wire leader sizes: No. 2, .011 diameter, 28 pounds breaking strength; No. 3, .012, 32; No. 4, .013, 39; No. 5, .014, 54; No. 6, .016, 61; No. 7, .018, 72; No. 8, .020, 88; No. 9, .022, 108; No. 10, .024, 127; No. 12, .029, 184; No. 15, .035, 258; No. 19, .043, 352.

BULL SHARK
(Carcharhinus leucas)

DESCRIPTION: The bull shark, belonging to the family Carcharhinidae, can be recognized by sharks. Shark meat can be a productive bait when fishing for the bull shark.

its heavy body, wide head and blunt, rounded snout. Upper teeth are broad, lower teeth thin. Coloration is gray above and white below. Adults have no conspicuous fin markings, but fins on the young may have darker edges. Bull sharks can attain lengths of 10 feet and weights of 500 pounds.

HABITS/HABITAT: The bull shark is a common inshore species in Texas waters. This shark normally is a slow-moving fish except when attacking prey, one of its favorite foods being smaller

One way to attract sharks to a baited hook is to chum, which means throwing some type of food overboard, as the food drifts with the current, sharks pick up the smell and come to the source. If possible, buy or bum trash fish from a shrimper, because it makes good chum. Cut up the fish and grind them to reduce the pieces to pulp; then ladle the stuff overboard. Chumming not only attracts sharks, it holds them in the area.

REMARKS: This fish is unusual in that it can tolerate water of much lower salinity than can other sharks. It is not unusual to find one swimming far up in a tributary river. The flesh is edible. STATE RECORD: 497 pounds. Galveston. July 3, 1971. Dale Harper, Houston.

WORLD RECORD: 490 pounds. Dauphin Island, Alabama. August 30, 1986. Phillip Wilson.

A shark has a keen sense of smell. This effective talent permits the shark to wander along until its scent-detection "radar" locks in on food. To get its attention, chum with blood, one of the most powerful of attractants. Go to a slaughtering plant and buy several gallons of cattle blood. Pour it into shallow pans and place it in the sun until the blood coagulates. Cut the blood into chunks and you have your chum, tossing a few pieces overboard right along as you fish, the blood weeping into the water to create a scent trail.

SANDBAR SHARK
(Carcharhinus milberti)

DESCRIPTION: Known also as the brown shark, the sandbar shark belongs to the family Carcharhinidae. Coloration of the fairly stout fish, a marauding shark will follow it up until the predator can move in and chomp down on the fish. Infrequently, a shark is even hooked this

body varies from gray to brown. The snout is broadly rounded and the eyes are quite small. The first dorsal fin is large for a member of what is called the sand shark or requiem shark family. The pectoral fins are also large. The second small dorsal is set just about over an equally small anal fin. The large tail has a long upper lobe. Average size is about 6 feet in length and about 100 pounds in weight, although the sandbar will grow to better than 200.

HABITS/HABITAT: Sandbar sharks, which like colder water, are not common to Texas waters. They will normally be found close to shore or just a few miles out in the Gulf, as they are more littoral (coastal) than pelagic. They roam in schools, moving around constantly, swimming and feeding on or near the bottom. When a sandbar shark is about 6 feet long, it will weigh about 100 pounds, but by the time it reaches 8 feet, about its maximum length, it will have more than doubled in weight.

REMARKS: Sometimes when a fisherman is reeling in a snapper, grouper, or some other reef way. But it is not normally landed because the tackle is inadequate; a shark is strong, with extremely sharp teeth that will sever any line but wire. A sandbar shark will typically stay deep to do its fighting, not coming to the surface until it is ready to surrender. The flesh is edible.

STATE RECORD: 226 pounds. Padre Island. March 21, 1975. James S. Wilson, Corpus Christi.

WORLD RECORD: 260 pounds. Gambia Coast, Gambia. January 2, 1989. Paul Delsignore.

Many saltwater fish such as redfish, sheepshead and tarpon have very tough mouths. A hook must be needle sharp to penetrate. A handy device for sharpening is the Hook-Hone-R, powered by rechargeable batteries. It is available from some tackle outlets or by mail order from Bass Pro Shops. Before you go fishing, sharpen your hooks, even new ones that haven't been used.

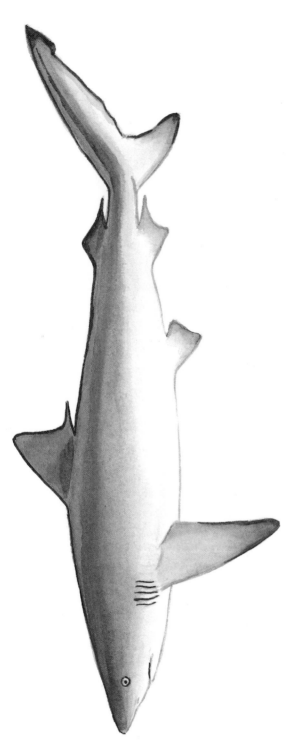

SILKY SHARK
(Carcharhinus falciformis)

DESCRIPTION: The silky shark is a member of the family Carcharhinidae. Its body is rather slender, with a coloration that ranges from dark off Padre Island. July 23, 1973. Wolfgang Buschang, Corpus Christi.
    WORLD RECORD: None.

to blackish along the back shading to off-white on the sides. Pectoral fins are long and narrow. The tips of the second dorsal and anal fin are also long. The head is fairly small, with noticeably small eyes, a moderately pointed snout, and teeth that are nearly symmetrical, with broad uppers. Average size is 200 pounds or more, with a maximum length of about 10 feet and weights exceeding 500 pounds.

HABITS/HABITAT: Silky sharks are offshore oceanic wanderers. Behavior suggests considerable up-and-down movement, since the shark can be seen idling on the surface, but it is also regularly caught at depths exceeding 100 feet.

REMARKS: The silky shark gets its name from tiny projections or denticles on the skin that create a silky feel when you run a hand along the side. The fish possesses both power and speed, and when a big one hits a bait with momentum, it can easily snap line testing more than 100 pounds. The meat can be eaten, but it is not normally utilized as food.

STATE RECORD: 556 pounds. Oil platform

For fish with sharp teeth, some anglers prefer to use a cable leader instead of wire because it is more flexible. The cable, either plain or with a nylon coating, isn't as strong as wire of comparable diameter, however. Wire of .011 diameter has a breaking strength of 28 pounds; cable of the same diameter breaks at 18 pounds.

You can get ready-made leaders, or buy cable in bulk and make your own. Loops in cable are made with metal sleeves. The cable is run through the sleeve, then through a hook or lure eye, then back through the sleeve, which is crimped tightly to keep the cable from slipping. Sleeves come in various sizes and it is important to select the proper size for the leader material you intend to use. Any tackle dealer on the coast should have a chart indicating the proper match of leader material and sleeve. The store also will have a crimping tool.

SPINNER SHARK
(Carcharhinus maculipinnis)

DESCRIPTION: The spinner shark, a member of the family Carcharhinidae, is grayish in color. The dorsal and pectoral fins along with the tail are black-tipped. The snout is slender and

Bay. May 21, 1989. David Lee Anderson, Hitchcock.

WORLD RECORD: 190 pounds. Flagler Beach, Florida. Gladys Prior.

very pointed, and the eyes are small. The spinner shark is often confused with its smaller cousin the blacktip shark, which has similarly marked fins, but the eyes of the blacktip are relatively large. Both the upper and lower teeth are slender and nearly symmetrical and not finely serrated as are those of the blacktip. Maximum size is about 8 feet long and 200 pounds.

HABITS/HABITAT: Spinner sharks roam both offshore and closer to shore, although the fish seems to be more of an inshore species. Food is mostly fish, although it will utilize almost anything it can catch or find. Little is known about its life history in Texas waters.

REMARKS: The spinner shark's name comes from its odd habit of jumping out of the water in a spinning motion. The meat is edible.

STATE RECORD: 184 pounds. Galveston

If you are fishing in deep salt water and you have a big fish on your line, listen for the captain's instructions. He might be maneuvering the boat to put you into better position to play the fish and any directional change might put a bow in the line. Reel furiously to eliminate the slack. This is when the fish can jump or shake the hook free. Another crucial time is when the fish is being brought to gaff alongside the boat. There is a risk of losing the fish, plus a risk to the deck hand or companion who is assisting. The person with the gaff or landing net should be in complete command. Do what he tells you to do.

DUSKY SHARK
(Carcharhinus obscurus)

DESCRIPTION: Sometimes known as the shovelnose shark because of its broad head, the dusky shark belongs to the family Carcharhinidae. Coloration is a darkish gray along the back and top of the dorsals, shading light on the sides

REMARKS: The dusky is one of the strongest of the deep-fighting sharks. The flesh is edible.

STATE RECORD: 530 pounds. Gulf of Mexico. March 1, 1975. Raymond E. Hein, Corpus Christi.

and white on the belly. In overall appearance the dusky shark resembles its close relative the sandbar or brown shark. The body shapes are about the same, although the sandbar might be a bit stouter, and the tails look alike. The denture arrangements of the pair are almost identical. Even marine biologists have trouble telling the species apart. The main difference is size; if the shark weighs more than 250 pounds, you almost can bet it is a dusky shark. The dusky's gill slits are slightly curved while those of the sandbar are straighter. Also, the dusky's small second dorsal is set farther back on the body than is that of the sandbar. The dusky shark attains lengths of 10 to 12 feet and weights of more than 300 pounds.

HABITS/HABITAT: The dusky shark is more pelagic in nature than is the sandbar, prowling almost constantly. A dusky shark is a deep feeder. As with most sharks, food is varied, with fish being the first preference—a fish of some substance, since a big shark has a big belly. (This is why fishermen after trophy-sized sharks use extremely large baits.)

WORLD RECORD: 764 pounds. Longboat Key, Florida. May 28, 1982. Warren Girle.

After taking their boats to the coast, most inland fishermen remember to wash their boats and flush the outboard motors with fresh water. But they often forget the trailer wheel bearings. They need repacking with grease at regular intervals, two or more times a year, depending on how often the bearings are submerged in saltwater.

To give a spicy flavor to fried fish, add a package of taco mix to about a cup of cornmeal. Dip fillets in beaten egg, then dredge them in the dry mixture and fry.

TIGER SHARK
(Galeocerdo cuvieri)

DESCRIPTION: The tiger shark, sometimes called the leopard shark, belongs to the family Carcharhinidae. The top of the head is flat, with a short, broadly rounded snout. It is distinguished from other sharks by the serrated teeth that curve backward, forming a notch midway from tip to

STATE RECORD: 1,128.98 pounds. Gulf of Mexico. May 24, 1992. Chap Cain III, Liberty.

WORLD RECORD: 1,780 pounds. Cherry Grove, South Carolina. June 14, 1964. Walter Maxwell.

base. The top lobe of the tail is long and pointed; the lower portion is much shorter. A tiger shark is slender when young but gets stouter as it grows older. The vertical brown stripes on the sides and tail—forming a tigerlike stripe pattern—are more pronounced on young specimens and fade away with age. The upper body is a darkish grayish-brown, while the lower part is a paler grayish-white. The tiger shark attains lengths of over 12 feet and weights exceeding 1,000 pounds.

HABITS/HABITAT: Tiger sharks might be encountered almost anywhere in the Gulf. This shark is among the most voracious of all sharks. Its diet consists of almost anything it can find, including stingrays, fish, crabs, squid, other smaller sharks—plus seabirds and carrion. Tiger sharks reproduce at any time of the year. As many as 80 fertile eggs may be carried by the female, and the young are about 2 feet long at birth.

REMARKS: This is the largest shark in Texas waters. The tiger shark is one species that is known to attack humans. The fish is edible, particularly the younger, smaller specimens.

Since the water on a shallow grass flat clears rapidly once the wind lays after dark, the best period for gigging flounders is often from midnight to daybreak. While some giggers still wade and use gasoline lanterns or spotlights, the popular method is to hunt from a shallow-running boat pushed along by what looks like a miniature airplane motor with a prop mounted on a steel frame above the outboard motor, which is used to run to and from the hunting territory. The air motor propels the flatbottom boat slowly through the shallows. Bright 12-volt quartz lights on the bow throw strong beams of light a few yards forward of the boat. The hunters stay poised with long-handled gigs, ready to stab any flounder they see in the illuminated water.

LEMON SHARK
(*Negaprion brevirostris*)

DESCRIPTION: The lemon shark, a member of the requiem shark family, Carcharhinidae, is the only shark in Texas waters with the combination of having a short, rounded snout; both dorsal fins almost equal in length, the first only slightly boats and also off docks and piers. Most come close to shore at night, and that is the best time to fish for them. Lemon sharks are voracious predators, feeding primarily on fish and crustaceans. Adults show a preference for hooks baited with

larger than the second, and straight symmetrical teeth with smooth cusps or points. The "lemon" comes from a yellowish tint in the color pattern, although it can vary. Most common is yellowish-brown along the back shading to a pale yellow on the sides. But the color also may be darkish brown on the topside, tinged with yellow or greenish-olive on the lower sides, and white or pale yellowish or light grayish-olive on the belly. The lemon shark grows to lengths of 10 feet or longer.

HABITS/HABITAT: Lemon sharks cruise both offshore and inshore waters and can be caught from fish or a large chunk of cut bait. The best fishing is during the warm-weather months. Young are born in the spring and summer in shallow water and measure 24 to 26 inches.

REMARKS: Because of its size and aggressive nature, a lemon shark is considered a threat to humans. The fish is edible.

STATE RECORD: 470 pounds. South Padre Island. August 28, 1987. Jim Blackburn, Harlingen.
WORLD RECORD: 405 pounds. Buxton, North Carolina. November 23, 1988. Colleen D. Harlow.

A cold norther pushes speckled trout into deep water, such as the well-known Army Hole at Matagorda Island near Port O'Connor. Another place to find trout when they go deep is in the turning basin of a harbor. To catch trout in the winter, fish a lure such as a shrimptail jig deep and very slowly. The trout's metabolism slows down in cold water.

Many fishermen listen to or read fishing reports for the wrong reason. They want to know whether or not a certain species is being caught, and where. More important is the condition of the water, whether the tide is high or low or normal, and water temperature. If conditions are right, your odds of success are much improved.

SAND TIGER SHARK
(Odontaspis taurus)

DESCRIPTION: The sand tiger shark belongs to the family Odontaspididae. Its most distinguishing feature is 2 dorsals that are almost equal in size. The nurse and lemon sharks are the only sand shark, but it was renamed sand tiger. Because of its size and tendency to prowl close to shore, the sand tiger is considered to be a potential threat to humans. The flesh is edible.

other species with dorsals of matching length. The flattened forehead slopes forward to a slender snout. Teeth are long but not serrated and unusual in that they are tricuspidate, meaning they have three "points." The upper portion of the tail is very long. Overall coloration of the fairly streamlined body is grayish, being darkest on the snout and along the dorsal surfaces and upper sides of the pectoral fins. The sand tiger has a maximum length of about 10 feet and a weight of about 300 or so pounds, although average size is less.

HABITS/HABITAT: Sand tiger sharks tend to roam close to shore, and they feed most actively at night, which is when they are most likely to be caught. The diet is varied, but mainly they prey on smaller fishes. This shark isn't thought to be present in Texas waters in any significant numbers.

REMARKS: There remains some confusion about this shark. At one time it was called the

STATE RECORD: None.
WORLD RECORD: 340 pounds. Buxton, North Carolina. June 3, 1990. Michael E. Seay.

Sharks do not have extremely poor vision and are not color-blind. According to marine researcher Dr. Samuel H. Gruber, the numerous sharks he has tested responded to light of all different colors. Also, the sensitivity to low light is very high. Unlike most other fish, which have no way of controlling the amount of light entering the eye, sharks have both an adjustable pupil and adjustable reflectors in the rear of the eye, allowing for sensitivity control, which permits the predators to hunt visually at night. This is why night is a prime time for catching them.

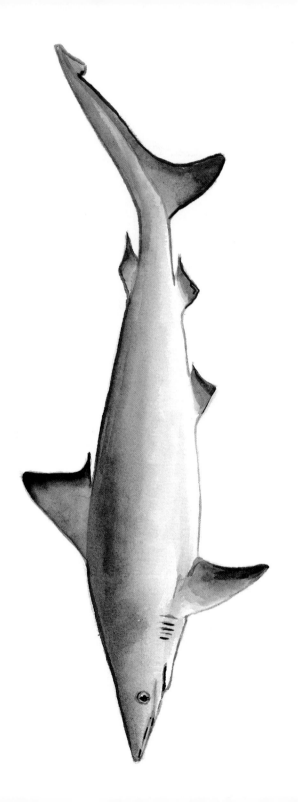

ATLANTIC SHARPNOSE SHARK
(*Rhizoprionodon terraenovae*)

DESCRIPTION: The Atlantic sharpnose shark belongs to the family Carcharhinidae, the

REMARKS: A shark is unique in that it does not have true bones. The skeleton is composed of

requiem sharks, or what are sometimes called the sand sharks. In fact, "sand shark" is this fish's common nickname. The slender body tapers to a narrow pointed snout with wrinkles extending around the corners of the mouth. Its teeth are notched and slanted to the rear. Coloration is grayish, usually with a few white spots on the sides, and the fins and tail have a dark trim. The second dorsal fin is set slightly back of the anal fin. The sharpnose shark is a small shark, about 36 inches or less in length.

HABITS/HABITAT: The sharpnose shark is one of the more abundant shark species in Texas waters. It is a predator, eating small fish, shrimp and mollusks, as well as being a scavenger. As with all sharks, the young are born fully developed. There is internal fertilization, with the male transferring sperm with a pair of claspers on his pelvic fins. The female carries her eggs internally until they hatch. Young sharpnose sharks are common in the surf and bays during the summer. Bigger sharpnose sharks are also caught far offshore.

a cartilaginous material which, unlike bone, is soft. The small sharpnose sharks that hang around close to shore are not considered a threat to humans. The fish is good to eat.

STATE RECORD: None.

WORLD RECORD: 13 pounds, 4 ounces. Galveston. May 28, 1989. Harold E. Denner.

If you are going to be in a standing position to play a big fish such as a shark, you should wear a gimbal belt, which has a heavy leather front section or a plate of covered, padded metal with a socket (gimbal) in which you place the rod butt in order to brace it. Otherwise, the butt will dig into your midsection, bruising or even tearing skin. Charter boats and most larger private boats have the belts aboard.

COMMON THRESHER SHARK
(Alopias vulpinus)

DESCRIPTION: The common thresher shark is a member of the family Alopiidae. Its most distinguishing feature is the very long, arching, upper

STATE RECORD: 133 pounds. Eight miles off Port Aransas. April 16, 1981. Bruce N. Hansen, Grand Island, Nebraska.

WORLD RECORD: None.

lobe of the tail, the length being almost equal to the length of the body proper. Coloration is bluish. The second dorsal is small and sits atop the body just forward of the anal fin. Teeth are abundant, numbering 20 on each side of the jaw. The common thresher is a big shark, maturing when it is about 12 to 14 feet long.

HABITS/HABITAT: The common thresher is not known to be present in any significant numbers in Texas waters, although as with most sharks, little is known of its life history. Unlike most other shark species, the common thresher feeds near the surface. It is known to range close to shore in its hunt for food, mostly schooling small fishes. It swings the powerful "tail" from side to side to stun and kill prey, the only shark known to collect food in this manner. The young, born live, will be about 3 or 4 feet long at birth.

REMARKS: The long upper lobe of the tail gives this shark a freakish appearance. The tail also serves as a propeller, the shark shooting forward in quick bursts of speed. The flesh is edible.

When fishing saltwater flats with fly tackle, you need a reel with an adjustable drag and backing line along with the fly line, since redfish, specks and other fish on the flats are strong and capable of long runs. Six- or seven-foot leaders are adequate for shallow-water fishing, but they should be tipped with short shock leaders, 20- or even 40-pound test, to keep sharp teeth of a redfish, speckled trout or flounder from severing the leader near the bait. Large streamer flies, 2 to 4 inches long, hook sizes No. 4 to 4/0, are the most popular artificials. Large popping bugs, either solid or hair bodies, are also good. Favorite colors are red, red and yellow, yellow, or white.

SHORTFIN MAKO SHARK
(Isurus oxyrinchus)

DESCRIPTION: The shortfin mako shark, or simply mako, is a member of the family Lamnidae. Coloration of the slender body is a deep blue-gray back with a white underside. The tail lobes shortfin mako brought aboard while it is still alive can be dangerous. The flesh is edible but not normally utilized as food.

STATE RECORD: 664 pounds. Offshore at

are of about equal length. The snout is sharply pointed, and the mouth can be opened to about a 90-degree angle, exposing an abundance of teeth that have no serrations but instead are knife-sharp. Average size is thought to be about 500 pounds or less.

Port Isabel. May 4, 1987. Donald Ewing, Richardson.

WORLD RECORD: 1,115 pounds. Black River, Mauritius. November 16, 1988. Patrick Guillanton.

HABITS/HABITAT: Shortfin mako sharks are nomadic and generally stick to the open Gulf, although they have been known to venture close to land on occasion. No one knows for sure, but they seem to be in Texas waters only in the warm-weather months. The young, usually 2 to 5 in a litter, are born live and are 2 feet long at birth. Fast-swimming makos prey on schools of mackerel, herring and other fishes.

REMARKS: The shortfin mako is not to be confused with the great white mako, which possibly isn't even found in Texas waters. The shortfin mako is a fine game fish, possessing speed, power and determination. Also, when hooked it jumps in high, acrobatic leaps, making it perhaps the most sporting of all the shark species. But the fisherman needs to be wary of the sharp teeth. A

Because the fly fisherman stalking redfish and other fish on the flats often needs to cast way out there with a single backcast, sometimes into a stiff wind, he needs a long rod with power. Fiberglass has the power but also the weight. After an hour or more of casting, arm and back muscles begin to protest. A graphite rod is lighter with better sensitivity. But more efficient and less tiring is an IM6 rod, which is sold under several major rod brand names. IM6 is smaller in diameter and reacts quicker than conventional graphite. Also, it is 17 percent lighter, and that can make a big difference.

GREAT HAMMERHEAD SHARK
(*Sphyrna mokarran*)

DESCRIPTION: The great hammerhead shark, known as the hammerhead, belongs to the great speed. The great hammerhead is sometimes confused with the scalloped hammerhead shark

family Sphyrnidae, the most distinctive group of sharks in the Gulf. The fish has that strange hammerlike head that gave it its name. An adult great hammerhead is a darkish olive color topside that lightens to a paler shade of the same color below. A young great hammerhead is generally brownish-gray along the back and also shades to a lighter version of the same color along the lower sides. Dusky fins have no noticeable edgings. The center of the head has an indentation, or notch. A great hammerhead can grow to lengths of 15 feet and measure 3 feet between the eyes.

HABITS/HABITAT: Great hammerheads wander both inshore and offshore. The fish often swims close to the surface with its fins showing. Its food includes fish, shrimp, crabs, stingrays and small sharks. The young are born fully developed.

REMARKS: A hammerhead's eyes and nostrils are located at the outer ends of the wide head, which affords a visual advantage for stalking prey. The head also serves as a planing device that allows a hammerhead to maneuver and turn with

(*Sphyrna lewini*), or what is called the small-eye hammerhead, since both have similar-shaped heads. The center of the scalloped hammerhead's head is not as deeply notched, however. Its color is lead-gray or brownish on the back shading to gray-white on the belly. The fish has no unique body markings. Fins are generally of the same color as the upper part of the body, being somewhat darker around the edges. Some specimens have black-tipped pectoral fins. The habits and food of these two hammerhead species are similar. Scalloped hammerheads grow to lengths of 10 feet. Hammerhead sharks are edible.

STATE RECORD: 871 pounds. Eighteen miles southeast of Galveston jetties. July 4, 1980. Mark A. Johnson, La Marque.

WORLD RECORD: 991 pounds. Sarasota, Florida. May 30, 1982. Allen Ogle.

State record scalloped hammerhead: 215 pounds (tie). Both Gulf of Mexico, both May 1992. Mark Duncan, Houston, and Pat Sconcl, Jr., Austin. (No world record.)

BONNETHEAD SHARK
(*Sphyrna tiburo*)

DESCRIPTION: The bonnethead belongs to the hammerhead shark family, Sphyrnidae. The along in the wakes of slow-moving boats to pick up discarded scraps. The fish is edible.

STATE RECORD: 22.81 pounds. Gulf of Mexico. July 13, 1991. Bill Kirschner, Pflugerville. WORLD RECORD: Same.

Eating fish is part of the angling experience. The way to fully enjoy the fruits of the catch is to eat the fish fresh. But for most of us, the fish, or at least some of it, will go into the freezer to be utilized later. Freezer life depends partially on fat content. Some saltwater fish such as tuna and mackerel have a high fat content. Most bay fish have a lower fat content. Those with the high content can be kept about three months; those with the lower content will be tasty after six months, longer if they are frozen encased in ice. To avoid keeping the fish too long, label each package as to what kind of fish and when it was put into the freezer.

shovel-shaped head with a rounded end and no notch in the center distinguishes this species from other hammerheads, which have a more hammerlike shape to the head. Coloration is gray or grayish-brown on the back and paler on the lower sides. Some are marked with a few small spots on the sides. A bonnethead matures when it is less than 4 feet long and a few grow to 5 feet in length.

HABITS/HABITAT: The bonnethead is one of the most common shark species in Texas waters, abundant in the surf and bays, but also prowling offshore, feeding on a variety of food: fish, shrimp, crabs and squid. The female gives birth to 6 to 9 fully developed young.

REMARKS: The bonnethead (also called the bonnetnose) not only is the smallest member of the hammerhead family, but it is the most sluggish. It will readily bite on most any bait but is not actively sought for sport because of its size and lack of spirit. Bonnethead sharks often follow

Index

Pylodictis olivaris, 94–95

Queen triggerfish, 277

Rachycentron canadum,
    194–95
Rainbow runner, *204*–5
Rainbow trout, *104*–5
Raja texana, 268–69
Rays. *See* Atlantic stingray;
    Cownose ray; Lesser
    electric ray
Records, applying for fish-
    ing, 41–43
Redbreast sunfish, 72–73
Red drum, *134*–35, 145,
    251; regulations on, 40.
    See also Freshwater red
    drum; Redfish
Redear sunfish, 68–69
Redeye bass. *See* Rock bass
Redfish, 3, 151, 167, 203,
    233, 235, 251, 303. *See
    also* Freshwater red
    drum; Red drum
Red snapper, 2, *240*–41;
    regulations on, 41
Reel. *See* Rod and reel
Regulations: boating, 31;
    fishing, 11, 37–41
Rhinoptera bonasus,
    270–71
*Rhizoprionodon ter-
    raenovae,* 298–99
Rhomboplites aurorubens,
    242–43
Ribbonfish. *See* Atlantic
    cutlassfish
Rio Grande perch, *128*–29
River sucker. *See* Northern
    carpsucker
Robalo. *See* Snook
Rock bass, 76–77. *See also*
    Green sunfish
Rock hind, *248*–49
Rod and reel, 14–16; down-
    riggers, 30; filling reels,
    17, 18, 19; importance

of balanced, in flyfish-
    ing, 73; lubricating,
    227; for saltwater flats
    fishing, 303; setting the
    reel drag, 23–26
Roundel skate, *268*–69

Sailfish, 2, *210*–11
Salmo gairdneri, 104–5
Salmo trutta, 104, *106*
Saltwater fish, 131–32;
    effect of temperature
    on, 5–6; inshore and
    offshore species listed/
    described, 261–307; in-
    shore species listed/de-
    scribed, 133–85; open-
    water species listed/de-
    scribed, 187–227; outer
    reef species, 229–
    59; regulations on,
    40–41
Saltwater gar. *See* Atlantic
    needlefish
Salvelinus fontinalis, 105
Sandbar shark, *284*–85
Sand bass. *See* White bass
Sand seatrout, *140*–41
Sand shark. *See* Atlantic
    sharpnose shark
Sand tiger shark, *296*–97
Sand trout. *See* Sand
    seatrout
Sarda sarda, 222–23
Scalloped hammerhead
    shark, 304–5
Scamp, *256*–57
Sciaenops ocellatus, 98–99,
    134–35
Scomberomorus cavalla,
    188–89
Scomberomorus maculatus,
    190–91
Scomberomorus regalis,
    192–93
Sea cat. *See* Blue catfish
Sea catfish, *156*–57
Seriola dumerili, 200–201